Christy

FROM ROUGH TO FAIR WAYS

JUSTIN DOYLE

Paperweight

First published in 2012 by Paperweight Publications, Level 4, Building 5,
Dundrum Townhouse Centre, Dublin 16, Ireland.

9781908813077
Christy - From Rough To Fair Ways

9781908813121
Christy - From Rough To Fair Ways e-book

Printed and bound in the UK by
CPI Group (UK) Ltd, Croydon, CR0 4YY

Paperweight Publishing Group, Level 4, Building 5,
Dundrum Townhouse Centre, Dublin 16, Ireland.

www.paperweightpublications.ie

Dedication

To my wife Ann, family, friends and loyal supporters
Christy O'Connor Jnr, October 2012

CONTENTS

The Warmup

CHAPTER ONE: *1st Hole – Early Skirmishes*   *p1*

CHAPTER TWO: *2nd Hole – Learning My New Trade*   *p13*

CHAPTER THREE: *3rd Hole – Playing The Tour*   *p27*

CHAPTER FOUR: *4th Hole – The African Rebels*   *p41*

CHAPTER FIVE: *5th Hole – Open'ing My Account*   *p53*

CHAPTER SIX: *6th Hole – Setting New Precedents*   *p65*

CHAPTER SEVEN: *7th Hole – 'Seve'*   *p83*

CHAPTER EIGHT: *8th Hole – Celebrating The Masters*   *p97*

CHAPTER NINE: *9th Hole – Drinking & Golf Don't Mix*   *p113*

CHAPTER TEN: *10th Hole – Sweet And Sour*   *p129*

CHAPTER ELEVEN: *11th Hole – An Irish Jersey*   *p143*

CHAPTER TWELVE: *12th Hole – Under Pressure*   *p157*

CHAPTER THIRTEEN: *13th Hole – One Shot*   *p167*

CHAPTER FOURTEEN: *14th Hole – Leaving My Pitch Mark*   *p183*

CHAPTER FIFTEEN: *15th Hole – Darren*   *p197*

CHAPTER SIXTEEN: *16th Hole – From Junior To Senior*   *p209*

CHAPTER SEVENTEEN: *17th Hole – Thirteen Pins*   *p221*

CHAPTER EIGHTEEN: *18th Hole – Taking Off My Cap*   *p235*

The 19th Hole – A Special Toast   *p251*

INDEX   *p253*

The Warm-up

When I was sitting down to write my book, someone said to me one day: "Why don't you call it 'Junior'?"

The very second I heard this I just shook my head in total disagreement.

Let us clear up one thing here and now at the very start. I have never been comfortable with that title, name, term, nickname or whatever you wish to call it.

I know that a lot of the public think that 'Junior' is my real name. Others are probably under the mistaken impression that it might be some sort of nickname or pet name given to me by a family member or school mate which, over time, became attached to me.

Nothing could be further from the truth. It was actually first given to me by the PGA back in the early 1970s when I was just beginning my golfing career on the European Tour. Ever since, it just became attached to my full name.

The governing body of the European Golf Tour – the PGA – decided to put 'Junior' at the end of my name in order to distinguish myself from my father's brother, who was already a big star in international golf.

The PGA had a very valid reason for doing so. Although my uncle Christy was a lot older than I, and he had been on Tour a lot longer, I did play in many of the same events as him. He would also be around for a good few years after my career began.

So, during those events and years, invariably people would often ask: "What did Christy O'Connor score today?"

The inevitable response was always: "Which Christy O'Connor are you talking about?"

Therefore, to tell the difference or to set the two of us apart, the European PGA labelled me Christy O'Connor Jnr and my much-loved uncle, Christy Snr. Essentially, it was all done for information and statistical reasons.

My uncle Christy O'Connor was always just that until I came on board and then he was immediately changed to 'Senior'. It is strange to think, and funny in a way, that he should always have been known by his own name but he will be immortalised as 'Senior'.

Even funnier is the fact that the title of my uncle's memoirs was 'Himself'. I do not know if he had issues with 'Senior' as I never really spoke with him about it but perhaps he did with a title like that!

In my own private life, the label has never, ever applied. Ok, there was some banter and occasional mickey-taking about it early on but as regards my mother, father, siblings and close family and friends, I have always been known simply as 'Christy'.

I didn't like it at the beginning and I have a couple of very good reasons to explain that. That word gives connotations of small, lesser in seniority or of less importance. In this instance, living in the shadow of someone senior like a father, grandfather or in this case, my uncle.

Along with all that you hear the typical Irish scenario of demeaning sayings like, 'oh, he'll never be as good as his auld fella' or 'his father was a great man'. You find it in all aspects of Irish life and at all levels of sport – particularly GAA.

Whether I like it or not, I am now tagged with it. It is probably a bit late now to be able to change that scenario but I still believe that when my uncle had retired from professional golf they could have dropped the 'Jnr' tag from the end of my name.

But anyway, there is an even more important reason for me not exactly loving it. I think it is terrible, in Irish life particularly, where you have males through several generations of the same family labelled with the same Christian name.

I am also critical of my own extended family here with the name 'Christy' and so on. That is why I made a conscious decision to name my own sons Darren and Nigel because I think it is quite tough being out there under the umbrella of somebody else.

It is so important for an individual to have their own identity and complete independence from everybody else. That should begin from the first day a person is born. Go out there and make your own name.

Make your own name – for yourself – like my son Nigel. Whatever he does in his life, it will be done by Nigel O'Connor. That is why I made a firm decision to never call any son of mine, Christy or Christopher.

God bless us and save us all if I did. We would then have a situation similar to the States where it is actually common to name three and four generations of sons the same. Two well-known US golfers spring to mind. Could you just imagine Christy O'Connor III?

So after having those few practice swings, and after finally getting that off my chest, I hope you will tag along and enjoy this round with me. I am Christy O'Connor and this will be the round of my life.

CHAPTER 1

Early Skirmishes

1st Hole: 'Tea Olive' 9.14am, April 7th 1977
I became the first Irish Professional golfer to play the US
Masters at Augusta

William Jefferson Blythe III, who is better known to all of us as
the 42nd US President Bill Clinton, was born on my birthday.
My own big day arrived in a suburban area of Galway City known
as Knocknacarra where I came into the world on August 19th
1948.

My mother was Elizabeth Noone and she came from a family of
four. They hailed from Riverstown in Sligo and she was also one
of twin sisters. The Noones were very hard-working people who
came from a coal-mining background. My mum and her sister
moved to England just before the outbreak of World War II.
Both worked as cooks and despite the later outbreak of hostilities
with Germany, she was very happy with her life.

She also fell in love with a very nice young man. But then
one day her world fell apart when she received news that her
boyfriend was tragically killed in the bombing of London. She
returned home and left England behind her forever.

It was at a 'Crossroads Dance' in the Taylors Hill area of
Salthill, just outside Galway, where my mum first laid eyes on my
father, John. In those bygone days, these dances were great occasions where the whole community would turn out at a junction

of four roads.

Once a week, at a certain crossroads, people arrived from all areas and all directions. Someone would play a mouth-organ; someone else would play an accordion and the music and merriment saw all sorts of people out swinging and dancing in the street. Almost everyone did their own little piece. There was a lot of set-dancing and singing. It is said that my father was an excellent step-dancer and he was also very good at playing the harmonica. Because of his talents, he was hugely in demand.

He was an older brother of my famous golfing uncle, Christy. By all accounts he was also a very decent golfer in his own right. There were five brothers in all — Michael, Stephen and Martin were the other three. My Dad's family were steeped in farming. Actually, he very nearly left farming altogether in order to go to America. Some people who were visiting Galway bumped into him and they asked him to go over there with the promise of work and a good life.

However, just as he was about to emigrate, my grandfather Michael begged him to stay. So he ran the farm instead. It was not a huge holding but it was very productive. That land would later become very expensive building land and a hugely valuable property. Its location was in arguably one of the most beautiful and scenic locations in the world on the foot of Galway Bay. Our own family did not have very much money at the time but we made up for that by having everything we needed with lots of different produce.

We owned cattle, pigs and even had a bog where we cut our own turf as well as hay and straw. Market gardening was also a huge part of our life so we were totally self-sufficient. But it was bloody hard work. There were chores for all of us and everyone was expected to roll up their sleeves to help. When I say 'us', I mean myself and my seven brothers; Sean, Frank, Albert, Eugene, Pascal, Vincent, Raymond and our only sister Maureen. There was little or no TV time.

When I look back on those early days it was the toughest period of my life. Just thinking about the hard work aspect makes me shudder. Sometimes I do not know how we got through some of the work. One must remember that we had to work without machinery. There were no big, powerful modern tractors to plough the land. Nor were there any modern balers to pack the hay into nice square bales. Instead, I had to work with two horses named Peg and Silver. I remember them fondly and it seems like only yesterday.

Peg was a hell of a character. On one occasion when we were working at threshing the straw, she actually picked up my brother Sean by the collar of his sweater and she hoisted him up into the air. She was so cute in that she held him so high, that my dad's outstretched hands could not reach sufficient to be able to let Sean loose. Then without any warning, she just tossed him over into the loose straw. All for a bit of devilment!

On the other hand though, she had a bit of a streak about her and she could be very narky. In that sort of mood, she was well able to bite hard. It was precisely because of this that my dad, following advice from my grandfather, decided one day that he had to sell her.

There was even high drama the day she was sold. On the way to the Fairground to be sold at the Galway Fair in Eyre Square, my father tried to put her into a carriage on the train. She put up huge resistance and she had never given any such trouble in transport before. When she was loaded, and as my dad cycled away down the road, he could hear her cries for what seemed like an eternity. My father was very upset by this. When he arrived home, he immediately went over to see my grandfather and he told him:

"Don't ever ask me to get rid of an animal again — especially when there was no need to."

As I already mentioned, the work was extremely hard and difficult. We were often asked to row in and do things that were far beyond what our strength or young bodies could handle.

One of the main chores was going out in all weathers in the morning before school to fetch the cows for milking. The same thing had to be done in the evening after school. In autumn and winter this meant we returned them to the land in the dark and freezing cold. There was one particular pasture where the cows grazed next to Gentian Hill. It was actually an island out in Galway Bay. It is quite well known and it is a popular area for walkers who can easily go out there when the tide is out.

Quite often we would be going about our daily chores in a brisk manner and all of a sudden there would be complete bedlam. My mum or dad would suddenly roar at the top of their voices; "someone go fetch the cattle as the tide is coming in!"

We would immediately scamper out the door knowing that this could lead to huge trouble. My brother Albert and I would fetch our donkey to help with bringing the livestock back in. However, on more than one occasion we were caught out. Several times we found ourselves quite literally up to our necks in four feet of salty sea water and we had to hang onto the donkey's tail in the strong current. Thankfully there were never any tragedies but it was a very frightening experience.

My first day at school was a day I will never forget as I never got there at all. That was because my brother Sean was a bit of a rogue (he is in heaven now, God be good to him). He brought me off that morning on the handlebars of his bike but instead of heading to school he cycled to the Galway docks. At the famous Spanish Arch, he set me up on a swing in an old shed while he and his friends went to the ships moored in the harbour.

Their aim was to try and get cigarettes from sailors. Fetching me later, Sean drilled into me everything that had to be told to my mother as he cycled me home. I will never forget that my first day, as told to my mother, was about our cow the family pet. Sean was so sharp. He told me everything that Mrs Reid would have asked us and spoken to us about on our first day at school. This was because he knew my mother would grill me on my first day and he also knew what questions she would be asking me.

If it was not the sailors he was seeking out, then he was off to the matinee with his friends. Poor Sean might have been able to get around my mum, but my dad was quite another matter altogether. He returned home late on so many occasions with the inevitable result that he would have to answer to my angry father. He would always pay dearly for his misdemeanours as his absence meant he was not pulling his weight on the farm.

Next day, Sean really did take me to school. Officially my first day at school began on my second day and fortunately for Sean, I was not missed by the teacher. I attended the 'Claddagh School' and it actually features in the world famous song, 'Galway Bay'. It stands there in the exact same spot and to this day it is still going strong. I know because I was actually asked to pay a visit to the school only very recently. I had an extremely enjoyable day meeting the teachers and pupils. Everything about that school was so idyllic and so surreal. If you ever happen to watch films and clips of old Ireland, then you literally see what I grew up with and what I experienced as a child.

Our lunch hours were spent strolling down to the harbour on the Claddagh where we watched fishermen with pipes in their mouths mending their nets. Or they would sell fish to women dressed in black shawls. ('The Galway Shawl' is another famous song).

As a child I was fascinated by all this. Anytime I see women in places like Africa carrying huge weights on their heads, I am reminded of days in Galway when the black-shawled women would carry baskets of fish on their heads to sell in the Galway market. The majority of the small homes in and around the Claddagh were thatched. In the streets outside, you would see small children running around with a stick which they used to roll the black tube of a bicycle tyre.

Part of the reason I was fascinated with all these scenes was because it was totally new to me. This was real inner-city Galway whereas I lived outside the city in the country and on a farm. It may not have been a huge distance from the Claddagh to Knocknacarra but they were worlds apart. All the different lifestyles, scenarios and games — in the streets and in the school yard —

were totally alien to me.

On the farm I was only used to chores and work but that is not to say that we did not enjoy many moments of fun. We did of course but just in an entirely different way. The fun we shared and enjoyed was almost always intermingled with our working lives.

A great time of the year for fun was when the neighbours came to help my dad out in 'The Haggard'. A haggard was a place where our yearly supply of turf, hay and straw was stored. When the neighbours arrived to help my dad tie and stack it all, they would bring their kids to help. This was an ideal opportunity for me, my brothers and sister to mingle and play with them. In those wide open places, there were always plenty of games to play. One particular game which is loved by kids the world over, and which we could not get enough of, was 'hide-and-seek'. The Haggard gave us plenty of places to hide and we all loved that thrill of hiding and finding someone. During those long and lovely summer evenings, I can fondly remember the shouts and screams of joy as we all scurried excitedly through the furrows between the stacks of hay and straw.

So, aside from the extremes of hard work, there were great times. Growing up on a farm also helped us to experience wonderful and glorious things that are now sadly departing this world. For instance, we cut seaweed to use as fertiliser and we spread it on the land. I can tell you that you have never tasted the bacon and cabbage that adorned my palate from back then. The seaweed certainly left its mark as some of the food served up by my mother was the sweetest and most succulent that I have ever tasted in my entire life.

My grandfather had a vegetable plot on the main road and not a day went by but there were at least 20 people staring over the wall into it. They may have been looking for a few vegetables but they also saw a fabulous two-acre plot with not a weed in sight. As a young kid I also enjoyed the many happy times when I ventured out to sea with my grandfather who owned a boat. Actually, his father, who was my great grandfather, used to work as a chef on board a ship which was based in Africa during the Boer War.

Stories were also a huge thing in our household. I would sit with my mouth gaping wide open listening to them. Grandfather told us all about the day he was on a boat which was caught up in a storm and they had to dock in Ballyvaughan.

They knew the storm was going to get worse and they needed food on board until it abated. That meant that someone had to walk from there to Galway to get supplies. My grandfather lost the toss and so he had to trudge off to do the shopping!

He was also a very good fisherman — as was my father. Fishing for 'Rock Salmon' was something they both loved and we were so lucky to be served up with some of the finest fish in the West of Ireland.

Sunday was a great day for stories. It was always seen back then as a 'rest day' and it was our only day of relaxation for the entire week. There was nothing better than listening to stories told by my Uncle Mick or my grandfather around a big blazing turf fire. Some of the yarns would have the hair standing on the back of my neck. Of course I now know that they are only fictitious but when I was a boy, I would be frightened out of my wits as rather innocently I believed in them. Ghost stories were very popular in the old days. There was the story of the 12-foot tall man or the Banshee whose wail and screech in the dead of night would signify that someone in the neighbourhood was at death's door.

****

Golf then came into my life. As it happened gradually, I had no idea just how big it would become and that it would shape my entire future. Although it must be said that it did not happen totally out of the blue or that it was a complete stranger.

After all, my famous golfing uncle was born right next door to Galway Golf Club and we lived only a stone's throw from it. Therefore as kids, there were always plenty of opportunities to 'sneak' a few holes to play. On one side of the road — the sea side

— there were four holes. The other 14 holes were on the other side. As evening drew to a close, and we thought we would not be seen, a lot of us kids in Knocknacarra would jump the wall to play as much golf as we could. We would take advantage of every bit of fading light that flickered. As the area was quite rural, there was not much street lighting around. However, there was just the faintest bit of light from the houses on the other side of the road.

Even without that small bit of light, and when it was almost pitch dark, we still had a trick or two up our sleeves. We would put a candle in an old empty tin can of peas or beans and use that as the target to play our chips or putts! In the fading light of dusk and then on into almost complete darkness, we would all be situated next to the green on the first hole. The candle flickering in the tin was our target and we would pitch and putt with the prize being a halfpenny to the winner.

The thing was that some of us kids did not even have a halfpenny in our pockets. I can tell you the Ryder Cup was nothing compared to that for pressure. When you lost, and you had to pay up, you would be lynched if you did not have it.

My golf really started in earnest when I began caddying. This was an enormous part of our young lives when our main aim back then was to earn some money from the members and especially from the influx of tourists. There were two main groups who caddied — the Juniors and Seniors. I began caddying when I was just nine years old and I would be paid 1shilling 3pence for my 18 holes of work. When I went up to senior level, I would be paid 2shillings 6pence.

A source of great delight to all of us was when the Americans came to town. Aside from the fact that it was a great opportunity for earning money and receiving tips, there was a great atmosphere and great razzamatazz generated all around the area.

The colours were so amazing and striking. Men, women and their children who were beautifully and immaculately dressed with an abundance of reds, yellows and blues were everywhere to be seen. More so than a circus, to us an Olympics had arrived in

Galway.

Even before the summer holidays neared, the excitement was palpable in school. We were all itching to get out there and caddy. There were plenty of caddies that should have been in school but who were in fact playing truant and their parents were none the wiser.

Many of the same touring faces would return year after year so you would become very familiar with them. This was also a great help to us as you got to know who the good tippers were and who to steer well clear of.

Most of the golfers we caddied for were sound and they would tip you at the end of the day. But if you came across a guy who was proven in the past to be a bit mean and you sensed he had not changed his attitude, then there were several ways to get back at him.

There was a particular spot near the seventh green where you did not have to caddy with your golfer to the eighth tee. You would just wait there with the bag of clubs near the seventh green, hand him his chosen club for the eighth tee and watch him go off to play his shot. While he was trudging away with his back to you, this was the perfect opportunity to reach into his bag and pull out a few brand new balls. You would then stub them into a bit of rough in a nearby mound and come back to collect them later!

One would have thought that this was a very cunning and well worked out plan. It often worked but then there were the times when the golfer got his own back with a very swift and effective counter-attack.

Going into the Pro Shop a few days later to exchange the new balls for a few shillings, the Pro behind the counter would look at the ball. His name was Bob Wallace and he actually turned out to be a real gentleman who was always good to our family.

You would get the impression that he was examining the ball for any 'smiles' (cracks) but you would soon be in for a real shock. He was in fact reading the brand name as well as any number on it. I laugh now as I think back on it but it was not funny at the time.

Then Bob would say: "Hold on here son, this ball belongs to the American tourist Mr. such and such. How did you come by it?"

What happened was that golfers, in response to their balls mysteriously disappearing, gave the local Pro a list of his balls and numbers before going out to play. In that way, balls that had vanished, and then suddenly re-appeared, would be returned to him.

Of course you could plea that it was a lost ball that you found stubbed in the side of a hill or wherever. The only problem arising from that situation might be that the golfer may have already told the Pro his ball was not lost but had been pilfered. A situation such as this could become really serious. You would be in huge trouble with the caddy master. I should know as I was up before him on many occasions. His name was Christy St George and he was related to the famous St Georges of Clarinbridge.

It would not be totally unknown for a junior or senior to be barred from life from a club but it would have to be very serious for that to happen. We would generally have to give Mr St George threepence from our working fee for the caddy as a fine.

Christy also had a real eagle eye and he was always on the lookout for misdemeanours. He would stalk the course and if he caught any non-members playing — which meant us — he would throw us off the course immediately. Severe cases were normally dealt with by barring the person or persons for a whole week. At the height of the tourist season, this could mean the end of the world for any poor unfortunate caught. In fact it was horrendous.

They say that 'for every action, there is an equal and opposite reaction' and this meant that Christy was not immune from our revenge. He was a chronic asthmatic and there was a simple and effective counter against any punishments he dished out. One act of revenge was to hide his inhaler in a shed in the clubhouse yard. You knew he had not found it when his groaning and gasping for air could be heard as he strode around the golf club looking for it. On another occasion, we peeled off the outer hard plastic skin from a golf ball to expose the elastic inside. You could easily have one hundred metres of the stuff. Wrapped around all the caddy trolleys, Christy would have had some job getting it all off!

As I matured though, the Club Professional Bob Wallace became a great friend and he was a huge influence on my career. He was our mentor, our guide — in short he was everything. I say 'our' because he took my uncle Christy Senior on board and then me.

I cannot speak highly enough of this man. He was not just a mentor to us in golf but in life as well. This was the person who brought my famous uncle to the standing in world golf that he so enjoyed and I was privileged to find myself under his wing as well.

He literally gave me my fist leg up in golf. I will never forget it. Bob and his assistants in the course golf shop handled thousands of different golf clubs. Any dud or broken clubs were dispatched to a rubbish tip close to the clubhouse in an old disused wood. Bob would allow me and my friends to sift through it for any clubs that we felt could be mended, put-together or might be of some use. He was always there to give helpful advice as well when I was trying to make a golf club.

Back in those days, so many clubs had wooden shafts. I would bring home some bits from Bob's tip and I would use nails to put a club together. In fact, one day I brought something home which could have meant that I would never have had a career in golf.

I found a round metal object in a drawer which was strikingly similar to a bullet. But I thought to myself that there was no way that it could have been a bullet as we had no guns at home. If it was a bullet, I was sure that it had been 'spent' and was not a live round.

So I decided to use it to fill an oversized screw hole at the base of the club. Then I got hold of a hammer to drive it into the hole. After a few blows — and without any warning — the club head blew to bits.

My Grandmother and I were in a state of complete shock. Thankfully we were not injured. Suddenly I realised that the object was indeed a 'live' round. I was mighty lucky that I did not lose my hand or even an eye.

By now I was spending more and more of my time immersed in golf. After starting out as a very young caddy, I was getting first-rate advice from a golf expert who started my famous uncle on the road to all his golf glory. Experimenting with discarded clubs and trying to put together a club to practise with showed that I was becoming heavily involved in golf. I was becoming fascinated by everything about it and I wanted to learn more.

Then an incident happened that left an indelible mark on me. It would be the turning point in my life. The point where I decided that golf was not just a game for me. It was going to be my ticket to earning a living and nothing would stop me or stand in my way. Working in the fields one day, from where you could see the first tee, I saw a golfer about to start his round. I got excited as I knew the man and so I shouted over to my mum if it was ok for me to go and caddy for a golfer. This man was no ordinary golfer. He was an excellent player. More to the point, he was a very good tipper. She was working away and I thought she heard me so off I hurried to the golf course.

Totally unaware that my father had spotted me from our land, I set off to caddy for the golfer. I had only just started the round when I spotted my dad coming towards me at a furious pace. I knew he was angry about something and that this was serious. He had clambered over five stone walls to reach me. When he came over to me, he grabbed me by the scruff of the neck and frog-marched me back to work the land. I felt humiliated and totally embarrassed by his actions in front of this golf club member.

From that very moment golf became the number one interest in my life. There was no going back now. I was determined to eke a living out of golf because after that incident, I vowed that I would never ever become a farmer.

CHAPTER 2

Learning My New Trade

2nd Hole: 'Pink Dogwood', 575 yards Par 5, Augusta
This is the longest hole at Augusta. In the 1977 US Masters I
made birdie to hold the lead briefly ahead of Jack Nicklaus.

In making that vow to myself, I was very lucky that I came from
a big family. I had six brothers, any one of whom could go on
and work the farm. It was not as if I was an only son or an eldest
son. If I had been, then that would have been difficult for several
reasons. It would have been very hard for me emotionally just to
abandon my responsibilities. Also my father would, without any
doubt, have been very much against it. So I was lucky and with
my mind made up, I threw myself whole-heartedly into golf.

Do not get me wrong. I do not mean to be disrespectful to my
family or those in agriculture by saying that I would never be a
farmer. I dearly love the land and sea, but for me it was a matter of
choice and a deep inner feeling that there was much more to life.
A seven or eight year old child should not be doing a man's work
from early morning to late at night. There were also very real
dangers to your health and well-being. I've already pointed out
the stories about our horses as well other things like dangerous
tides. My family are not to blame for my hard upbringing. That
was just the way it was during those times past. Nevertheless, that
does not make it right. I believe that everyone has a conscience
and choices in life and that does not mean everyone doing the

same thing.

Subsequent events in my life and career would prove that I made the correct decision. More to the point, it was probably made for me. It was written in stone as they say and golf was to be my destiny.

Once a year there was a Caddies' Tournament and, for this event, some of the more generous members lent us their clubs. On one of those occasions, my brother Frank was given a loan of a full set of clubs from a priest. He was having a few practice swings when all of a sudden he took a huge lump out of the head of the driver. Frank was swinging under the eaves just outside the clubhouse but he swung back too far and the head of the club crashed through a slate above him.

We did not know whether to laugh or cry. In fact some were in hysterics of laughter saying to Frank that went he went to the priest with his confession, he would be cursed by him for ever more.

Getting a loan of clubs was a real luxury because so many of today's professionals are brought up with everything at their beck and call. They can have the longest titanium drivers and the best irons and putters all with lovely ping sounds.

In my day, everything was so hollow and hard. Many professional golfers from my era probably began their future careers in their childhood with 1-irons; 2-irons or most commonly of all, 9-irons. But there was no such title on the clubs that I started off with. Mine were makeshift. They were an amalgamation of shafts, grips and heads joined together with small nails and glue. All thanks to Bob Wallace's rubbish tip outside the clubhouse.

It helped me so much though and it would prove to be an invaluable experience as my game improved. When the caddy tournaments came around, I found that when I used a proper set of clubs it was like stepping into a Ferrari after being in an old Ford Escort.

My game progressed rapidly. So much so, that I found members coming up to me asking for tips on this or that. It seemed like whenever I went out to play, someone approached. Some of the members were far too mean to go to the club professional to buy lessons. They were for the most part, poor players with high handicaps. By playing those four holes on the sea side of the road over and over again, with a makeshift club, I progressed to an 8-handicap by the time I was a very young teenager.

Another reason why my game improved was that I caddied for excellent players. I learned so much from watching members like Tommy O'Connor, Sean Hosty and Kevin Wallace, the son of Bob.

One day I approached Bob to ask him if he could make a proper set of clubs for me. I remember we came to an agreement that it would cost me £2 10shillings, which was an awful lot of money back then. Part of the agreement was that I would pay Bob back instalments of 5shillings per week until the cost was cleared. It was really a 'hire purchase' scheme and the way almost all sales were made in those days. Inevitably, I missed the odd week or two of the deal.

By this stage I had also become a full member of Galway Golf Club. The membership fee was paid for by my poor mum. God bless her as she was so supportive of me. Although she no doubt wanted me to study at school like most mothers, she really understood me. She knew what I wanted and she would prove to be my biggest supporter in my golf and other quests. My father was opposed to it all. I firmly believe that he wanted me to take over the farm.

As I already mentioned, I was very lucky that I had brothers who were more than capable of running the farm. Four of them were younger than me. My father would have to realise that in Eugene, Pascal, Vincent and Raymond he had no worries on the farm front.

With my mother's belief in me, I now had the time to concentrate seriously on golf. Moreover, I now had freedom. The world was mine to explore and I would start out on that journey by initially making frequent visits to two of my favourite courses.

I love Lahinch in County Clare and Rosses Point in County Sligo. I have played them so much that I have lost count. They are two of the world's greatest links courses with the strong breeze coming in off the sea making for a true test of your game. To get to those places, I needed transport. That meant that I needed to make money or to get a job. I could not rely on letting my mother pay my membership. I had to pay her back and I had to pay other people, like Bob Wallace, back.

Making money seemed to come naturally to me ever since I played for a halfpenny and also in my work as a junior caddy. Even when I was much younger, and away from golf, I was always thinking up ways in which I could make a few shillings. There was the time when my brother Frank and I made a little barrow with wheels. We would then collect sticks or steal the odd bit of turf which we would place in the barrow. We wheeled it around and sold it so that we would have money for sweets or a matinee.

Then, just when it seemed as if my whole world was evolving around golf, I almost abandoned all thoughts of a potential career in it forever. It looked like I would never follow in my uncle's footsteps when my mum and I went into business in 1961.

We had a building which we used as a dairy for the farm. So after weeks and months of planning, we decided to upgrade it and turn it into a shop. The work started on the project but we soon realised we had overlooked the whole aspect of planning permission.

One day the Head Planner from Galway paid us a visit. The situation became very serious when, after producing paperwork for my father, he told him that we would have to knock the entire building because we did not seek permission to build in the first instance. It looked as if all our work and plans and dreams were about to crumble into a pile of rubble. I can tell you that there were a lot of sleepless nights. The worry and torment was huge. It seemed incredible that this could be happening to us. It was an awful time. The whole sorry situation should really have been a matter of simple procedure. It was entirely our fault and our predicament had resulted from a stupid mistake of not seeking planning permission. Thankfully the situation was sorted. My parents left no stone unturned in speaking to some of the most influential people in the know around Salthill and Galway and it worked. The whole thing was overturned and we were free to start our dream shop.

An essential reason for setting up a shop was the caravan parks springing up within a stone's throw of where we lived. We resided in a magnificent building at the top of a lane just in front of the sea. It had, without doubt, huge potential. We could see that as each year passed, there was a huge increase in the number of visitors and tourists to the area. So we stocked the shop with all the main requisites in groceries. In summer, ice cream and dairy produce was the main seller. When the tourists arrived on a Friday for the start of their holidays, they would have to stock up their caravans and tents with food and beverages. So our shop would supply and deliver.

My whole life was about to change enormously and it could have changed forever. Every morning I would bring to the nearby caravan park, 20 crates of milk which I can tell you were extremely heavy. Back in those days pints of milk came in bottles and each crate held around 20 bottles. So you can imagine how heavy they were. I delivered them on an old cart with wheels which I had made. Each evening, I then had to return to fetch the empty bottles and sort out the orders for the next morning. You could say that I was a milkman with my own delivery rounds.

I worked from 7am to 11pm seven days a week and all through the summer. I did so because I got a great buzz out of it. I enjoyed meeting people from all areas and all walks of life. Of course at this stage, I was also very independent and making good money.

Salthill was like a mini Blackpool. The atmosphere was incredible and it was growing rapidly from just a quiet seaside area to a place full of hustle and bustle. The cafes, pubs, dance halls and singing bars were thronged. With the hectic activity and demands on my time, there was little or no time at all for golf. I was busy scurrying around to meet demand. Because of that, I knew that there was no time to waste and I had to learn to drive.

Just as soon as everyone arrived in Salthill, and the place was buzzing, it then died down as quick. In late August and early September when the kids had returned to school, the area became very quiet. This gave me the chance to drive a car. My moment came behind the wheels of a Volkswagen Ice Cream van! The routine of driving and selling ice cream around Knockncarra soon became monotonous to the driver. I discovered that he had a penchant for comic magazines so I sort of bribed him. I supplied him with an endless amount of comics. While he sat back and was engrossed by the latest escapades of those characters like Desperate Dan and Gnasher in the 'Beano', I would take to the wheel. Thankfully, I was never caught.

Totally against the will of my parents, I went and bought my first car when I was 14. I went to College Road in Galway — where Connacht play their rugby at the Greyhound track — to a very busy garage called McCairns Motors. It was 1962 and today that garage is no longer there. I pestered their mechanic to find me something and eventually, he came up trumps. My first car was a Ford Anglia. I paid £130 for it and although she was not perfect, I fell in love with her. The handbrake was gone and the bodywork was in a two-tone colour of black and rust but the bumpers were so strong. I would use those back and front metal bumpers to park it by letting the car bounce back off a wall thereby coming to a halt! My first car could not have come along at a better time. I got a fantastic order from the local nuns in a convent at Seamount. They required ice creams for their post-lunch desserts and I was asked to deliver 50 of them.

Costing 4pence each, that was some order for me. They had to be delivered punctually at 1.55pm. That was a very important stipulation. The ice cream had to be delivered at not 2pm, or 2.05pm, but at 1.55pm which was the end of their lunch.

The ice creams were cut in our shop and a wafer was placed at each side of them to make it look like an ice cream sandwich. I put them all on a tray and then placed them on the back seat of the car. I made sure to drive very slow and carefully to the nuns. I cannot state enough how important that order became. With an order like that, I can actually recall going into McCairns and paying off the first two months' 'Hire Purchase' payments on that car.

My first drive to Dublin is something I will never forget. A friend of mine who is now deceased, Bernard Conlon, tagged along. He had an incredible laugh and he laughed so much that day as he could not believe we were going to Dublin for the first time.

Bernard was a lot older than me. He laughed when we drove through red lights. We were unsure of what the lights meant so we just kept on going. But the fun only started when we went in search of a hotel room for the night. I parked the car on that inclined North Frederick Street which runs up by the side of the old Gate Theatre at the junction of Parnell Street. It is quite a steep hill there and with the state my Ford car was in, I should have known better. As we both walked off to find a hotel, the car started to roll back. There was a beautiful posh car just behind it. We both sprinted back and quickly put our backs to the bonnet. We literally just stopped it in the nick of time.

Paddy Conlon, who is also deceased and was a brother of Bernard's, was a great friend of mine. He was also a mechanic and the car was ending up in his workshop on so many occasions that it began to break my heart. His garage was situated on his farm out in the Kilcolgan area of Galway near Clarinbridge. Every time he worked on that car, and if it was not finished, I would have to walk home. On one occasion, I had to start out walking that 12 mile slog at 1am.

September meant that it became a very lean time in the shop right through until May. With this in mind, along with the fact that I was now driving, the golf bug began to hit me once more. So I began to play once again with my brothers Frank and Albert.

Of more pressing importance however, was the fact that there was no money coming in and I had debts to pay. I had to repay in

19

the region of 5shillings per week which was £2 a month. The tank was running on empty and then I heard about a golf event. There was a competition down in Lahinch Golf Club in County Clare. It was known as an 'Alliance' and these events are still very popular today. I drove down with Albert to play in it. I laugh to myself now because of the amount of fun I had in that car. I wondered if it would conk out on the way there and back. It was so wet that the rain was blowing into the car from all directions along the windswept coast road. You could even taste the salt.

I drove down to play for the first prize of £5 and it was all in aid of the car. The drive was worth it and it paid off as I won. The £5 equalled two months repayments so as well as being happy, I was very relieved. Another very important thing happened in that event.

My partner in that competition was the then professional at Lahinch, Mr McCavery. He is the father of current professional, Robert McCavery. Afterwards, I can remember how I was amazed at how he knew every single shot I played for to record on my scorecard.

He also told me about some of my shots later and I just stood there in disbelief. I quizzed him on how his memory was so good in knowing all this. It was a trick that I would learn to perfect myself. In later years, I in turn would amaze my friends and partners with very accurate details of their shots and scores. To some it was a sore point as they did not liked having a bad shot or a short missed putt pointed out again.

Playing competitions and practising hard became very beneficial to my game. From an 8-handicap I soon got down to a handicap of four. In truth, I knew there was an awful lot more improvement left in me because I was not playing as much golf as was required. Improving my game to a four-handicap was all down to the experience of learning and playing with a man by the name of Tommy O'Connor. This is a guy who was a Scratch golfer for 45 years.

Tommy who is different from another Tom O'Connor mentioned in these pages, came from another great O'Connor golfing family. His brothers Peter and Patrick were also renowned golf teachers. On the subject of O'Connors, I used to play against my very good friend Tony O'Connor through those winter months. We would play for 2shillings and nine times out of 10, I would beat him and he would pay up.

That was until that terrible day when he beat me and I had not a shilling in my pocket as I never expected him to win. Understandably, he was furious with me. He was so happy at beating me for the first time and I had no prize of 2shillings for him.

Very irate, I told Tony to calm down and that I would get him his money. So I told him to hang about for a while and I would be back with it. I went to see the Assistant-Pro Gus Murphy and times were so tough that he did not have 2shillings either.

Tony did not give up that easily. If anything, that made him even more enraged and he insisted on going to my parents. The fun did not stop there. My parents gave me the 2shillings to give to Tony but not without being very cross with me on three counts. Firstly I did not have the money; I should not have been betting and also, I could not afford 2shillings. It also instilled into me the fact that you can never get too cocky. There is nothing certain in life – least of all, golf.

Every single day around this time, I pestered Bob Wallace in the Pro shop. I begged him to help me turn professional. My two brothers Sean and Frank had landed jobs as professionals in golf clubs. The years were passing and I was desperate to follow suit.

Sean was up in Bundoran in County Donegal as Assistant to my uncle Christy. I will never forget the day he left to take up that position. I was so envious and jealous. He gave his bicycle to my brother Frank and his leather gloves to me.

As I mentioned earlier, he was such a rebellious character. But he was a loveable rogue. When he was leaving the school, in front of everybody he gave the teachers the v-sign! We were all amused but again very jealous when he said: "I'm off."

Frank went a very different route. He became Assistant to Bob at Galway Golf Club before becoming Christy Senior's Assistant. Senior was by this stage in the Royal Dublin Golf Club and Frank took over from Sean who landed a really plush job elsewhere.

Sean ended up as the Head Professional in the Cotton Bay Club in Eleuthera Island, The Bahamas. It is one of the most beautiful places I have ever seen in my life. Frank would later land a plum position as a teaching professional in Oslo, Norway.

Meanwhile I was becoming more and more envious. All this only increased my desire and I kept pestering Bob until I had almost given up hope. Then one day out of the blue he called me over and said: "Son, go home and tell your parents that you are leaving for England tomorrow."

I could not wait to tell my parents. If it was my desire, or my decision, I would never have been allowed to go. But coming from Bob, it carried so much more weight especially after what he had done for Frank. He was our judge and jury. In those days you read about great Irish soccer players going over to sign as professional footballers with the likes of Manchester United and Leeds United. This was my ticket to a career in professional golf. Only a teenager, I was so excited.

I was also about to board my first flight. It was a propelled aeroplane. I can vividly recall the propellers on it. As you looked out the window on each side of the plane, you could see the big blades rotating furiously.

On board, I sat with a priest. By some sort of divine intervention, he only happened to be a member of South Shields Golf Club in Newcastle, County Durham where I was to take up my new job. As the plane straightened out on the runway, I could feel no forward motion. I felt a few 'chucks' or sudden vibrations and I thought that it had come to a halt. As I wondered why, I asked the priest: "Have we stopped?"

He chuckled to himself and looking at me with a huge grin on his face, said: "No, that is only the plane travelling up through some thick clouds."

I arrived in Newcastle-Upon-Tyne in April 1966. I was 17 years old and four months short of turning 18. It was an era known as the 'Swinging 60s' and as I arrived, The Beatles were No.1 with almost every single record that they brought out.

There to meet me on my arrival was Kevin Wallace, Bob's son. Kevin had just returned from Sweden to take up a position running not one but three golf clubs in the North of England. I stayed with Kevin and his Swedish wife Barbro. He sat me down and explained the terms and conditions of my new job. I would be paid £3 per week for a seven-day working week.

I would also work between those three golf clubs which were South Shields, Beamish Park which was close to Newcastle city centre and Whitburn which was very near Sunderland. It all sounded great until he mentioned my teaching fee.

My hourly rate would be 7shillings 6pence of which Kevin would take 4shillings from that. This would prove to be very difficult to live on. It would also prove frustrating as when it eventually came down to it, I got very little time to teach. Teaching means that you can get out there and actually play while teaching newcomers and this was really what I wanted. Instead, I found myself in the club shop repairing clubs, putting grips on clubs and selling merchandise.

There was very little in South Shields for me. I also had to walk from where I was staying to a village called Cleadon and then to the golf club. There were many shops and sights along the way but only one particular place interested me. It was a coffee shop. As I passed by, I would spot mince pies and Cornish pasties and they would really whet my appetite. But very often, I did not have the money in my pocket to buy any. So I would purposefully walk past there just to get the lovely smells. I remember it so well.

****

I played small professional tournaments and Pro-Ams around the Newcastle area. During the teaching lessons part of my contract, I got to meet some big celebrities and I was also privileged to give them golf tuition. The hugely popular Welsh singer Tom Jones was given his first golf lesson by me. I also taught Freddie Garrity of well-known 60s band 'Freddie and The Dreamers'. A lot of actors and musicians visited Newcastle to perform in the 'Latino Nite Club' in South Shields.

During my stay in the North of England, the World Cup was also being played. Qualifying matches were played at Sunderland's Roker Park ground. My luck was very much in as I got to meet some of soccer's all-time greats. Sir Booby Moore and the great Portuguese player Eusebio as well as many other soccer stars came to play golf at Whitburn in their off-time. The members were delighted with me as well and for another very good reason.

I used to get complimentary World Cup match tickets and I would pass them on to people. In later life I would actually come to regret one major thing about that World Cup.

On 30th July 1966, I had tickets for the England v West Germany World Cup final at the twin towers of Wembley but I never got there. I ended up giving them to one of the members.

This was caused by my frequent trips to the Casino in South Shields. As I said, the area was a lonely place to be and I would often walk the streets at night just to get out. The casino probably gave me a feeling of a close affinity to the razzamatazz of Salthill. However, I was often broke by the time I came out of there.

With 2/6pence in my pocket (half a crown), I would play roulette and gamble it all on either black or red in an attempt to double my money. After losing on so many occasions, some of the croupier ladies felt pity for me. They would hand me back my 2/6pence under the table! Foolishly, and despite several warnings from them for me to stop, I would continue. When I lost under their ultimatum, they would then keep my money. Many a sad night was spent walking home from there with no money to keep me going for the rest of the week. I would keep walking around as the alternative was to stare at my four walls.

You were left praying on a Monday that you would get a lesson.

In all honesty though, if I sold some golf merchandise the next day, I would hold on to a few pence with the intention of paying it back out of my wages.

Then out of that gloom came a turning point in my golf career. I will never forget the day in 1967 when a quite stunning set of golf clubs arrived for me. It was part of a new contract I had with Leyland and the golf bag in front of my eyes took my breath away. It was a black and gold striped bag in the Leyland company name. The name 'Christy O'Connor' was emblazoned down the side of the golf bag in white script. When I took out the gleaming silver coloured clubs, I also noticed my name on each of the club heads.

Without any doubt, it was the most beautiful thing I had ever received in my life. I was so proud of myself. At that moment I could remember thinking that if only my family and friends could see me now. It was also the moment I had officially turned professional.

My sudden urge was to go out and immediately play a round of golf with them. But being in the shop meant that I could not always do what I wanted and this was always frustrating. I did not want to be in a shop any longer. I was just bursting to go and play. So every available hour that I did manage to get, I played with those clubs. They were amazing. Perhaps it was this newly-acquired feelgood factor but I really did begin to make huge progress using those new clubs.

My time in the North East was made very special by my after-noons of Sunday lunch at Whitburn with the head green-keeper and his wif. The roast beef and Yorkshire Pudding were scrump-tious and oh how I wished for Sundays to come along.

Another lovely person was a man by the name of Harry Evers. He was the Secretary and after the President's Prize he said to me as I stood with Kevin in the shop: "I suppose we will be seeing you tonight at the President's dinner Christy?"

"No Sir, I'm not invited", I replied.

As it was a dress dinner, I counted myself out as I could not af-ford to rent a suit. He said: "Christy I'll give you one of my old suits. Take it home and be there as my guest tonight." I will never forget Kevin Wallace's face when I tried on that over-sized suit.

My brother Albert had by this stage joined me for a stint as Assistant Pro for the summer. But true love soon brought him back home. I missed his company dreadfully. We used to go for a beer or a walk around the area in the evenings. Soon, my stint was also to end.

One of the saddest days in my life was when Kevin said to me in the shop one day: "Christy, things are very quiet so I'm afraid I'm going to have to let you go."

Rubbing salt into my wounds he continued: "There is somebody coming today to buy your clubs."

Tommy Woodhouse later came into the shop. He was a 4-handicapper. After checking the clubs and agreeing a deal with Kevin, my specially designed clubs were his. I was gutted. I shall never forget that day for the rest of my life. With no job and nowhere to go, I went to stay with my Aunt Ann who was my mother's twin sister. She and her husband Mike looked after our family any time we were in London. I am indebted to her and I will always owe her a great deal of gratitude.

It was a gruelling seven-hour bus journey to her in London. All the way there I cried.

CHAPTER 3

Playing The Tour

3rd Hole: 410 yards, Par 4 at Royal Birkdale, 1983.
In my four rounds played at the Open that year, at the third
I made two birdies and two pars

Soon after returning home, my uncle Christy offered me a job as his assistant in Royal Dublin as my brother Sean vacated it to go to the Bahamas. This was a completely new sphere for me because he was now away on tour most of the year leaving me in charge. I was to work for him for almost 18 months. The golf shop was always busy with Americans and so many other visitors coming in to pay their green fees and buy merchandise. I was to learn so much from my uncle — particularly in the line of discipline.

He was very strict and everything had to be done properly and by the rules. In particular he was always fussy about appearance and practising. He expected the exact same from me and he had no bother in telling me in no uncertain terms. Above all, I was now my own boss with the run of things while he was away. In Royal Dublin you got to know the times when it was not busy and I availed of this to play as much golf as I could.

It actually got to the stage where I valued his opinion and his experience so much that I missed him being away so often. When he would return home, the first thing I would strive to do was to have a game of golf with him.

While he was playing in the 1969 British Open at Royal Lytham

& St Annes, which is just across the Irish Sea in Lancashire, his father died. That was my grandfather Michael and it was a sad time for the entire O'Connor family.

Christy went out and shot a magnificent second round of 65 that day. His round was well publicised throughout Ireland in the newspapers as well as on television and radio particularly in light of his father passing away. The BBC covered it as well and a measure of how great that round was can be gauged through the exploits of Gary Player. When the little South African legend won the British Open on that same course five years later, his best round was 68.

My uncle's round put him into second place just one shot behind the great left-handed New Zealander, Bob Charles. But it looked as though he would return to Ireland for his father's funeral so it remained to be seen if he would now pull out of that British Open. All the emotion and inner torment that surrounded his father's death no doubt contributed to his shooting another 74 in the final round. He finished fifth overall with Tony Jacklin winning the title.

When my uncle flew into Dublin on the Sunday, he asked me to drive him to Galway to see his father in repose. But on the way into Galway, he suggested that we stop off in Salthill to have a drink in memory of Michael before going out home to pay our respects. As it was after 11.30pm most pubs at that time were shut and the bar would have been closed for the night. I decided to chance my arm anyway. I knocked on the door of the Oslo Hotel (as it was known then) which was run by the Hanlon family.

One of the Hanlons came out and asked me what I wanted. I told him that my uncle Christy O'Connor was sitting outside in the car and because his father had passed away, he would like to toast his memory with a drink.

With that, he replied:

"I don't believe you as I was watching him playing today on the television in the British Open over in England?"

"Do you want me to go out to the car and bring him over?" I

asked.

When I brought Christy up to the door, the guy said to him:

"Whoever you are, you have some nerve. Get the hell out of here. Christy O'Connor is a much bigger man than you."

We were all set to go away licking our wounds when all of a sudden a customer, who was trying to squeeze his way out the door on the way home, spotted Christy and said:

"My God, how are you Christy? Well done on that great round of 65 in the Open."

With that, we were invited inside and the Hanlon family insisted there would be free drinks on the house!

****

Sometime after the funeral, my brother Frank who had now moved from Norway to Holland suggested that I should come over to him. After thinking about it, I decided to go over to him and it would prove to be another defining moment in my career to that point.

Christy Senior was very upset when I decided to go to Holland. But it was something I knew deep down that I had to do. England had given me a huge degree of responsibility and I met so many wonderful people there and I got to know the place. This would be much the same. It was a chance to see a bit more of Europe and above all, I would have my own independence. With respect to my uncle and my family, if I had of remained in Ireland they would always have had a certain hold over me.

From a very young age, I had always liked the idea of being my own man. Also, my brothers Frank and Sean were experiencing different parts of the world and they were not complaining. It was an invitation I could not refuse as I had nothing to lose in going over.

Frank was the Club Professional at the Kennemer Golf Club in Zandvoort. Situated in the North of Holland very close to Amsterdam and Haarlem, the course has been re-designed very well from the original state it was in shortly after World War II. Over 100 German war bunkers as well as anti tank walls were constructed on the land and they all had to be cleared for the construction of a new golf course. For historical purposes, some of them still remain there.

The course reminded me very much of back home in Ireland. Even though it is a mile away from the North Sea, it is classified as a links course. The telltale signs are there for all to see. It is a very rugged and hilly course with the small hills probably old and ancient sand dunes reclaimed from the sea. There are gorse bushes and the long grass in the rough would not look out of place on some of the links courses in Ireland and England. As Frank was teaching every day on the course, I had very little to do. With what little savings I had brought with me, I soon found that I was running out of money. That is when Frank came to my rescue again. He had a meeting with the members and the Committee and they agreed that I could practise and play as much as I wanted. This was music to my ears. For the first time in my life I could play as much golf as I wanted when I wanted.

Then one day a man named Piet Hein Streutgers offered me enough money to live on if I would look after and teach his son Peter. I was also asked to allow him and some of his young golfing friends to tag along with me during my round. This was an unbelievable offer. He paid me the equivalent of £40 per week in Dutch Guilders. Not only was this more than enough for me to live on it also meant that I could improve my own game by paying to enter golf events.

Soon after this, I finished third in the Dutch Close Championships but there was a bit of a sting in the tail for me. I had to forfeit the prize-money I won as I was an 'Unaffiliated' player. But I knew from that experience that I had what it took to play and win on tour.

****

One of the biggest shocks of my life also befell me when I was in Holland. Out of the blue one day, the Secretary asked if he could speak to me for a few minutes. I knew from his face that something bad had happened.

Initially I hoped that I had not done something wrong. But then all I could think about was my family back home and I prayed nothing had happened. Little did I know then that it actually concerned my brother Frank. The Secretary informed me that he had been in an accident. My heart was in my mouth. This hit me like the thud of an electric shock and I could hear my heart beating rapidly. I prayed to God that he was not going to say that it had been a tragic accident.

Frank had been knocked down by a motorbike which was driven by a son of the club professional. This was very hard news to take but when I heard it was a motorbike and not a car, I thought that perhaps the injuries were not too severe. But when I was brought to the local hospital, I could not have been more wrong. I was reduced to tears when I saw Frank in front of me. In fact, the injuries sustained by both the motorcyclist and Frank were so bad, I could not tell who was who. Frank's face had swollen up very badly due to the extent of the bad bruising and there was also blood everywhere from deep gashes. It would take him some time to be able to move in his bed without feeling extreme pain from all the bruising on his body.

It was a very traumatic and trying time for us and one which will live with me to the end of my days. Both men were on trolleys and it was a very gruesome sight to witness. Someone as young as I was, at that time, should never be in a position to see such things. Furthermore, it was made worse because there was nobody that I could turn to for help and advice. I wanted to reach out to my mum and dad or even to another family member like Sean or Albert but there was nobody to share my anxiety and grief with.

Poor Frank was also in a dreadful state and I felt so helpless and lost in a foreign hospital. But I had to pull myself together for his sake and for my parents, whom I rang each day with an update. Thankfully, Frank made a full recovery in the end. I say 'full' but that is not entirely true and I will get on to that in a moment. He was in the hospital and then a convalescing home for three months and during that period I took over his position in the golf club.

When he had recovered fully, and he was up and about again, he returned to the club. But one day he was called into a meeting and he was told by the club authorities that he would be best advised not to pursue damages through the Dutch legal system. I do not know for sure if it was Frank's intention to do so. However, it is commonplace for most people involved in such accidents to sue for compensation and/or damages. What I do know is that he suffers great pain from his injuries right up to the present day.

After almost two years in Holland I returned to Dublin. A friend of mine named Michael Murphy told me one day that there was an opening in Carlow Golf Club for a club professional. He asked me if I would be interested. I said to him:

"I would Michael but where is Carlow?"

If I did not know where Carlow was back then, and I truly did not, then this beautiful place would become hugely influential in my life. Among many other things, I would eventually end up meeting my future wife there. I also have a home in Carlow to this day.

To my utter delight, Carlow accepted me as their club professional. A most wonderful golf course, it is without doubt the place where my golf finally got the chance to mature and blossom. They say that hard work reaps rewards and the old saying goes, 'you only get out of it, what you put into it'. This was so true regarding Carlow. The hard work ethic which I was brought up on was really put into practise and full swing there.

I needed a little push and a helping hand to get started though and it arrived in a most unlikely way. Not too long after arriving in Carlow, and totally out of the blue, I fell in love with a beautiful local girl. She was a very striking blonde and her name was

Ann O'Boyle. Her father was well known in the town as he was an Army Officer who had served with the Irish Peacekeeping division of the United Nations in The Congo. Rather than have a detrimental affect on my game, Ann helped my game enormously. For six years, I played and practised for almost 10 hours a day on so many days a week. She was as regimental and disciplined as her father in that regard.

Up until this point, my life and my game had been so unsettled. I did not know where I was going next. One minute I was in England and the next minute I was in Dublin and then onto Holland. It could have kept going like that until everything fell into place in Carlow. Ann was a nurse in the local hospital. She worked until 6pm in the evening. If I was trying desperately to become dedicated to my golf, then I had just found myself a dedicated partner and caddy. After her work she made her way out to me on the course. Whether I was putting balls, chipping balls or driving, Ann was there for me. Not looking to go to a pub, a café or to see a matinee, she would very often remain out there with me until 10pm. I will give you a very good example of the kind of thing I am talking about.

Before the last round of the British Open, you may see the BBC in their 'live' television coverage, send a reporter to 'the range'. In the background, you can see a whole host of professional golfers all lined up and striking maybe 30 or 40 golf balls. It can help you so much if there is someone at the end of those shots — especially the shots that go astray into the rough. So I would tell Ann to go down to a given point on the course between say 200-300 yards. Then I would practise my shots by striking them down towards her. It would be her job to round them all up. In comparison to modern times, we could not afford to lose too many golf balls back then as they were expensive enough. Ann was fantastic for me.

My brother Eugene joined me in Carlow as my assistant in 1970. He was also a great help to me. His arrival meant that I could play tournaments at home and abroad safe in the knowledge that there was someone in charge of things back home in the club. Every-thing was fitting into place. Eugene's arrival was crucial. In 1972, the modern European Tour officially began. It was lucky that I had everything in order because from 1972 onwards, I would cre-ate a record that would be the envy of many.

Back in those days and unlike today when the Tour can begin in December and January — the season began with the US Masters at Augusta on April 6th in the States. This was followed by the start of our Tour a week later on April 12th — the Spanish Open in Girona.

The following week, Jimmy Kinsella won the Madrid Open beating Jose Maria Canizares into second. A great win for Jimmy and many years later Jose Maria would become a good friend and team-mate of mine in the 1989 Ryder Cup team. Three Balleste-ros brothers were also in that field — Manuel, Vincente and Bal-domero. A younger Ballesteros by the name of Severiano would come along and dominate the game a few years later. Seve and I had some craic but that is another story for later on.

My first big event that year came a month later when I travelled to the South Coast for the Penfold Tournament in Bournemouth. This was an event run by a well known business tycoon named Dick Penfold who also sponsored various tennis events.

How ironic that Peter Oosterhuis landed himself in hot water before the event even began. Peter and I would end up right in the thick of things at the business end of the tournament. He was fined £25 for playing more than one ball in practise for the event. Peter had been warned along with Tony Jacklin for a similar of-fence at the Piccadilly Medal event a fortnight previously. Peter would later appeal the fine but his 30-minute hearing failed.

I could not have wished for a better start. I hit the ground run-ning when I opened up with a great three-under-par round of 68. Anything under 70 on the European Tour back then was a very good score. It is hard to believe now but it gave you a great chance of winning. But I almost ruined my big chance of success when I hit a bad round of three-over, 74 the next day. However, a good level par score in the penultimate round had me on top of the scoreboard going into the final day's play.

What happened next has never been fully investigated. I was still in front by two shots when I teed off at the Par 5 13th hole. I hooked my second shot to the left of the green and into a small forest very close to a road running alongside. The ball went into an area of pine trees with the ground covered in pine needles. Crowds swarmed around searching for it. I was not alarmed as this is a common enough occurrence in golf and at any moment someone would soon shout that it had been found. But the search went on and on until my allocated time for looking for a lost ball was almost up. I was baffled and it was a real mystery to me as I hit what seemed like a good shot. Even though it went slightly left, this was a Par 5 with plenty of margin for error.

I did not know what to do. Paddy McGuirk and Christy Senior as well as others were helping me look for my ball. They had come out to support me and follow me in my final round as they knew I was in with a great chance of winning my first title. Rules state that you have five minutes in which to find your ball and play your shot. As we were trudging around for a good few minutes looking for it, Christy Senior suggested that I better go back and play another ball. A little voice in my head was yearning for me to call the referee. My mind was in a quandary. Time was almost up so, a little reluctantly, I agreed with Senior but I was very disgruntled going back to play again.

After hitting my spare ball on the green I got down in two putts for a bogey six. Peter Oosterhuis playing through our group, made an eagle to go a shot ahead of me. My two shot lead was gone and to add salt to my wounds I found out why my ball was 'lost'. Several spectators approached me just after bogeying the hole and said that they had seen a young boy riding a bicycle out on the road nearby. He jumped off his bike, grabbed my ball and made off with it!

At that time Crawley Boovey was the referee. But because these guys were so fussy and stiff-upper-lipped, as well as having to be brought out of their way to solve a problem, he could quite possibly have disqualified me by finding some other rule infringement. For instance if I found out about the boy stealing my ball and I delayed longer than the five minutes in order to find the ref, he could have said that there was no firm evidence of a boy stealing my ball and then disqualified me. In those days there was just the one Rules Official and he had enough on his plate and had so much to deal with. You did not mess with these guys as the fining of Oosterhuis before the tournament illustrated.

I fought back to tie the lead by birdying the 15th. At the 18th hole we were still tied so we had to go to a Play-Off to determine the winner. Typically, and to compound my misfortune, Peter birdied the first hole in the Play-Off to beat me and win the event.

All hell broke loose afterwards. I saw one paper the next day talking about 'the kid who stole the golf ball' but there were also rumours and counter-rumours. Some even asked where the referee was but the Bournemouth Echo paid generous tribute to me with the headline:

'LOST THE GAME BUT WON CROWD'S HEART'

Having slept on it, the newspapers only compounded the agony I felt next day. However the Bournemouth newspaper report revealed that I might have received a free drop and that I was very unlucky.

The following paragraphs made me feel a whole lot better: 'Young Christy O'Connor won the hearts of the spectators following a tragic final round incident in the Penfold golf tournament at Queens Park. Christy was forced to declare his ball lost at the 13th and he took a six including one penalty stroke.

The young Irishman had the added torment of watching Oosterhuis hole an eagle putt to take the lead. Moments later O'Connor learned that his ball had in fact been stolen by a small boy who scampered away. Had this been known earlier Christy could have had a 'free drop'. This undoubtedly cost him the tournament but O'Connor showed he possessed a fine temperament under extreme pressure and will no doubt be heard of again.'

All said and done, I had to be happy with second place and a cheque for £1,000. That was huge money back then. It was also no disgrace to lose to Peter. He ended up as the leading Money Winner that year. But whenever we meet, we laugh about that incident.

****

Two weeks later I finished 14th in the John Player Trophy played at Bognor Regis thanks to a third round of 69 which earned me around £150. The following week, another 69 in the last round gave me a finishing position of 25th in the Martini International and £100. Despite another sub-70 round of 67 in the French Open in July, the rest of 1972 turned sour after getting that taste for victory in Bournemouth. I watched my uncle win the Carroll's International at Woodbrook because I missed the cut with rounds of 78, 75.

More missed cuts followed at the Scottish Open in Carnoustie; the Swiss Open and the WD & HO Wills in Edinburgh. What was most disappointing for me was that since the excellent 67 in France, I would not hit another sub-70 round in six remaining events. Nevertheless, on the all important money scale, I did earn £500 from three of the last four events of the 1972 season by finishing inside the top 40 in all of them.

Along with a certain Sam Torrance, I finished joint 30th in the Benson & Hedges at Fulford in York. Back on my old stomping ground of Newcastle in the North of England, I also finished 38th in the Dunlop Masters. If I thought these events were signalling a return to form, then I could not have been more wrong. Worse was to follow in the 1973 season.

The Tour teed off a week earlier in '73 with the Madrid Open at the end of March. Jimmy Kinsella made a valiant attempt to defend his title from the previous year. A joint best of the week 67 gave him fourth.

Jimmy and I went on to contest the final of the Irish Matchplay in Kilkenny later that year, which I won. On the way to the final I beat David Jones from Northern Ireland, John O'Leary and Peter Townsend. When I received my £1,000 cheque, a very funny thing happened.

Some of my suppliers including Slazenger, Dunlop, Wilson and Leyland were all lined up waiting for me. Instead of paying them their dues from the shop in Carlow, I was using the money taken in for their sold goods to put towards my own Tour expenses. Now they were all lined up and looking for their rightful cut of my prize-money.

Another funny incident happened regarding my Bank Manager in Carlow. He was constantly ringing me to tell me that my account was in the red. As I got off to a good start in my professional career finishing second in the Penfold and then winning smaller events like the Irish Matchplay, he called me in one day. He said: "Christy, we have a situation here."

"I know, I know but I'll pay off those debts when I start winning", I told him.

"No, unusually you are £1,000 in the black!"

I could not believe it. When my suppliers were queuing up for me, I thought they had cleaned me out. The very first thing I did after that meeting was to go back to the club shop, close it and bring my brother and assistant Eugene out on the town.

We went into Hanley's Menswear in Carlow where I purchased a much needed overcoat for him. Then we went on a monumental piss-up around the whole county. All I can say is that it was a good job the drink driving laws were not as enforced back then as now. I had a little Fiat car at the time. It was in an awful state from travelling around England — and to the British Open which I will talk about in another chapter. So I decided to buy a new car.

Michael Reidy, a friend of mine, showed me a beautiful blue Opel Record and I fell in love with it at first sight. I could not wait to show it to my girlfriend Ann and we spent many a day and night hobnobbing around the Carlow countryside in it. However, it cost £1,500 and that was way over my budget. Having slept on it and digested the situation a few days later, a horrible realisation dawned on me. How was I going to pay Michael Reidy?

While this worry was going through my head, I received a call one day from Tony Gray. He was an official on the European Tour and he was one of life's true gentlemen. He asked if I would like to come over and play in a Pro-Am. I thought about it and accepted. Another great friend of mine, John Morrissey, said it was ok to stay with him while I was over there. Anytime I was playing near London, he would always insist on Ann and I staying in his very popular pub in Twickenham, 'The Winning Post'. He was a beautiful and very generous person.

So I decided to repay him somewhat. I invited him to caddy for me in the Pro-Am. He accepted and we drove to the event in Walton Heath. It turned out to be a fantastic day as I won. No prizes for guessing how much I won - £1,500! Tony Gray was a godsend.

I could now afford to pay off that debt on the Opel car in full which I did. Before that, we enjoyed the most fantastic celebration party in his pub. It was always a popular establishment anyway with rugby crowds but on this occasion it was thronging.

Back on the main Tour however, things were not going so well. My season kicked off in 1973 at the Spanish Open in La Manga but it was to be a very poor start. I finished +16 but it was great to see Paddy McGuirk (he of McGuirk's Golf Shop fame) finish 12th. It was then off to the Italian Open in Rome the following week but again I had a few days to forget. I finished +10 with rounds of 73, 81. My appetite was whetted with a return to Bournemouth for the Penfold. But things dried up with another +10 finish of 80, 72.

So it went on and on right to the end of the season. My game on Tour was in turmoil and I could not quite put my finger on what was happening. My new career on the new European Tour had started brightly but now there was a dark shadow looming over me.

I only hit one sub-70 round all season and that was a 68 in the German Open in Dusseldorf. What made things worse was the fact that fellow Irish golfers were enjoying the fruits of their labours and playing great golf. Eddie Polland won that Penfold event; Paddy McGuirk won the Carroll's at Woodbrook by two shots from Christy Senior and my uncle was also very consistent by acquiring so many Top-10 and Top-20 finishes. Therein lay the key perhaps.

Because I had hit the ground running the previous year, I was maybe expecting everything to come easily. I had to remind myself that this was my uncle's 22nd season on the Tour whereas I was only in my sixth and in the second of the new tour format.

I could only hope that things would get better for the 1974 season and what better way to prepare for it than a bit of African sun and safari.

CHAPTER 4

The African Rebels

4th Hole: Par 4, Royal County Down at Senior British Open 2000.
The turning point in my tussle with John Bland as I hit 4-iron to 15ft
for birdie

In stark contrast to exotic places like Asia, Dubai and Qatar where professional golfers like to ply their trade today, Africa was a hugely popular destination for us in the 60s and 70s.

As a precursor to the main European Tour, many top players ventured to Africa after Christmas - not primarily to get a nice tan or to warm-up ahead of the main tour - but to try and make money to put towards their season's golfing overheads.

Tournaments in Africa presented fairly good opportunities of winning some decent prize-money. Any monies gained would very much help towards the exorbitant costs of hotel and travel expenses through the long year on tour in Europe.

Of course with the temperate climate of Europe and its wet and windy weather, there is also no doubt that many golfers embraced Africa as a holiday. Some would bring along the wife and kids knowing they would be apart from their family for most of the season.

Visiting Africa was the fulfilment of a lifetime's ambition for me as it is for most people. Growing up on a farm and close to the sea, I was always close to wildlife and the outdoors and so this was a dream come true.

During my childhood I had often wondered about Africa as from time to time I watched wildlife programmes on television. Back then we also watched the adventures of 'Tarzan' (and Jane) in the jungle and 'Elsa' the lion in that great series 'Born Free'. But the film 'Zulu' starring Michael Caine also showed a very violent side of the so-called 'dark continent'. I would experience both the dangers and delights first hand.

In 1974 I visited and fell in love with Africa and thus began a 20-year love affair. Kenya, Zambia and Nigeria were the countries I played in. I am not being flippant in saying that Nigeria was like something out of Zulu. It was extremely dangerous and some of the gory things I saw there were akin to medieval times and not part of modern society.

One night myself, Liam Higgins and Eamonn Darcy were late returning from a day out shopping for souvenirs to bring home. We were aware that at the time there was an 8pm curfew because of so much unrest in the country. All the golfers stayed with the locals as you did not dare stay in hotels. In a country with such strife, hotels were very often targeted by rebels or government forces and many white people were known to have been abducted.

Suddenly, in the dusk we saw the lights of a vehicle speeding towards us. Guessing that it could have been an army truck carrying rebels or soldiers, we dived into a ditch which might well have been snake infested. We just did not have any time to think about that.

We lay there on top of each other in that filthy ravine and we heard the engine getting nearer and nearer. It then slowed down and our hearts were in our mouths. I remember we all looked at each other and we thought they had seen us when it stopped beside us.

What made things even more worrying was that in the preceding days, one of the golfers had told us all about a 'shoot to kill' policy that he read in the local papers. We did not move a muscle. In any case we could not as we were frozen to the spot.

From their voices we knew that they were indeed armed combatants so we had made the right decision to dive for our lives. I honestly thought when they pulled up next to us that we were dead and gone or that we would have been thrown into the back of the truck.

Luckily, they pulled out of there a couple of minutes later. The relief was enormous. In a country with such unrest and where we had broken a curfew, the consequences could have been serious. Sprinting the last few hundred yards to where we were staying with our hosts, we were even more relieved that we made it indoors. When we told the locals what had happened they were shocked and frightened.

I suppose they also felt unwarranted attention might have been brought upon them. The situation became even worse. Driving from Lagos the capital, to Port Harcourt, we lost count of the number of bodies we saw along the sides of the road.

It was desperately sad to see. Words cannot really adequately describe your feelings. At those times, we often wondered what the hell we were doing there. It was like a scene from 'Apocalypse Now'.

We also wondered why the bodies were just left there to rot. Our driver told us that it is a tradition that only a family member can touch or remove a body. Families were probably scared to go to the scene or were unaware that a loved one was missing. It was so sad.

Zambia was totally different and I had a wonderful time there. I say it was different but I suppose when you have a leader in power for so long, it only takes a spark to ignite or flare up a serious disturbance or even a revolt.

President Kenneth Kaunda was in power when I arrived in the country in 1974. In actual fact, he had come to power in 1964 and he would rule until 1991. To my mind he was a smashing character. He was charming and I had the privilege of meeting him twice.

That year was actually very important in Zambian history. It was the year they officially adopted a Constitution. The country also played in the Africa Cup of Nations which was staged in Egypt.

Their soccer team are known as the 'Copper Bullets'. That had nothing to do with violence or war. They were so named because of the history of copper mining in the country.

Unfortunately they failed to fire in that final in Cairo losing to the Zaire Leopards. They also lost in the 1994 final but it was good to see them beat the Ivory Coast on penalties to win the cup in 2012. I would say the celebrations over there were mighty.

I was involved in my very own 'penalty shootout' in Zambia '74. After finishing on a score of 282 (-10) at the Zambian Open in the mining town of Mufulira, I found that I had finished in a three-way tie with Eddie Polland and Englishman, Mike Ingham.

Again I had to go into a Play-Off which I was delighted to nail at the very first hole. I was the only one of us to birdie the hole so the title was mine. It was an incredible feeling and it more than made up for losing my first final on the European Tour in a Play-Off.

Winning outside of Ireland was so sweet particularly since there were so many good players in that field. A lot of them were playing in Europe regularly. Beating the likes of Eddie Polland also gave me great inner confidence that I could finally win on the tour. I became the first Irish winner and the only Irish winner until James Loughnane won it 23 years later when the event was part of 'The Sunshine Tour'. Loughnane would go on to win it for a second time in 2000.

There were huge celebrations especially since the first prize was a very impressive £5,000! Money like that was precisely why so many players took time out to play in Africa. A smiling President Kaunda also presented me with the winner's trophy.

The Guinness fairly flowed that night I can tell you. Yes there was always plenty of beer and spirits on hand. You name the brand and we had it. Players used to bring out a supply and it was not unknown for a quantity of booze to be flown out for various celebrations.

Take St Patrick's Day for instance. The Zambian Open usually co-incided with the 17th March and even if one particular year did not fall on that date, we would celebrate it anyway. Zambia, or Northern Rhodesia as it was known to some of the golfers before 1964, will always be special to me because of my first win away from home. But it is such a beautiful scenic country as well. However, the memories are so many and varied.

We endured it all. We had the happy times, turbulent times and sad times. Probably the happiest memory of all, quite apart from my win, was being in the company of the great Harry McQuillan and his wife Nelly. Harry would be known to many Irish people from all golfing backgrounds. He was a pure gent. Eamonn Darcy and I stayed with Harry and his wife as their guests. Without doubt he was one of the greatest golfers I have ever seen in my life.

His greatness had so much to do with his very unorthodox style. A +5 handicapper, he was one of those extremely rare golfers who played with his left hand gripping the shaft below his right hand. In the trade we call it 'cack-handed'.

In other words he was the complete opposite of the vast majority of golfers regarding the way he gripped the club. This belied his immense talent. He was such a great golfer that my uncle brought him over to play in the British Open. He thought Harry could win it.

But there were sad times in Zambia too. In 1976 we all mourned the death of British golfer David Moore. His body was found in the courtyard of Mufulira General Hospital with a gunshot wound. He was only 21 and nobody knew exactly what had happened.

This beautiful country was therefore not at all immune from violent times of its own and I was to witness and hear about some more tragic incidents as well. The most common tragedies were almost always the result of robberies or break-ins. Our night-watchmen in Mufulira were Zambians who used bow and arrows as their weapons. I remember one particular afternoon, after playing one of our rounds, some of these security guys allowed us to practise with their bow and arrows.

There were a couple of big thick trees nearby so we practised for almost two hours. We had great fun shooting the arrows into the big tree trunks. Like everything else in life, some of us were dab hands at it while others were pretty awful. Next morning, one of the golfers opened his window to let in some air when he spotted a gruesome sight just outside in the grounds. The body of a black man was lying on the ground with an arrow protruding from his chest.

It transpired that he had been killed by a night-watchman as he was fleeing from an attempted robbery. We also found out that many robbers coated their entire bodies in oil so that they could not be caught because they would be too 'slippery' to catch.

Perhaps that is the reason why this poor man was killed. If there is one thing that Africans detest it is thieves. In many African countries, people will run together and chase a thief for miles. It is not uncommon for thieves to be beaten to death when they are caught.

All golfers were constantly reminded about robberies on trips to Africa. We were told to put all our valuables in a hotel safe. If there was no safe, the best place used for hiding one's personal possessions was up the chimney.

Over the years, Paddy McGuirk reminded us all on more than one occasion about the time he was robbed in his room while asleep! He woke up to see the shocking sight of the iron bars outside his room window bent wide enough apart for a body to squeeze through. When he looked around his room he found that clothing and other items had been stolen from him. In such circumstances possessions do not really matter. He later acknowledged that it was a blessing he did not wake while the thief was in his room.

Even when things seemed quite normal and totally relaxed the whole situation could change in an instant without any warning. Just such a shocking incident happened one day when I was with Ian Woosnam. We both feared for our lives.

We were driving from Zambia's third largest city Ndola to the capital Lusaka. In hindsight it was a mistake for us to be out driving on the open roads. The roads were in an awful state and we should have employed someone with local knowledge to drive us. Arriving at a checkpoint we were ordered out of the car by soldiers. They spoke in English and they asked us to step off the road into tall bull grass. To where they were pointing in the grass we could see a furrow or pathway cut through it.

My heart was beating furiously as there were a lot of mysterious abductions around this time. It was only then that I became aware of flashes travelling across my mind from newspapers and from what other golfers and locals had told us.

A guy by the name of Ray Uyazi who was a flight engineer with Zambia Airways had 'died in a tragic accident' on the Great East Road; a Lusaka Governor 'died tragically on the Kafue Road'; a Lusaka Policeman also 'died tragically on the Kafue Road'.

Perhaps the most chilling, in the predicament that we now found ourselves in, was the case of a local rock icon. He was shot dead in the bushes of Solwezi by armed forces. I was frozen with fear and then unbelievably, Woosie lost his temper with them. I could not believe it. At the best of times he looks and acts like Hollywood tough guy Joe Pesci and suddenly he *was* Joe Pesci! I feared for our lives and there he was arguing with them for tossing our luggage and bags out on the road and searching the contents.

Then came a brainwave and I do not know who thought of it first but it seemed to make matters worse. We told them that we were golfers and guests of President Kaunda and that only served to make them more aggressive. Later we would find out that not all of Kaunda's men were loyal to him. All of a sudden in the distance a car came over the brow of a hill at great speed. The soldiers turned around and move slowly towards it as if to wave down this car as well.

As they did, we gathered up our bags, threw them into the car and high tailed it out of there without ever looking back. It was yet another heart-stopping moment on an African road and just when I thought it would never happen again, it did.

Another year in Lusaka I was staying with Eamonn Darcy on a street which was full of Embassies. We were coming back to our lodgings from the golf club when we turned into the wrong driveway. The houses all looked very similar but when we turned in to this particular residence, men with machine guns raced over to our car doors and pointed their weapons in our faces. Darcy and I put our hands up and begged them not to shoot. I do not know what it was that made me certain they were going to pull those triggers. Perhaps it was the way they were jerking them rather violently at us.

By this stage we were screaming at them and begging them not to shoot. We told them we were staying next door as we were here to play a golf tournament. Like security men with their loud tannoy-like walkie-talkies, they made some calls and then waved us on.

Huge relief yet again but it must be said that these sad and scary incidents in Zambia were well out-numbered by all the great times we had there. A fitting end to my recollections on Zambia concerns the charming President Kaunda.

He was a fantastic host and each year we arrived, he would throw a huge party at his Presidential Palace. On his private golf course, he would then ask us professional golfers to play golf with his staff and his friends. There was a sting in the tail though. When the scores were calculated at the end of the day, we would always find that they would scribble down a few shots less in favour of themselves. In other words, we never won.

It mattered not one bit because the party had to be seen to be believed. The sound of African music abounded throughout the palace. There was wine, beer and spirits from across the globe while full-bodied deer and wild boar turned on roasting spits.

Kenya was a completely different experience with no hint of trouble at any time I was there. How strange it was then, that after two decades of my experiences of Africa, huge trouble flared up in Kenya which threatened to spill over into all-out war.

Thankfully I was not there because I never want anything to take from my memories of Kenya. It was like a surreal experience in Heaven. When I think back to it now I feel a lump in my throat because I am so glad that my son Darren got to share and enjoy it all.

The Masai Mara National Reserve and Wildlife Park is something everybody should see. It is truly awesome and it is not just about the wild animals and birds. One thing I marvelled at was the beautiful flowers which blossomed in such sweltering heat.

My hosts for many years in Kenya were a beautiful couple — Mr & Mrs Roberts. They were employed by Peugeot to look after many golf professionals. Tommy Halpin and I were the two lucky golfers to enjoy their hospitality on many occasions. What I really loved about that couple was that there was no airs and graces about them. They did not care what they said to you and they treated you just like they would their own children. They even gave out to me like parents scolding their children.

In 1990 when I made my entry for the Kenya Open, a very good friend of mine asked me to take in an extra week. He suggested I take my wife Ann, our daughter Ann and my two sons Darren and Nigel so that we could all go on Safari.

It turned out to be the week's holiday of a lifetime. We all stayed in a well known lodge called 'Noah's Ark'. It was very impressive with all the windows three inches thick and for very good reason.

At night you were able to view all the various animals coming to a watering hole from behind the safety of those windows. It was common through the night to hear a bell sounding. This signified to anyone interested, that there was activity at the waterhole.

On another occasion our driver John Ladedi drove us to the world famous Lake Nakuru. There we witnessed the most wonderful sight of flamingos in their thousands as they fed on the salt water lake. Looking back, I am so glad we took Darren and the kids along.

Just prior to our leaving Kenya, we got to see some more of that beautiful country. We were given a private flight where we could view the splendour of the Kenyan bush from the air.

When we were coming back in to land the pilot had to swoop the plane down in order to startle the herds of elephant and particularly the buffalo. This had to be done in order to get them off the runway and clear our path for landing.

During our last couple of nights we stayed in camp along the river.

When the lights went out you could see the Hippos come out of the water. I enjoyed it all immensely but not so my wife Ann regarding the Hippos. They were massive creatures. They were so heavy that you could feel the pounding vibrations from their feet and their loud cries echoed everywhere. Ann had a hold of me right through the night and she even said a prayer or two to St Anthony.

I returned to Kenya again some years later. Before jetting home and instead of going on safari, I took in a spot of fishing with an old friend of mine and an ex-Tour player, Gary Cullen.

Gary was an Englishman and today he runs a hotel in Malawi. These were no ordinary fishing trips. We went out on a large boat to fish and I was so thrilled to catch a whopping Marlin weighing 700lb!

It took me almost two hours to reel him in and I was strapped to my seat on the side of the boat. Thank goodness I golfed in defence of my title before this as I could not move my arms for two days after that fishing trip.

To celebrate the catch a huge party was thrown. Chefs went around with trays holding slivers of swordfish marinated with the giant marlin I had caught. It went on into the early hours and there were some sore heads next day. Then a near tragedy unfolded.

As I had never experienced 'snorkelling' before, I decided to try it by going out on a special motorboat with Gary and his wife. This boat had a glass bottom in it where you could see all sorts of exotic fish swimming below you in such beautiful hues and colours.

Gary was a very good swimmer and fully trained at snorkelling. I think he expected me to be just as good but I had never done this sort of thing before. Then we became separated and I could not see them anywhere. Soon I began to panic in the water. Not knowing what to do, I started to kick the flippers I was wearing in a sideways 'in and out' sort of motion. For those who know how to do it, I was so obviously doing it wrong.

My head started to go under and I used as much energy as I could to keep popping my head back up over the surface. I tried to get a glimpse of the boat or to see if Gary and his wife were anywhere around it but I was alone.

Using up so much energy I began to weaken. I could feel my legs become heavy and things were looking very bleak. I honestly thought that I was going to die. Then I said some prayers and all of a sudden I saw the boat about 50 yards in front of me.

I summoned up one gargantuan last effort and slowly but surely I reached it. It seemed like it took me forever to climb in and when I did manage to get on board, I collapsed through total exhaustion.

When Gary and his wife returned, they were shocked at what I told them. In fairness, they thought I was well able to handle the sea. Thinking that I was fine fending for myself they let me off to explore as they swam away under water for huge distances.

That is why I could not spot them anywhere. They used some technique whereby they chewed on the mouthpiece of the snorkel pipe. This blocked any water from coming in and they could dive and swim great distances. They thought I had done the same. News spread and later the local press were swarming around the hotel like a plague of mosquitoes searching for a story. They got it. I saw one sensational headline which read:

'IRISH GOLFER ALMOST DROWNS'.

As beautiful as it was, there was never a dull moment in Africa. There was always something or someone around the next bend. When I returned home after the Zambian Open win, my one burning hope was that my first win in Europe was just around the corner.

CHAPTER 5

Open'ing My Account

5th Hole: 568 yards, Par 5 at St Andrews 2000.
In the four rounds I played in my last British Open, at five
I made three birdies and par

My 1974 Zambia Open win suddenly catapulted me into the limelight and propelled me right up the golf charts. Little did I know then what lay in store for me but suffice it to say that my win in Mufulira led to all sorts of doors opening for me.

No matter what sport a team or competitor plays, a winner exudes tremendous confidence. If you look back at results in all sports the evidence is there to show this. In golf, soccer, tennis, rugby or whatever, when a win is achieved the form is most always continued.

When I arrived back to play the 1974 European Tour after my successful winter in Africa, I was buzzing. I was proud to tee off knowing that I was a winner at last. I cannot emphasise enough the huge importance around that feeling and the sense of higher status. The Portuguese Open in Estoril outside Lisbon was where I made my seasonal bow in early April. I began with what looked on paper to be an impressive first round 68 but back then the course played Par 69 so I was -1 under. Nevertheless it was a promising start.

Next day I shot a disastrous +6 round of 75. With the way the event was to unfold, I felt that bad round cost me a chance of winning as my game showed up superbly. I finished strongly with rounds of 68, 67 to finish in the top 10 and a cheque for £800.

Whereas I could hardly hit a sub-70 round during the whole of the previous year, I was now peppering the flag and hitting rounds in the 60s. Without winning, my good form and my game held firm and it stood up right through until the end of the season. Later when I would evaluate that year, the statistics showed that I only finished out of the money in three or four events. The importance of this can never be underestimated when you are seeking invites to major tournaments or trying to obtain Ryder Cup points.

I very much hoped to continue my rich vein of form into 1975 but it got off to what can only be described as a very embarrassing start. I still cringe and blush when I think back about it now. Our season teed off in Portugal, the same as the previous year. This time we played the Portuguese Open in Penina the first week in April and I was staying with my late and great buddy, Andy Murphy. The morning after I had arrived, I got a phone call at 8am from someone claiming to be Jimmy Bruen. Jimmy was an Irish amateur golfer of some renown and a great player.

I had heard so much about him but I had never met him so I said: "Whoever you are ringing me at this hour of the morning, feck off and don't ring again. Jimmy Bruen has been dead for a good few years now."

I slammed the receiver down but I was soon in for an almighty shock.

Andy asked me who I had been angry with on the phone so I replied: "Oh some prankster saying that he was Jimmy Bruen but I told him to feck off because he had a cheek to ring me with poor Jimmy dead and gone."

Andy then informed me that Jimmy was not dead. Furthermore, he was here at the Portuguese Open as a guest of his very good friend Henry Cotton - the legendary Sir Henry Thomas Cotton. Henry Cotton won three British Opens and was placed in its top 10 a further 17 times. In one of those winning Opens he shot 65 which led to the golf manufacturer Dunlop naming a golf ball after him – the Dunlop 65.

I was mortified. I did not know what to do. It was one of those moments when your entire body is hit with a gigantic thud of embarrassment and you can feel the shock take over you. I got myself spruced up quickly and I went off to the course to find Jimmy Bruen.

When I tracked him down I grovelled so much that I did everything bar kneeling down in front of him to beg for his forgiveness. He was well and truly alive and thank God for that because he turned out to be one of the nicest people I have ever met in my life. We ended up playing together in the Pro-Am before the event and although we did not win, we had great fun that day. Jimmy was a monster hitter. In fact when he was only 18 years old he was the longest hitter in Europe.

****

A funny thing happened that year after I had won the Irish Dunlop Masters at The Hermitage for the second time. I sank my winning putt on the 18th and my playing partner Jimmy Martin, who played in the World Cup and Ryder Cup, congratulated me. When we were walking off the last green to the recorders hut, Tom Cryan, who was a very well known sports writer at that time, came over to me and said:

"How did you get on 'Tommy'?"

Now Tom Cryan was a true gentleman so I knew he was not up to any prank but I still wondered why he called me Tommy. Then I realised he had mistaken me for Tommy Halpin so I replied:

"Ah I'm afraid I didn't do very well Mr Cryan".

Journalists are usually on top of things and have their facts right. I could not get over this major slip up from Tom – and this after I had just won the event. I chuckled to myself all the way back to the changing room.

Now that I think of it, an even funnier thing happened on my way to play the Martini International in Westward Ho! in Devon. My wife and I went over a week before the event in early June to stay with John Morrissey and his wife Bridie. On the Sunday before the Martini teed off later in the week, Bridie asked us if we would like to go to mass. There was nothing strange about that after all we Irish are very good Catholics and great mass-goers. But on this occasion I was in for a huge surprise. Halfway through the mass Ann nudged me. Apparently Bridie had arranged for Ann and I to walk up the aisle to the altar together holding the gifts for communion!

Later that week we set off for the Martini International in the south of England. We stayed in a mobile home which belonged to one of the members of the club. It was beautiful as it overlooked the sea. The occasion felt more like a summer holiday rather than going to play in a professional golf tournament. In actual fact the sea air was so good that I was feeling in great form and in my practice round on the links course I felt I could win. I told Ann just that.

Once again I must stress that these events were also very important for accumulating Ryder Cup points for late September. I remember I desperately wanted to make the team particularly since my best golfing pal Eamonn Darcy looked certain to make it. Eamonn was in brilliant form that year. Before the Martini, he played very good golf in the Sun Alliance tournament at Royal St Georges. It looked like he would win but he was beaten in a play-off by Neil Coles.

I had a great draw for the first two rounds in Westward Ho!. The start times were favourable as was my playing partner, Ronnie Shade of Scotland. My first round score was a decent if not spectacular round of 71. A second round 68 put me bang in contention on 139, but I was still two shots behind Eamonn, who continued his excellent form with great rounds of 69, 68. Shooting a steady 70 in the third round put me in with a great chance of winning.

Darcy ruined any chance he had of winning the event by having a really off day in the final round. He shot 75 to fall out of contention. Just when I had gotten the better of Guy Hunt, who I felt was the big danger, out of the pack came Australia's Ian Stanley. After shooting 69 in the penultimate round, Ian followed it up with a fantastic 67 on the Sunday to force his way to the top. I had been three shots in front of him going into the last day so now he was the leader in the clubhouse. Provided I did not do anything stupid or make elementary errors, I knew I would not lose because it was all in my hands. As it transpired, I did not lose nor did I win as we were both tied for the lead at the end.

Normally this would have meant yet another Play-Off. However the rules for the Martini International dictated that the title would be shared between us. The first and second place prize money was shared between us and we would each get the trophy for our mantelpiece for six months.

The result was also something of a coincidence. Twelve years earlier, my uncle Christy won the same Martini International. But he also had to share that 1963 prize as he finished level with Coles. I should add that he went on to win it outright in

'64.

There is always a great sense of anti-climax at sharing a prize and title. Yet I suppose we both played very well for all four rounds so it would have been harsh on the loser. Because the prize money was also halved, I decided to throw a huge party. Ann and I travelled back to London to stay with John and Bridie. Rather tongue-in-cheek, both women were very quick to remind me again and again that going up to receive communion at mass the previous Sunday was what won the title for me.

John closed his Twickenham bar to the public. Instead we called fellow golfers and caddies on their way back from the tournament and asked them to pop in for a few celebratory drinks. They did not have to worry about anything else as I was paying. We also invited a host of Irish friends and we danced and drank until early morning. It was a marvellous session full of singing and it was a very fitting way to celebrate my first European victory.

Just a few days before writing this I got word that John's brother Jimmy Morrissey passed away. He was a tremendous character. He had many friends like legendary hurlers Joe Hayes and Nicky English. They were at his funeral as was soccer star Niall Quinn.

Referring back to '74 and one of the highlights for me that year was my performance in the British Open. This is a very special event that is so dear to all golfers in Britain and Ireland. It is 'our' Open and we all want to qualify for it and to do as well as we can in it.

After a very poor start when I shot a +7, 78, I really improved after that and ended up finishing in a tie for 24th and collecting some decent prize money. Gary Player won that Open at Royal Lytham & St Annes but it had been a good British Open return for me.

Monafeith near Dundee in Scotland was where I attempted to qualify for my very first British Open three years previously in 1970. I was among many other hopefuls at that Scottish venue hoping to pre-qualify for one of the biggest events in the world of golf.

Qualifying was over just 36 holes and there were only a handful of British Open spots available so it was a bit of a lottery. It was also 'dog-eat-dog' golf and in such circumstances I was expecting a very tough and rigorous test of my golf and my nerve.

Things could not have started any sweeter for me when I holed my second shot to the 10th hole and after the first day I was sitting pretty after a round of 69. I had a very good local man on my bag. He was a real canny Scot who literally knew every yard of the course.

In fact he was so cute that even though I got the better of the golf course, he got the better of me. Rather stupidly, I was so naïve that I paid him his agreed wages for the two days after that first day. He never turned up next morning. His going AWOL left me in a real quandary. I felt hopelessly lost. Getting away from what he did to me, he was actually an excellent caddy. His expertise in yardage; his knowledge of the terrain and his lining up putts were invaluable.

A local schoolboy was the only person I could find to carry my bag next morning. However, I shot another round of 69. When I went to check the scores afterwards, I found that I had finished level with four other players. I was in a five-way Play-Off! Vicente Fernandez of Argentina; Tomas Lopez of Spain; England's Malcolm Gregson and Kita of Japan all lined up with me on the first tee. We all shook hands and muttered various pleasantries.

The situation on any other given day may well have been a bit humorous and plenty of laughter would have ensued. But this was serious. What focussed our attention even harder on that tee was the fact that there were only two spots to be won. Five men lined up for a stab at two treasured places in the British Open at the home of golf in St Andrews. Now it really had boiled down to a lottery. Three men were going to be dejected after all their efforts in getting to a wet, windy and wild Scotland. The best two would win – or to be more precise where a ball is bouncing around lottery-like on a rough and ragged links course – the luckiest two would prevail. There was no luck involved with regard to the excellent tee-shot played by Lopez.

On what was a possible driveable Par 4, he opted to take the bull by the horns and he drove a superb shot on the green. His fantastic shot gained the win as he two-putted for birdie while the rest of us made par. Lopez was in the Open and there was just one spot left.

As the Spaniard packed his bags and headed off to the clubhouse with his work done, the rest of us were left holding dockets with a price of 3/1 to land the booty. Which one of us remained to be seen but by the law of averages all bets would be settled on the next hole. It looked like it rested between Fernandez and Kita who played brilliant second shots very close to the pin. I was looking every inch the straggler bringing up the rear. If I had to give myself any chance then I needed to hit my second shot very close as well. The other two looked like they would hole their putts. If I did not manage to make a three, then I was packing my bag as well.

Concentrating even harder, I focussed all my attentions on getting close to make a three and have another possible chance on the next. I holed it for a two! The other guys picked up their balls and when I went up to the green they came over to shake my hand. I could not believe it. Lightning had struck twice as for the second day running I had holed an approach shot for an eagle.

St Andrews, the home of golf, was beckoning. I was thrilled. I had made it to the British Open and would play alongside the greats of the game. I would play a course that has been played by legends and which I had heard so much about from my uncle.

Christy Senior had played there many times and at that very moment in Monafeith, I was about to follow in his footsteps. I was cock-a-hoop for the next few days. I could not wait to get there and even that would turn out to be something of an adventure.

Travelling by ferry, Ann and I drove our little Fiat 850 from Carlow to Morecambe & Heysham which is across the Irish Sea in Lancashire. For the life of me, I still scratch my head to this day as I do not know how and why we made this silly mistake. All we had to do was drive up to Belfast and then get on the short crossing to Scotland. Now we found ourselves not far from Manchester and we had to drive several hours up to St Andrews.

When we eventually got there we were exhausted. I then parked the little Fiat in the Clubhouse car park alongside the MGs, the Triumphs; the Bentleys; the 'Beemer" and a 'Roller' or two. That was some sight I can tell you. Going inside to register my name was like going in to a Royal residence. I was afraid to touch anything. Everything was pristine and polished from head to toe and everybody seemed to be walking around dressed to the nines or in uniforms.

Then I made my way to the locker room after registering. I was given a key to my very own locker. It just took my breath away and I had to pinch myself to believe that I was actually in there. Everywhere I looked in that changing room there were reminders of famous golfing names. Inscribed on those lockers were the names of Nicklaus, Palmer, Player etc but it was nothing compared to the sight of the names Tom Morris and Tom Morris Junior. At that moment I just shook my head and looked elsewhere around that room. I believed I had died and earned my passage to Heaven. That somehow, as a golfer just qualified for the British Open, I had earned my ticket through golf's Pearly Gates to be here.

When I went back out to Ann I was like an excited kid. I told her what I have just related here and I showed her the credentials I had received. Included in the itinerary was a guest pass for her.

Then, at such a late stage, we went off in search of accommodation. As you can imagine, British Open week in the small tiny area of St Andrews is crammed with literally thousands of people. Golfers; their entourages; golf fans and the media converge on the place and it is generally the same with all of the Majors.

I admit that everything was very foolishly planned on our parts. I suppose that I was still only learning the ropes back then. With great difficulty we eventually booked into a little place and I actually enjoyed a great night's sleep as I was exhausted from all the travel.

Boy I strutted my stuff next day. John Travolta had nothing on me. I was as proud as a peacock as I arrived on the practice grounds very early next morning. I had to find a 'bagman' and that was common practice with so many caddies offering their services. It was always a case of bargaining the best price amongst them when selecting a caddy. When this was finalised, I walked with a putter under my arm over to the practice green. In truth, I ventured over to see the world's best golfers rather than practise my putting.

I walked among some giants of the game that morning and I felt like I had been there all my life. Maybe it all got to me and quite possibly it proved a bridge too far because when the tournament got under way, I did not play well. Perhaps that was because I was paired alongside a certain Jack Nicklaus. I do not think I created a favourable first impression with him. I was a very green 21-year-old just a few weeks short of my 22nd birthday and pitted with 'The Golden Bear'.

After the wayward journey to St Andrews and trying to find accommodation, I then arrived on the tee without any tees. I got the shock of my life as the announcer called my name only to find a total absence of tees. I felt like a calamitous Frank Spencer. Jack was not impressed. As I felt around for tees in my front and back pockets as well as my golf bag, he gave me a ticking off. With a sharp look and slight mock he said to me: "You mean you haven't brought any tees with you!"

In the circumstances it was no surprise that I missed the cut in my first visit to St Andrews. Afterwards I consoled myself with the smug thought that there would be many more British Opens but therein lies a valuable lesson.

I would indeed play many more British Opens but always make the most of any opportunity as I would not play St Andrews again until 2000.

Ann and I decided to remain on and watch the action and I am so glad I did. We witnessed one of the most famous or infamous moments in the history of the game. Poor Doug Sanders missed a 2ft putt to win it on the last green. Who else but Jack Nicklaus then beat him in the ensuing Play-Off. Incidentally Tomas Lopez, the guy who won my own Play-Off in Scotland with a birdie on the first, got off to a very good start. He was in the top 20 at the cut and although he faded thereafter, he did at least qualify for the weekend to play all four days of the Open.

****

So 1970 was the beginning of my adventures at the Open. By 1975 I did not have to pre-qualify as I was now a winner and I was performing well enough on Tour to make the Open on my own merit. I finished just inside the Top 50 at Carnoustie. Again I stayed on to watch the climax of that event.

I was blessed as once more I was to witness an historic moment in the annals of the British Open. Like Nicklaus before him, Tom Watson had to rely on a last gasp moment of high drama on the 18th to triumph. The unfortunate Jack Newton must have felt he was about to be crowned the Open champion. Watson was a shot behind as he stood over a 20ft birdie putt. He had to hole it to tie Newton. He did and just like Nicklaus he went on to win the Play-Off. Watching all this unfold only served to make me more determined to try even harder in the greatest of all golf events. A year later, the 1976 Open would turn out to be one of the highlights of my career.

In the meantime there were still some big tournaments to play for in what was left of the '75 season. I had my eye on one particular tournament for sometime during the entire season. It was a brand new event on the tour calendar and I could not wait to play it. The Summer's Martini victory had instilled huge confidence in me ahead of the all new Irish Open.

CHAPTER 6

Setting New Precedents

6th Hole: Par 4, Lahinch, Co. Clare
One of the most beautiful and scenic golf holes in the world
with the Atlantic Ocean appearing in front of you in all its
splendour. The beach guards a tricky green

Woodbrook Golf Club on the Dublin Road in Bray, County Wicklow is one of the most beautiful courses in Ireland. It is an artist's dream with the course built on 100ft high sea cliffs and beautiful landscapes all round. The name 'Woodbrook' was constantly mentioned in our various O'Connor households down through the years and for a very good reason.

My uncle Christy could virtually play the course blindfolded as he won there so many times. He won the Irish Hospitals Sweepstake tournament there in 1962 when a total prize fund of 5,000 Guineas made it one of the biggest events in Europe. It later became known as the Carroll's International which he won on four occasions – '64, '66, '67 and '72.

In 1975 the event became the inaugural Carroll's Irish Open and I drove up to Woodbrook with high hopes of doing well and so carrying on the good O'Connor tradition. My brother Sean had also spent a lot of time there as an Assistant Pro. With my game in excellent shape, I had every reason to feel confident. I remember getting that feeling once more. That gut instinct which I felt before the Martini International and which compelled me to tell Ann "I'm going to win it."

Thinking about it now, everything about Woodbrook was so professional and above all so full of class. The avenue leading up to the course looked resplendent and I would say that it was even more beautiful than the famous 'Magnolia Way' in Augusta, Georgia. A few days before the event in late August, Christy Senior wished me luck. In so doing, he presented me with a brand new driver with a graphite shaft. Back then these were totally new to the Irish golf scene. When he gave it to me, he told me that it had formerly belonged to the great American Gay Brewer. The late Brewer won the 1967 Ryder Cup with the US team and earlier he triumphed at the US Masters after previously losing in '66 to Jack Nicklaus in a Play-Off. Therefore I felt very privileged to be in possession of this club which he had traded with my uncle. Not alone was it a treasure in terms of its origins but it was also very special to me as it gave me instant 'fade'.

For those of you who are not sure what I mean by fade then let me explain: The vast majority of golfers worldwide stand with their feet in a position relative to the clock of 9.15 when addressing the ball to strike. In other words, they stand with their legs slightly apart and with their left foot positioned at '9' and right foot at '15'. In theory you should hit the ball straight and directly down the middle of the fairway. There are many golfers like Phil Mickelson, to use one example, who like to use fade and I am one. I like to fade the ball from left to right. Any golfer wishing to do that must stand at 9.10 or even 9.05. In other words you position your left leg slightly behind your right.

When I was practising with my new driver coming up to the Irish Open, I found that it gave me instant fade. I liked it and this new driver felt much more comfortable and smooth. More importantly I felt that my new club would give me an added and distinct advantage over most of the field. That was not just because I had played and knew Woodbrook more than most of the other golfers but I would also be able to employ my fade tactics. Any golfers familiar with Woodbrook know that there are three tight holes on the closing back nine that are perilously close to the cliff edge. I knew from experience that other players would be wary of these threats but I could not wait to play them.

Whereas most players would drive normally down the middle or slightly right to avoid the danger, I would send the ball out left towards the cliff or even over the edge of it and watch it fade back on to the middle of the fairway. Many players hitting straight would see the wind carry their ball further right and into the rough. I knew this would happen to other players during their rounds but even those playing with me and watching what I did, could be put off or intimidated by my shots.

That is not to say that I am being smug or gloating. I am merely pointing out a tactical and knowledgeable advantage that I felt I would have over most of the field. I had played in the old Carroll's International and I had plenty of experience playing the course.

How ironic that JC Snead was my playing partner for the first two rounds of the Irish Open. He was a nephew of the great American legend Sam Snead who was known as 'Slammin' Sam' for his lengthy drives. More than that, Sam was known for his accuracy off the tee and many tried to copy his style. He was a true legend of the sport as he won 82 PGA events including seven Majors but never his beloved US Open. He lived to the ripe old age of 89.

JC was a great partner to have. Make no mistake about it

but the draw is of huge importance. It is a fact of life on Tour that there are some players who do not like each other and so being drawn with each other could put one or the other off their game. There are also golfers who can be intimidated by the play or drives of playing partners and by the sheer size or physique of other golfers. Above all, there are those who are intimidated by the reputation of a class golfer paired with them.

Not so JC. He and I were very relaxed in each other's company. So much so that I went out and shot an -8, 66 in the opening round. However, it must be stressed that the course played Par 74 back then. Today it is Par 72 as they shortened two Par 5s to long Par 4s.

My new graphite driver had worked like a dream and it was just the start I had wanted. Looking up at the scoreboard at the end of the round I thought I would have a handsome enough lead but a little known American matched my round. Kentuckian Bob Wynn also shot 66. I think throughout his career Bob only had the one win on the US Tour but he was very consistent with a string of top 10s and 20s to his name. Tragically he died from lung cancer at a relatively young age some years ago.

But I was joint-leader of my home Open with a two-shot lead over the rest of the field. Italian Baldovino Dassu was in a group who shot 68 with a large number of players on 69 including Eamonn Darcy. My playing partner JC also shot a good round of -5, 69.

Next day I shot another steady and consistent round of -4, 70 and I had a fair idea that this would keep me at the top or even increase my lead. Scoring had proved that bit more difficult than the previous day as evidenced by JC Snead shooting 73. Imagine my surprise therefore to find that I had been relegated to second place as that man Ian Stanley was on fire. Ian, with whom I had shared the Martini title, shot a magnificent second round 66 which, added to his initial 69, put him a shot in front of me.

Scoring was so low that the cut came at -3 with legendary New Zealander Bob Charles one of those to miss out on that mark. Sam Torrance also missed out. As Ian was on -13 the '10-shot rule' came into play to determine the cut-off point for the weekend.

I was a shot behind him so we were both paired together for the third round. Scotland's Harry Bannerman was a further two shots behind me and alone in third place. Knowing the course so well, at this stage it looked like another duel between Ian and I.

Precisely what I had envisaged and what I talked about earlier came into play like a well-executed plan on the penultimate day. I played extremely well. So well in fact, that Ian made many mistakes in a round that he would wish to erase from his memory.

The turning point came on the very last hole of that third round. On a very challenging 18th, with out of bounds down the left and right sides of the fairway, Ian sliced his ball down onto the railway tracks. He finished with a level par 74 which was a very disappointing return on such a course.

I shot -5, 69 which put me alone at the top and with a seemingly-unassailable three-shot lead.

As is so often the case though, so many more elements come into play and nothing is ever certain. Not least the nerves and the pressure of playing in front of an expectant home crowd reaching 10,000 strong and with RTE television covering the event.

Harry Bannerman and Peter Butler of England were my closest pursuers. Ian Stanley was a shot further behind and four off my lead in joint-fourth position. I also cast a wary eye over a certain Tony Jacklin who had also moved into fourth after two good rounds.

I was paired with canny Scot Harry Bannerman and I can tell you I was nervous. The enormous Irish crowds had gathered and this did not help. Something else that did not help was my new playing partner. Earlier I touched on the 'intimidation factor' that all golfers have to endure. Harry was a perfect example of what I meant. Some players did not like Harry and many did not like playing with him.

He was an extremely cocky individual but hand-on-heart, I liked him. In fairness, he had a right to be confident as he was a damn good player. So good that he halved his singles match with Arnold Palmer in the 1971 Ryder Cup in St. Louis, Missouri. He won 2½ pts for Europe that year so he was formidable. If anything I felt that with the pressure cooker swell of support heaving on me, he might actually help my game. Perhaps I might also be able to take him down a peg or two on a course that I loved.

He may have been my nearest challenger but there were also two other serious threats. Tom Watson had won the British Open a few weeks before and Jacklin was also in the mix.

Bannerman, like a typical gutsy and bonny Scot who could smell the generous Irish punts on offer, was really up for the task. I fully expected him to throw caution to the wind. What I did not expect was for him to wholly outplay me and teach me a lesson.

Before I began my final round on a glorious sunny day, there was great excitement up ahead as not one but two players made a hole-in-one at the 17th. My uncle was one of the players and John McTear from Glasgow was the other.

Harry made birdies at the first and second holes and then he actually took the outright lead after a bit of a disaster for me at the 4th. He made birdie but after hooking my drive I made bogey and from three ahead, I found myself trailing Bannerman after four holes.

I battled back to draw level after hitting a wedge to 18ft at the 5th where I made birdie to his par. The lead changed hands again but when he bogeyed the 8th I went back in front and the turning point came at the 11th. I pitched to 3ft for birdie and a two-shot lead.

For any neutrals it was a riveting match. Both of us birdied the 12th and then at the 17th Harry looked like reducing the lead again when he hit a superb 9-iron to 5ft. However I holed my 18ft putt to knock the stuffing out of him. Even then there was more drama.

On the 18th and final hole, my caddy Tom O'Connor, with a concerned look in his eyes, asked me not to take out the driver. There was 'out of bounds' down the left and right. He advised me to play a 3-wood which he knew I could use to great effect with fade.

Taking his advice I hit the ball out left as usual but it did not fade as much as I would have liked. For a brief moment my heart was in my mouth as I thought I had just blown my lead and my chance of winning the title. Then I saw it catch the left rough. I was relieved as I knew it was not OB. However, from where I was standing I could not see the white ball so I was hoping and praying that it was not buried in thick stuff. But as I approached I felt a great relief and a little satisfaction as the ball was lying ok.

Tom had stopped me on the tee from taking out the driver. He knew that I was pumped up and that the adrenalin was flowing fiercely within me. It would not leave my system and thinking it was all over I tried to finish in style. The crowds were spurring me on. I tried to be smart. I tried to be a little too clever and perhaps even arrogant. Thinking that the 'Fat Lady' had sung her song I played to the crowd.

It was like the British Open down that final fairway. I thought I was going to be stampeded. I stooped under a security rope drawn across by marshals and with plenty of back-slapping and shouts of 'Come on Christy', the occasion and adrenalin got to me.

Taking a 7-iron to my ball in the semi-rough, I connected with it perfectly. I hit it sweetly on the smooth spot. As I looked at it in the air I thought that I was indeed going to finish in style.

After pitching right next to the pin my heart leapt back up into my mouth again. Through gritted teeth I called on it to slow down and stop. It disobeyed and flew through the green and into the spectators at the back.

I could not believe it. When I got to my ball I realised that I had to take a drop to the front edge of the green. As it transpired, I got a 'free drop'. I managed to chip to 8ft from the drop zone and when Bannerman missed his putt, I took two putts for a one-shot victory.

From having the cushion of a three-shot lead, a gallant Harry ran me very close. His round of -6, 68 bettered mine by two shots but I clung on for the win and a near £5,000 first prize.

To win my home country's Open was just a dream. My uncle was waiting for me at the Scorer's hut with a bottle of champagne. I thought that was a magnificent gesture from him and I felt so proud. It was also my second victory on tour in the space of three months. Even after it had been all done and dusted, there was to be high drama which made even bigger headlines in some quarters than my Irish Open win.

While the victory podium was being set up, word went around that there was a bomb nearby! The 'bomb-scare' sent everyone scurrying for the exit gates which was a real shame. An hour later the official presentation ceremony took place on the 1st tee. The cheque, a gold medal and a beautiful Waterford Crystal trophy were handed to me. There was no happier or prouder man in Ireland at that moment. I was in the mood to celebrate. The earlier bomb scare had been a hoax and that did not surprise me one bit.

People felt that as it was common for various paramilitaries to issue bomb warnings back then, it must have been something to do with that. I disagree and I have a fair idea who was responsible. Out of sheer and utter jealousy, I am convinced that a certain individual made a nuisance phone call. That person had nothing whatsoever to do with any paramilitary group and it was done out of spite, jealousy and ill feeling towards me. I will say no more on the subject other than if the purpose of making that outrageous phone call was to ruin my day then it failed on every front.

After the presentation I went off for one huge party and a long night's journey into day.

David and Brian Lavin, the famous Dublin pub proprietors, threw a huge party for me at their plush home in Rathfarnham. I had an absolute ball and it was one of the best parties I ever experienced. A mention should also be made to my caddy Tom O'Connor who was there. He was a Garda based in Dublin and I do not know how he managed to get so much time off. This was his first major win with me and he would be on my bag for eight wins in total.

At the party I also had a lovely time with one very famous golfer. Jack Newton was there having finished in the top 10 and I really enjoyed his company. At the time Jack's Play-Off loss to Tom Watson in the British Open was still fresh in the mind and he also famously came second in the US Masters in 1980.

But I feel a huge sadness come over me when I think of what happened to Jack later on in life. He walked into the propeller of a plane in his native Australia which resulted in the loss of an arm and multiple injuries. It took him out of the game he loved so dear.

That sobering thought makes me realise how lucky I am. So what if Ross Fisher won at Killarney 35 years later and received €500,000 in comparison to my £5,000. Money means nothing when I think of two very important factors. Mine was the very first name on the Irish Open trophy which has many illustrious golfing names engraved upon it. I was also the first Irishman to win it. Incidentally, money does not come into it where Shane Lowry is concerned either.

When the Offaly man won it the year before Fisher at Baltray in Co Louth, he had to forfeit his half million first prize. As an amateur, Shane could not receive a penny under rules. Robert Rock was the luckiest runner-up as he received the winner's cheque.

Prouder still was seeing my name as a 'double winner' on the roll of honour for that 1975 European Tour. The list of winners was a real 'who's who' of the greatest players the game has seen. I also finished seventh on the money list.

There were two other double winners that year. The great Arnold Palmer won the Spanish Open and the Penfold PGA while Bob Shearer won the Madrid Open and the Piccadily Medal. Other winners included Tom Watson in the Open; Maurice Bembridge in the German Open; South African Hugh Baiocchi won the Dutch Open; Vicente Fernandez lifted the Benson & Hedges; Bernard Gallacher won the Dunlop and American Hale Irwin captured the World Matchplay in Wentworth.

The season climaxed with the 1975 Ryder Cup at Laurel Valley Golf Club in Ligonier, Pennsylvania. After a hugely successful season I made it into the side fairly comfortably by finishing seventh on the European Order of Merit. It was to be my very first Ryder Cup representing Great Britain &

Ireland.

In actual fact it was to be the penultimate time that anyone would represent GB & Ireland as the team for the 1979 Ryder Cup became known as Europe. I remember going over to England for my Ryder Cup fitting and I will never forget the day my gear arrived. Everyone in Carlow must have seen my Ryder Cup bag and uniform when it arrived at Carlow Golf Club. I remember my brother Eugene and my family were very proud when I tried on the four different uniforms and the blue golf bag looked stunning.

Captain Bernard Hunt selected three Irish players in his team which was: Tony Jacklin, Peter Oosterhuis, Bernard Gallacher; Tommy Horton, Brian Huggett, Eamonn Darcy, myself, John O'Leary, Guy Hunt, Brian Barnes, Maurice Bembridge and Norman Wood.

The USA was awesome. It was a real dream team. Captain Arnold Palmer's team was: Bob Murphy, Johnny Miller; Lee Trevino, Hale Irwin, Gene Littler, Billy Casper, Tom Weiskopf, Jack Nicklaus, Ray Floyd, JC Snead, Al Geiberger and Lou Graham. En route to the States from Heathrow we took part in the World Open which was played at Pinehurst's No.2 course. It was a fantastic set-up and we mingled with the American team. This was a very good introduction for us and it helped us to relax ahead of the Cup.

None of us had any success in that World Open. We really treated it as a holiday because we had bigger fish on our plate. During that event Bernard Hunt held several meetings with us at which we discussed formats and tactics along with the Vice Captain Dai Rees.

Welshman Dai had an impeccable Ryder Cup record so we would look to draw on his experience which was invaluable. We knew the powerful Yanks looked down on us and viewed us as a soft touch. Dai had the vast experience of playing in nine Ryder Cups and in 1957 he inspired the team to beat the Americans at Lindrick. Up until 1985 and from the pre-War years, that defeat for the USA in '57 was the only one that they experienced in 53 years.

So it was easy to see why American golf viewed Europe as easy prey. Jack Nicklaus even gave several interviews to the media where he stated words to the effect that the Ryder Cup would become obsolete unless European golfers were brought in.

He was right. GB & Ireland players were all predominantly club professionals who held down jobs in the club shops on course. Without being disrespectful, in effect we were 'journeymen' professionals.

When we arrived at the course in Ligonier, we were introduced to the American team and then we began practice rounds. In the evening we attended a variety of functions and parties and looking back I can recall that these were becoming a real pain in the arse. By this stage we just wanted to get on with the competition. At many of these functions we bumped into future US President George Bush Senior. He was there in his capacity as a patron of the Ryder Cup.

Some of the stuff we had to contend with was typical American fanfare and way over the top. The big official party was where we were all assembled with the US team at the residence of the famous Mrs. Mellon.

She was one of the wealthiest ladies in the world. We all travelled by coach to her estate and I tell you no word of a lie that driving up through the grounds it took us over an hour to find her mansion!

A safari in Africa was nothing compared to this. We had to cross so much terrain it was unreal. We passed through her off-limits shooting range; her exclusive golf course and even her very own private racecourse. Upon disembarking and walking up to the massive doors of her residence, we were met by an orchestra. A full string orchestra who were all lined up in perfect symmetry and playing excerpts from famous composers like Tchaikovsky and Mozart.

It was unreal. I remember Eamonn Darcy looking at me and he was blushing red in the face with embarrassment. I just burst into laughter and he likewise. We had only ever seen things like this on television or in Hollywood movies. All of us – the Americans in tow as well – were shown around the various rooms in the house. I say house but some of the rooms were the size of a small Irish house within a massive fortress.

Mentioning the word 'fortress' I remember seeing Nicklaus and Palmer fascinated with a set of guns from her private collection. You could hear the pair of them guffawing at a hugely valuable set of 'Purdy's' they came across.

Later when we sat for dinner we were served by staff who all wore white gloves and were splendidly attired in immaculate suits complete with dicky-bows. There were so many staff on duty that it seemed as if we had one each.

The evening finished with Lee Trevino requesting that I get up and sing 'Danny Boy'. To get away from all the rigmarole I did not need a second invite and so I readily agreed. I first met Trevino when I was paired with him in the British Open at Carnoustie. When the evening's entertainment eventually drew to a close it was a relief. I was exhausted and I probably fell asleep within minutes of retiring to bed. It was just as well as my first taste of the Ryder Cup awaited me next morning.

Today's European Captains see the pairing of Irish players as an essential part of team selections. Padraig Harrington with Paul McGinley and Graeme McDowell with Rory McIlroy are evidence of that.

Bernard Hunt saw fit to do exactly the same thing. He left me out of the Morning Foursomes but pencilled me in for the

Afternoon Fourballs with Eamonn Darcy. GB & Ireland got off to a disastrous start and were whitewashed 4-0 in morning play.

In the top morning match, Bernard Gallacher and Brian Barnes, who were seen to be our strongest pairing, were hammered 5+4 by Jack Nicklaus and Tom Weiskopf. John O'Leary and Tommy Horton had their chance but lost narrowly to Trevino and JC Snead.

Tony Jacklin and Peter Oosterhuis gave us the perfect start in the afternoon session with a relieving 2+1 victory over Ray Floyd and Billy Casper. Then it was my turn to enter the arena of waiting lions.

Eamonn and I faced a daunting task against Tom Weiskopf and Lou Graham. Graham may not be universally known to golf fans but he won the US Open and finished second and third in it as well.

Weiskopf was a giant. He stood 6'3" and was perhaps the best golfer in the world at the time. He won the British Open but he also had an amazing dozen or so top 10 finishes and was runner up on half a dozen occasions in majors.

Not to be overawed, Darcy and I started with fire in our bellies. You could sense the arrogance from the American quarters. Against those giants we slung everything at them and after the first few holes they knew that these 'Davids' were not going away.

Eamonn birdied the first and second holes. I birdied the third and we both birdied the fourth. The utter determination inside us had to be seen to be sensed. Here, in the Ryder Cup on Pennsylvanian soil, we were displaying our 'A Game' to the Yanks. We hit the ground running with no US Airbase capable of dealing with our flights. On the ground our cabin crew were willing us on. They could not believe what they were witnessing.

One man stood tall and swatted away these pests with his caveman-like club. The giant Weiskopf stood up to the barrage through those opening holes. No invader from across the Atlantic was going to come in and trouble his kin.

We were 1 down after four holes!

In those days the driver and the fairway woods were just that – wooden. If Weiskopf had the technology golfers have today he might well have come away from the fourth hole with an 'albatross'.

Measuring 560 yards it was seen as a huge Par 5 back then. Not so for Titanic Tom. He launched a massive drive and then found the green with another massive hit. The Americans eagled it to take the advantage.

Something like that really knocks the stuffing out of you. We were deflated after all our opening efforts. It went on like this right to the end. Eamonn and I knocked sparks off our clubs and played brilliantly but lost 3+2.

It was easy to see how Weiskopf had won his morning match 5+4. You had to give him and Lou Graham great credit. They played for their country like you would expect. Graham was inspired by Tom's efforts and it proved to be too good for us.

Another match was lost that afternoon and the other game was halved. At the end of the first day's play we had put a bit of respectability on the score-line but we trailed by 6 ½ pts – 1 ½ pts overnight. In what is traditionally our strongest format, we failed.

Next morning trumpeted a similar story. I was to be paired in the afternoon with John O'Leary. Before that the Americans won the morning matches 3-1 and so stretched their lead to 9 ½ - 2 ½ with Eamonn Darcy and Guy Hunt winning a ½ pt v Floyd Geiberger.

There was still hope but it was not looking too healthy. Tony Jacklin and Brian Huggett won their match in the afternoon to give GB & Ireland another point and renewed hope but then along came Mr. Weiskopf.

For the second day running I faced up to Tom who was paired on this occasion with Johnny Miller. What a combination. John O'Leary and I were faced with some task and so it proved. We were well and truly beaten 5+3.

USA won two more matches that day to leave us with what we now virtually accepted as an impossible task. Going into Sunday and the final day's singles matches, we were a whopping nine points in arrears, 12 ½ - 3 ½. When the singles format was posted on the notice board the next morning I was gutted. Bernard Hunt left me out. Such a situation does not arise today as every player gets the chance to play in singles.

Looking at the format it showed that Jacklin, Oosterhuis, Gallacher, Barnes and Horton would play in both the morning and afternoon singles. I felt very disappointed and when I further examined the posting I felt belittled.

John O'Leary and Eamonn Darcy were pencilled in and this was very hard to deal with. People would no doubt wonder why two Irishmen were put in and I was left out. There was a certain stigma and sense of shame about it. I was angry and I wanted to confront Bernard Hunt and ask him to explain his selection. But I knew there was no point. What was done was done. For the sake of the team and not wishing to make it personal I let it be but it rankled with me.

The singles were also lost 8 ½ - 7 ½ meaning that America retained the Ryder Cup once again on a final score of 21-11. However, that day will be forever remembered for an episode involving Brian Barnes and Jack Nicklaus.

Big Brian was a fantastic character. He was Scottish and nothing ever seemed to fluster him. He took everything in his stride and he was one hell of a great player throughout his long career.

In the morning singles he handed out a real good beating to Jack Nicklaus. Probably feeling a great sense of embarrassment at losing to a member of the greatly 'inferior' GB & Ireland team, he asked Brian Barnes to play him again in the afternoon singles. It was not his call to play Barnes. His emotions were running so high that he immediately went in pursuit of his Captain. Wanting to stamp and seal an afternoon rematch with Brian Barnes, he told Arnold Palmer of his intentions before Palmer famously replied:

"Jack, I'm not sure if you are playing as I haven't picked the team for the afternoon yet!"

Not surprisingly because of his immense standing in the game, Jack got his way. But Brian pulled him down a peg by beating him for the second time that day!

I flew back to Britain with the rest of the team. There was no great sense of sombreness or sadness. Truth be told we expected it and we all knew that we gave it our all. I then flew back home and got prepared for the Irish Matchplay Championships in Lahinch.

In the first round I got a real scare against Tony O'Connor from Greystones. I was -4 for my round and playing really well but Tony played brilliantly. It went all the way to the final hole where I eventually won 1 up.

Tommy Halpin was a really good competitor in this sphere and I managed to beat him by 2+1 before getting the better of Paul Leonard in the semi-final by the same score.

Peter Townsend from England was my opponent in the final.

My game was in splendid shape. So much of that had to do with a new-found confidence from playing against the world's best at the Ryder Cup. I reached the turn at Lahinch in 34 shots but found myself 3 down! Peter was playing out of his skin.

Not to be outdone, I played excellent golf coming home. I

made birdies on that back nine to finally beat a player who
had an illustrious amateur and professional career. He won the
British Boys twice and the British Youths. As a professional he
won events worldwide in Colombia, Venezuela, Zambia and
South Africa. On the main European Tour he won the Dutch
and Swiss Opens, the British PGA as well as the Hassan
Trophy which Michael Hoey won in 2012. It was a great scalp
to have and Peter and I would have many more battles in the
future. In fact that first Matchplay was just the beginning of a
long-running saga that would unfold between us.

'Irish Matchplay Champion' was the perfect end to what
had been such an eventful year for me. As always I celebrated
in boisterous fashion with family and friends. Overall it had
been a fantastic year to be savoured because in golf it could
not and would not last.

CHAPTER 7

'Seve'

7th Hole: 150 yards, Par 3 at Royal Birkdale 1983.
Of the four rounds I played in the British Open that year, at
7 I made three birdies and par

The biggest and proudest day of my life arrived in January 1976 when I finally made an honest woman of Ann and she became my wife. The wedding lasted for five days! Brendan Bowyer was the singer at our wedding and he stayed the full five days too!

My brother Eugene was best man and after the long celebration we went to Tenerife on our honeymoon for a week. There we bumped into Charlie Chawke and his wife who were also honeymooning. What a coincidence. My office in Goatstown in Dublin is a few hundred metres directly down the road from Charlie's famous pub, 'The Goat Grill'. We have been firm friends now for 36 years.

After winning the Irish Matchplay at my favourite course of Lahinch the previous year, I was in the clubhouse celebrating afterwards when I was approached by Myles Murphy (who would later become my manager), Paddy O'Rourke and Paddy Casey. They asked me if I would consider moving to Shannon where they were members and would I consider becoming their 'Tour Professional'. Along with that they dangled the extra carrot of offering the 'Club Professional' position to Eugene.

At the time I was feeling in need of a new change and direction in my life. I felt that it would be the ideal place to start a family with Ann. As regards travelling abroad to play on tour, the International Airport in the village was also a huge incentive for me. I went to seek the advice of my uncle a few months before my wedding. He told me:

"Have you gone crazy? You were seventh on the European Order of Merit this season. If you move down there you will finish 47th next year!"

At the back of my mind though I had an urge to move and when I went back to the members, they kept on convincing me to join them. There was something else about Clare that was attracting me – the craic down there was mighty.

The members went out of their way to be kind to myself and Eugene. They were far too kind. It was a totally different lifestyle and an antidote to the slog and huge pressures of Tour life. It was monotonous whereas down in Clare I could relax and let my hair down. I took the plunge in 1976 and purchased a beautiful home on a hill in Shannon. For a while it was idyllic. But windswept Clare with thousands of miles of sea air sweeping in from the East Coast of North America can be a pretty rural and isolated place.

So I took to some serious socialising in Shannon. Every evening following our afternoon round of golf, I would take to the bar with Paddy O'Rourke. After a few drinks the cover on the piano was then swept aside and the music began. The Clubhouse bar became like a Parisian music hall. Piano keys were belting out notes accompanied by myself and a dozen or so other voices all singing along. This would go on for maybe

On the 18th at the Belfry after beating Fred Couples in the Ryder Cup in 1989 and (inset) the famous 2-iron shot to within a few feet of the hole

In conversation with my pal Tom Watson at the British Open at Royal County Down and (below) doing all I can to chip out of a dreaded bunker

Shining in the intense heat and celebrating a fantastic success with the silverware at the State Farm Senior Classic in Baltimore in 1999

Getting into the swing of things at the US Senior Open in 2002; (below) talking golf with Fred Couples

Discussing playing tactics with Prince Andrew and (below) with the Claret Jug following my win at the British Senior Open for the first time in 1999

Proudly hoisting aloft the famous Claret Jug once again after retaining my British Senior Open title in 2000

Pitching my way out of trouble at the Irish Senior Open; (below) collecting my cheque after the Foremost Insurance Championship

Showing my respect to Tony Johnstone after my nervewracking British Masters Play-Off success over the Zimbabwean in 1992

three hours and then we would all go home for dinner and resume later.

It was usually the case that we would start drinking in the clubhouse bar which is affectionately known to all golfers as the '19th Hole'. Then when we returned later for the 'other round' we would meet in 'Dirty Nellys' across from Bunratty Castle.

Soon we would find ourselves travelling to other hostelries. We regularly brought our 'travelling musical road show' to Paddy Casey's in Sixmilebridge or even further a field to bigger towns like Ennis. Even then we were not finished as we would always make the Shannon Shamrock Hotel our very last port of call. We loved listening to the splendid voices of the Bunratty Folk Singers who would entertain us until our eyes were almost shut. As you can imagine, Ann had to suffer and put up with all this. Deep down inside I also felt that this could not be good for the '76 Tour which was about to tee off. Needless to say my game was great in Shannon but I was worried wondering how it would be on tour.

****

On that 1976 European Tour a new star was born. He burned so brightly for the whole world to see and for decades to come thereafter. The arrival of this golfing 'messiah' literally changed every single facet of international golf and I witnessed it all unfolding.

Severiano Ballesteros Sota from Pedrena in the Cantabria region of Spain was nine years younger than me. But he came from a remarkably similar background to my own. His parents were also farmers and he too began his career with makeshift golfing equipment.

When I read his autobiography entitled 'Seve', I was intrigued to find all the similarities between us. It was amusing to read his caddying adventures as a youngster as well as his sneaking in some practise holes under the cover of darkness at the nearby golf course.

I entered the '76 season after winning three tournaments the previous year and making my Ryder Cup debut on the strength of that. I felt that my game was getting better and still open to huge improvement. But after my wedding and move to Shannon, I had major worries that my game might not stand up to professional competition. There was no doubt it was very rusty. This was not helped by my intensive and exhaustive socialising.

It is fair to say that players from the European continent up to this point were seen as a bit inferior. Perhaps there were one or two good Italian or other European players but the tour was largely dominated by players from the UK, America, South Africa and Ireland. European players at that time just did not have the experience of playing the types of courses we played from a young age. They did not have links courses nor did their sun-baked countries have the damp and wet weather that we receive right through the year.

Seve entered the year as something of 'a second season novice' to coin a well-known horse racing phrase. He first began to get noticed during the previous year when he was a real 'hungry hombre'. Though it must be said he was no overnight success. In fact, in his very first event of the '74 season in his own backyard, he experienced an ignominious end to the Spanish Open at the end of April. He missed the cut with a +15 score and rounds of 83, 76. I finished just ahead of him on +11 and scores of 81, 74.

However, in the very last tournament of the season Seve signalled his emergence. In just a handful of opportunities he obtained, he finished 17th in the El Paraiso Open on Spain's Costa del Sol.

I first got to know Seve in a pub! There were so many tournaments played in and around the south of England back then. I would stay with John Morrissey and his wife and it was during one of these occasions that I had the pleasure of meeting Seve. One night in 'The Winning Post' in Twickenham, we had a great session going with the drinks flowing and the music drowned out by loud sing-songs. I was in the company of my uncle Christy and another golfer, Hugh Jackson.

Amid all the noisy chaos, I was introduced to a couple of bronze-skinned individuals. With smiles on their faces I could tell they were having a swell time and enjoying all the revelry. It was Seve Ballesteros and he was present with his brother Manuel. In his own inimitable speaking-through-his-nose type Spanish accent, he would tell everyone who cared to listen that his name was not S-e-v-e-r-i-a-n-o and furthermore it was not B-a-l-l-e-s-t-e-r-o-s.

His name was pronounced Sevranjo Byasteras (bias-tare-ass). When Seve was having a drink or when he was in the 19th Hole it could be quite funny and sometimes hilarious listening to him trying to explain all this. Perhaps that is why his name was shortened.

To save him the anxiety of having to explain the pronunciation of his name every time, and to save golfers the embarrassment of getting it wrong, someone decided to call him 'Seve' for short. He seemed to accept that. As for Manuel, well he was Manuel. But I can tell you he occasionally received some ribbing over the character 'Manuel' in the comedy Fawlty Towers which was at the height of its popularity. He was not too dissimilar from the character either.

Seve and I would become friends over the following decades and our paths would cross in many ways on many occasions.

He annoyed me and I will refer to that later but I will always treasure that particular memory when he let his hair down with me in London.

The Portuguese Open in mid-April was where we all congregated for the start of the 1976 season. I got off to a very bad start shooting a first round 79 and I finished well down the field. Seve finished in fifth. I had good cause for my apprehension concerning my game. A week later in the Spanish Open, things did not get any better for me. I opened with a 76 and followed that with a miserable 80 in the second round. I had missed the cut. In his home Open, Seve finished sixth with victory going to our own Eddie Polland.

Come to think of it, the Spanish Open has proved to be a very happy hunting ground for Irish players over the years. Not so for me and I flew home and took a break for the next couple of events. I needed time out to try and sort out my game. During this time Seve's fantastic start to the year continued with a top-20 in the Madrid Open and then he finished eighth in the French Open. I returned for the Penfold Championships at the very end of May.

That year the Penfold was staged at the British Open venue of Royal St George's better known as Sandwich. A links course, it brought about an improvement in my game and I showed a glimmer of a return to form. Things did not look good after my first round when I shot another poor 76. But I knuckled down and worked hard with great results. Rounds of 71, 69 and 71 lifted me up into a share of 14th place. But spare a thought for poor Eamonn Darcy. He ended up in a three-way tie for the lead with Gary Player and Neil Coles. Yet another Play-Off ensued with Coles coming out on top to win.

The Irish monopolised the scoreboard that day with John O'Leary just a shot behind that trio in fourth and my uncle

Christy finishing in a tie for fifth with Arnold Palmer and Eddie Polland. There would be a huge consolation for Eamonn when he paired up with me to win the Sumrie Better Ball in Bournemouth. A full calendar event on Tour, it was a sort of 'doubles' tournament in Fourballs and a very big win for us.

People might have forgotten all about this but another new Irish event became part of the tour calendar in the mid-70s. The Kerrygold International Classic was first staged the year before in the Co Kerry golfing hotbed of Waterville.

In the first week of June, Tony Jacklin took the second staging of the event when he edged out Eddie Polland by a shot. Still not entirely happy with my game, I came home in 20th for a bit of money good enough to pay for expenses. GAA legend Mick O'Dwyer comes from Waterville as does local professional golfer Liam Higgins. Liam put his knowledge of the course to good use by picking up a decent cheque for sixth place.

He went on to do even better the following year by winning it. Alas, that third staging of the Kerrygold International turned out to be the last. After just three years of it, the sponsors and organisers pulled out of the tour which was a shame.

Defending my Martini International title in mid-June proved frustrating for me as I was struggling to fire a sub-70 round. A final round of 70 moved me up to just outside the top 20. Sam Torrance won it — his second victory in a month.

A week later and I could finally say that I was happy with my game. After a few signs in the previous weeks, things seemed to have turned the corner and clicked into place at the Greater Manchester Open. I felt that the cobwebs were now gone from my game.

I finished sixth after shooting a 69 in the final round. Special mention must be made here to that curly-haired and ever-smiling gentle giant John O'Leary. He shot a splendid first round 64 on that Par 70 Wilmslow course. His Ryder Cup appearance no doubt inspired him.

John kept it going as well and deservedly won the event by four shots. When you think that today Ireland has the best golfers in the world in McIlroy, McDowell, Harrington and Clarke, then we were not a bad lot back then either.

My uncle Christy, Eamonn Darcy, Eddie Polland, John O'Leary and others showed that we could more than hold our own with the best. Do not forget it was at a time when true legends of the game like Palmer, Player and Jacklin all played on our tour!

Then it finally all clicked into place for me. It was as if my game was being fine-tuned for one particular event. Perhaps it was peaking and maturing like a fine wine and it just so happened that it all came together at one of the biggest sporting events of the year.

On July 10th 1976 my name appeared up in lights across the entire globe. In the British Open at Royal Birkdale, I shot 69 to hold the first round lead. By the end of the day I was still at the top but I had been joined by two other players. Norio Suzuki of Japan and that young, determined and dashing Seve also shot -3, 69. There is no doubt about it, the feeling is fantastic. When you are a young boy you dream of playing the Open and you dream about winning it but leading is not so bad either.

It actually feels special. BBC Television and Radio; RTE; the daily newspapers all carry details next day of who is leading the Open. All around the world — in Australia, South Africa, Japan, the States and South America as well as across Europe — they follow suit.

Very few people realise that even today it is a victory of sorts and it is a huge prize in its own right to lead the Open. You can see that by the way the media have attached labels to so many golfers over the years as 'the man who led the Open'.

More importantly, this can lead to tournament invitations and even lucrative contracts. By shooting my way to the top, I had also joined a very unique club of Irishmen to have led the British Open. In the modern day, not too many have achieved that feat. Paul McGinley became the next Irishman to achieve it when he led 31 years later at Carnoustie in 2007. This signalled the start of an Irish domination with Padraig Harrington going on to lift the Claret Jug twice and then Darren Clarke won it in 2011.

My own scaling of the heights was not to last. I shot a +1 round of 73 the next day and followed that with a 75 in the third round for which there were excuses. Typical of the Open, the wind got up on the penultimate day with almost every player struggling.

Ballesteros shot 73 and Nicklaus did not fare much better. There were only a handful of players who broke par and just one player shot below 70. How Vicente Fernandez went round in 69 that day I will never know.

Contrast that with the final round when almost everyone shot under-par including my good self who returned a -1, 71. That lifted me right up into a share of fifth place with Americans Tom Kite, Hubert Green, Mark James and Tommy Horton.

American Johnny Miller won it by a whopping six shots on a great score of -9 from Ballesteros. I finished level and picked up a cheque for just over £3,000. Not bad when you consider that first prize paid £9,000.

In his autobiography 'Seve', the late Severiano Ballesteros quite openly reveals that he had little time for both Miller and Kite. Now I miss Seve and I had so much time for him but I have to say that I was very disappointed with the revelations in his book. His memoirs are packed with so many 'pops' at everyone from referees and officials to a whole host of players. Some of the players are absolute legends and I feel he showed a certain lack of respect.

Although Ballesteros was loved by so many, it has to be said he was a difficult and fiery player. He was confrontational with players and officials and his temper would not abate. This meant that he would often halt play and call for an official to sort out the problem.

It is important to add that little bit of balance here. Absolutely everyone knows that Seve was fiery. So when he says things about people in his book, people should realise that these players do not have a chance to respond and are no doubt hurt and disappointed.

Thankfully I have a chance to respond here to events that happened between us. I do not wish to do so in a childish tit-for-tat 'he said this and I said that' type scenario. I merely wish to point out that I no doubt speak for scores of golfers who fell foul of his outbursts.

When I was going head-to-head with Seve in a Spanish Open some years later he was walking around the green surveying his putt. I was doing likewise and then as he was walking near to me he looked at me and then looking away said to me in broken English:

"An I always sink you just a good putter."

This remark made me so angry. It was said to intimidate me but I felt it was insulting in a game where we pride ourselves on gentlemanly behaviour. It was totally uncalled for.

A lot of things were said on the golf course in those days in the heat of the moment and perhaps Seve should have just left it at that. People move on and decades later those things had been long forgotten and should have been rendered meaningless today.

****

Back to golf and after finishing joint-second with Nicklaus in just his second Open what Seve did next was sensational. In early August he won the Dutch Open by a whopping eight shots! He then finished fifth at the Irish Open. In defending my title, I was dejected at missing the cut and I handed over the trophy to 'Gentle Ben' - American Ben Crenshaw who won by two shots.

While my game hit the doldrums again, I seemed to steady the ship again at the Benson & Hedges when I finished in the top 30. Immediately following that I finished in the top 20 at the Dunlop Masters and in the season ending Italian Open I was again in the top 30.

Today those finishes would be seen as very consistent and would earn any golfer nice money. But on the whole, the season was a big disappointment with the exception of my great showing at Royal Birkdale. After getting used to winning, I was trying desperately to get back to doing just that. Perhaps I was trying too hard or maybe the chickens were at last coming home to roost concerning my new move to Shannon.

I just did not know at that precise time. But there was only one golfer who was on everyone's lips in '76 and that was Seve. His consistency and his play was simply awesome. It was out of this world and before the season drew to a close, he did it again, capturing the lucrative Lancome Trophy in Paris. A wonderkid of a golfer had arrived.

A Spanish Armada arrived on the European tour and a huge change was about to take place. In 1976 Francisco Abreu won in Madrid, Manuel Pinero won the Swiss Open and the tragic Salvador Balbuena set it all in motion that year by winning the Portuguese Open.

Balbuena was only 29 when he died suddenly in a restaurant

in Lyon just three years later before the French Open. Ironically he was second there in '77. He was dining with fellow Spanish players Pinero, Antonio Garrido and Jose Maria Canizares when he collapsed and died.

They immediately withdrew from the event but a few others like Ballesteros decided to play on. They promised to donate any monies earned to his wife and family. All seven of the conquistadors who played finished in the money with Seve third. They passed on £5000.

****

Regarding my game, the words of my uncle rang true. He said that if I moved to Shannon I would finish 47th on the European money list – I finished 46th! I knew that my lifestyle in Shannon, for the sake of my health and my game, could not continue.

On 28th October 1976 Ann gave birth to our first child — a daughter whom we decided to name Ann after her fabulous mother. After the season I endured, it was another very proud moment in my own life but it also compounded my growing worries and problems.

I had a battle on my hands to get back to where I should have been — in my opinion to where Seve was. My game's natural progression had stumbled because of events in my life that were solely to do with choices I made. It was my fault that I was lagging behind.

Other hungrier and younger golfers were coming through the ranks and like Seve they had no fear or respect for their peers. Things would only become much harder for me unless I knuckled down and fought to get my game back.

With the extra responsibility on my shoulders of an extra mouth to feed, I got a huge shock one day when I went to catch an Aer Lingus flight to an event. In attempting to withdraw money from my Bank, the manager told me that my account was empty.

Going back home to Ann to tell her of my sad tale was highly embarrassing. I will never forget that day and how we tried to find ways to make ends meet. Into the early January winter of '77 things looked bleak with burdensome bills of outstanding balances arriving.

Then a flashy-looking envelope arrived one day with an American postage stamp.

"Who do we know in America?" I enquired of Ann.

As I opened it, the words inside gave me a huge fillip and a cure for my winter blues.

On beautiful glossy paper, with a bright yellow logo, a letter addressed to:

MR. CHRISTY O'CONNOR JUNIOR

officially invited me to the 1977 US Masters in Augusta, Georgia.

CHAPTER 8

Celebrating The Masters

8th Hole: 175 yards, Par 3 at St Andrews 2000
Another Par 3 which I love and I made birdie in the first
round of my last British Open

The US Masters invite was a bolt out of the blue. There is no doubting the fact I was cock-a-hoop and it was fantastic news to receive. When the dust settled however, I actually began to have second thoughts about accepting.

We Irish are great for trying to celebrate any bit of good news. Typical of my situation at that time, I soon found myself perched back up on the bar stool. Armed with the Masters invitation in my back pocket, I went to the pub in Sixmilebridge. Paddy Casey was behind the bar when I went into his premises. I took out the letter and gave it to him. As he was reading it I asked him:

"What do you think Paddy — should I accept?"

This was an indication of how times had changed in my life and career within such a short space of time. Two years earlier I would have jumped at the chance with no second thoughts but so much had changed in that short intervening period. My game was simply not up to the huge standards expected of invitees to such a prestigious event as the Masters. I was socialising and drinking far too much and I had a baby daughter to feed and clothe with not much money coming in.

There was no point in asking my uncle for advice on this one. He turned down so many invites to play in Augusta. Over the years there have been all sorts of rumours and speculation as to why such a great golfer never played the first major of the year. It sounds incredulous but it is very true to say that my uncle was quite happy with his lot in Europe. He had a routine whereby he played all the events on tour that he wanted to play and he omitted events from his schedule that he saw as getting in the way. He was unbelievably consistent in Europe, finishing in the money in almost every event he played. The tour had become his valuable little nest egg and there was nothing going to get in the way of that.

Quite simply the US Masters was of no great benefit to him. In fact he could only see it as being more of a hindrance to his schedule. That was the way he felt and when you look at it a little closer who is anyone to argue with his view. Between practise and getting himself prepared for travelling to the States, that could take up perhaps a week or more of his time. Then after playing the event and getting home for a few days, he could have missed playing two or three events in Europe in that time. The potential income earned from those few weeks in Europe far outweighed all the hassle involved in playing the US Masters.

He saw Europe as money in his hand whereas the States was a gamble which was simply not worth taking on.

Christy was not the only golfer to shun the Masters and it was not necessarily golfers outside of America who turned down invites. The great Lee Trevino by all accounts was a really complex character. I had the great pleasure of being paired with him in the Open and to all and sundry he looked like a really fun guy. Looking at him he was always laughing, cracking jokes and he seemed a real extrovert. To his adoring public he was known as 'Super Mex'.

Away from the spotlight however, there are many who say he was a strange character and a bit introverted. He turned down the chance to play Augusta every time an invite came through the door until eventually the pressure grew on the American PGA. They in turn put pressure on Clifford Roberts to get Trevino to play Augusta. Roberts was a former New York investment banker who took over the running of the Augusta Masters from its founder, and his former partner, the great Bobby Jones. Although many felt that Trevino's game was not suited to the course, Roberts eventually succeeded in getting him to play. But Trevino was never entirely happy there. He spent most of his time in his room mending clubs and putting on grips rather than socialising.

As a boy I had always heard about the great events like the British Open, the Masters and the US Open and now I was off to America. In truth I was thrilled with the opportunity to play one of the world's greatest golf courses no matter what I said to Paddy Casey. We Irish are great at downplaying something we are excited about. This was a boyhood dream about to come true. I had always embraced the chance of exploring far away hills from Knocknacarra and I always found that a lot of that scenery was as green as ours.

****

Augusta, Georgia, was like one beautiful and very colourful dream. It had to be seen to be believed. It was 'Wizard of Oz' stuff as I made my way to 2604 Washington Road and then up through the splendour of Magnolia Drive. The flowers, the birds echoing their beautiful song right around the course, the wildlife and of course Augusta National itself. The entire golf course and greens were like a brand new carpet that had been rolled out for the occasion with not a divot to be seen anywhere. I could have dropped dead right there and I would have gone straight to Heaven because that is where I was. That whole experience is something that I will never forget. With my head held high I felt like an Irish king at an assembly of golf's world leaders.

Tommy Horton and Seve Ballesteros also made their Masters debuts with me that year.

It was customary at the Masters 'Dinner' for newcomers to be introduced into the event by another golfer. Gary Player stood and introduced me to the entire Masters field assembled at the function. It is 35 years ago and so I cannot recall exactly what he said. There was the usual small talk and plenty of laughter and no doubt one or two references to my uncle. What I found very amusing though was Gary Player himself. Anyone familiar with Gary will know that he is never short of a word or two. But he went on and on as if he had known me all his life. In reality, I hardly knew this golfing great at all.

We really made up for that the next day as I played with Gary in the famous 'Par 3 Competition'. This infamous little event has gained notoriety over the years as no winner of it has ever gone on to lift the Masters itself.

I had such a laugh that day and I enjoyed myself immensely. The laughter and banter continued to the practise round. Ben Crenshaw came over to us and I can vividly recall him saying:

"Well Gary you know what, I've just found the secret."

I burst out laughing when Gary replied:

"Well Ben if you ever do, please let me know because I never did!"

Then I decided to spend a little time with my fellow Europeans. I practised with the late Seve and Tommy Horton. Seve was so serious about his debut and eager to get going.

It was easy to see he was at his peak and why he was a multiple winner at home. That did not stop us from having a real light-hearted moment on the Par 3 16th green which is that famous closing hole over water. Tommy Horton said to Seve:

"Seve, you know I don't think these greens are as fast as they are made out to be."

In his squeaky-nose Spanish accent, Seve replied:

"You sink (sic) so? Try putt from a fron lef of green to back right."

So with that, Tommy crouched over his putt and struck the ball. His ball was never going in as it was off-line. It went a few inches past when all of a sudden it stopped and then it started to roll back. Seve was in tears of laughter as Tommy's ball travelled back to a few inches past his feet.

In his broken English and literally bursting with laughter, Seve quipped:

"An you say greens no quick!" Well I laughed so loud.

For my week in Augusta I accepted an unusual invitation. I decided to accept an offer of accommodation from two Irish priests who were from Wexford and Cork. When I agreed I thought to myself that they were going to be rather boring hosts. I was so wrong.

The first thing they requested from me each evening was to drive my splendid courtesy car. It looked superb with the name 'Christy O'Connor Junior' displayed on the front, back and sides. They changed into Aran sweaters and drove off into Augusta each night. That left me in the company of the cook and housekeeper and I remember her name was Tilda. She was a very big lady and she was very jolly and hearty. Her cooking was out of this world.

Tilda would literally stand over your shoulder when serving her dish of the day. She would not leave until she was satisfied you had eaten every morsel. She would say:

"Come on eat up! You have to be a big strong man for play-ing in those green fields."

On the first tee next morning, at 9.14 on the 7th April to be exact, I stood tall as a very proud Irishman. I was the first pro-fessional golfer from the Republic of Ireland to play the US Masters. Joe Carr had played previously as an amateur.

Doug Ford was my playing partner and what a man to have beside you. They talk about legends but this person is, without doubt, the forgotten man of golf. What a golfer and what a life he enjoyed. It was a privilege to be playing with him. Aged 54, he was a lot older than me. In fact, he turned professional the year after I was born. Doug was a golfer to enjoy my round with and to learn from. He had won two majors including the Masters but he almost took an entirely different career path.

In the pre-war years, the New York Yankees offered him a contract to play baseball with them. So he went home to his father to tell him the great news. But his father asked him how long he expected to play with them. When the young Ford replied "about 10 years", his father told him that he could expect to play golf all of his life. Today, aged 90, he still plays the game he loves and he is the oldest surviving winner of the US Masters.

He won it in 1957 by holing a bunker shot on the last hole to pip Sam Snead. A few years before this, he and Snead were involved in one of the most amazing episodes that ever hap-pened in golf. At the end of the Jacksonville Open, they both finished tied at the top. There was to be a Play-Off next day. Snead turned up next morning and offered his hand to a shocked and perplexed Ford telling him that the title was his.

Apparently Snead had asked for a ruling the previous day concerning his ball which had finished behind a stake. His playing partner told him that the ball was out of bounds but when they called for the referee he could not be found.

However, a secondary rules official ruled that his ball was fine and to play on. Snead could not sleep that night. His conscience told him that he had made a mistake but when he offered his hand to Doug Ford next day, his generous offer was refused. So in an all-round spirit of great sportsmanship, and one of the greatest golf acts ever witnessed, Ford accepted Snead's explanation and told him that he was a huge man for doing it. But with the slate wiped clean, they should now play off to find a winner.

Snead was now the baffled one and was very taken by what his gracious opponent said. Ford explained to him that an unclear rule would only taint his 'win' forever. Sam shook his hand again, told him he was the rightful winner and walked away.

Needless to say I thoroughly enjoyed my day with Mr Ford. As so many people never get the chance to play Augusta, come and share with me that very first round from an Irish professional at Augusta...

I got off to a steady start on the notoriously difficult Par 4 first. In the all-time records of Masters it ranks as the sixth most difficult hole on the course. It measures around 450 yards but there is a bunker 290 yards from the tee which guards the fairway. In choosing to 'lay-up', I left myself with a long and difficult second shot to a very undulating green. But in making the green I two-putted to secure a safe par and solid start.

The second hole is the longest hole at Augusta. A Par 5 named 'Pink Dogwood', it measures almost 580 yards but it is one of the easiest on the course for making birdies. Although the green is guarded by two bunkers, I made the green safely with my second shot.

Again I two-putted but this time it was for a birdie. I was delighted to be under par for my first two holes. The third

hole 'Flowering Peach' was a fairly short Par 4 and I made par
without any difficulty.

It was around this stage when I remember smiling to myself.
Looking up at the giant scoreboard I saw:

1. CHRISTY O'CONNOR -1; 2. JACK NICKLAUS
EVEN.

You know, looking back now I wish I could have cherished
it forever by snapping the image on a Polaroid camera. That
photo would have been framed and copied and I am sure it
would have hung proudly in several pubs around Shannon –
and Casey's bar.

Perhaps I should not have peered up at it. All sorts of
thoughts were running through my head. I was beginning to
get ahead of myself and lose focus. Perhaps I began to feel that
I was now a little imperious and that Augusta was easy. She
would prove me so wrong.

The fourth hole in my day was 30 yards shorter than it is today. When I stood on the tee it was only a 200-yard Par 3 but
today it ranks as the fourth most difficult. I secured another
par but then I was in for a very rude awakening on the fifth.

'Magnolia' is a fairly long Par 4 which has a dog-leg swing
to the left. In fact the entire hole seems to swing left with the
green sloping and bumpy. I avoided the bunkers to the left off
the tee but the fast sloping green caught me out. A bogey five
ensued and I was back to level par.

The second Par 3 was up next and it could not have been any
easier. It measured 180 yards and so a medium iron off the
tee was required. 'Juniper' is elevated as you stand on the tee
looking down on it in the distance. You can see a huge bunker
in front of the green but it should not really pose a threat.
Although the green is a little undulating, you just need to find
the centre of the green. I secured par.

On the seventh hole, it is essential to find the fairway as it is very narrow. It is an uphill hole and although there are three bunkers in front of the green, it was pretty easy. In 1977 it was a short enough Par 4 and again I secured par. I remained level after seven holes.

Going into the Par 5 next hole I was confident of getting back under par again. Although playing uphill, 'Yellow Jasmine' was shorter than the difficult and longer Par 5 that I had birdied earlier. It is essential to keep straight and avoid the large bunker on the right. However there was a bigger problem. All along the left, the fairway has pine trees. My natural draw could not be employed here. Off the tee, my ball went further right than I wanted and I found trouble in the rough. I signed for a bogey 6 and dropped to +1.

The ninth caught me out as well. There is a notorious slope at the front of the green which is also fast and undulating. It is treacherous. I hit a good drive on this long Par 4 but my second shot rolled 50 yards back off the green. I ended up taking five and fell to +2.

From a very bright and promising start the wheels were beginning to come off and I did not do a whole lot wrong. That is Augusta for you. Just one mistake can ruin your round as we saw with Rory McIlroy who found the same sort of trouble in 2011 as I did.

Things were looking bleak for me with the famous 'Amen Corner' to come on my turn for home. Worse still was the very next hole. 'Camellia' is a monster 490-yard Par 4.

On the back of consecutive bogeys I now had to negotiate Augusta's most difficult hole.

You have to witness this 10th hole first hand to believe it. Standing on the tee you are looking right down the barrel into a steep valley and it is also a dog-leg left. At first sight it looks impossible to get from the tee to sinking your final putt in just four shots. There was one big advantage for me. Hitting left or middle of the fairway was the place to be so that suited my fade. I hit a beautiful drive right into the centre and followed that with a lovely shot to the green which gave me a birdie chance. I made par.

The start of the infamous 'Amen Corner' was next up with the monster 11th Hole known as 'White Dogwood'. Today it is an unbelievable 505 yards Par 4. Thank goodness it was much shorter back in '77. Downhill left-to-right suited me again here and provided I avoided the pond to the left of the green I was fine. I hit one of my best drives of the day to set up a nice straightforward second to the green. I found the centre and two-putted for another safe par.

Part Two of the dreaded triumvirate comes in the shape of a very short Par 3 known as 'Golden Bell'. All golf fans should know this hole from seeing it on television down through the years. 'Rae's Creek' runs in front of that green with the pin usually in the front and near to the water. You have two bunkers at the back right. Year after year you see most golfers find the centre some 50 or 60 yards from the pin and putting long across the green.

Others hit too hard to avoid the water and you see their ball hitting the bank at the back. Sometimes it will bounce back into light rough or onto the front fringe. But if it stays in there among the flowers and fauna you are faced with a definite bogey or worse.

If the wind is blowing it makes things even more hazardous and you need a stronger club. I took just a 9-iron off the tee and left it about 25 feet from the pin for another outside birdie chance. I made another par to safely negotiate two of the three – Amen.

With just six holes left in my round I was feeling different emotions. I was disappointed to have slipped from -1 to +2 and frustrated with some of the mistakes I made. But still I felt reasonably happy and confident that I could learn from those mistakes next day. The last leg of the difficult corner proved to be the undoing of my round. 'Azalea' is a short enough Par 5 and a great birdie chance. However there is danger lurking everywhere and unfortunately after a good drive, I found Rae's Creek.

I came away from there with a bogey six and followed that with yet another bogey on the 14th. My round was unravelling and I was now +4. The frustration was building up in me because some of these holes were easy enough but it was mistakes that were costing me.

'Firethorn' the Par 5 15th was a perfect example of what I was feeling and it proved to be the total ruination of my round. It is ranked as the all-time easiest hole at Augusta and I should have been looking at a routine birdie or even an eagle. In attempting to get back on track I was hell-bent on trying to make eagle. After a good drive the plan was taking shape. Looking up ahead for your second shot, all golfers have a choice to make.

A huge pond faces you in front of the green which is intimidating to say the least. You either lay up short of the water for a pitch and good chance of birdie or go for the green leaving a putt for an eagle or resulting tap-in birdie. I had to make something happen.

There is danger up there and it is staring back at you in the face. It is looking at you and you are looking at it and then comes the time to draw. No time to blink, you have to hit.

I chose to go for it in two. The reward is there for you if you make it. It looks easy. It is a great birdie chance. I hit it too hard. The ball went through the green. When I reached my ball I found that it was down in a gully. I had no view of the pin from where I was. Faced with a very tricky situation I tried to get back spin on it as I lofted it up. But the green slopes wickedly towards the water and there was no stopping my ball. It finished in 'the drink' as they call it in the States.

Tommy Horton's words of fast greens had come back to haunt me. Playing my fifth shot from in front of the water I tried to get it as close to the pin as possible for bogey putt. I missed and tapped in for a double-bogey seven.

An ugly round was now manifest in my +6 score and with three holes still to play it was now a case of damage limitation. There was little consolation in the fact that I managed to do this and I completed my first round at the Masters in +6, 78 shots.

Welcome to Augusta!

There was really no way back after that. The following day I teed off at 1.19pm with Roger Maltbie. I knew very little about him at the outset. He was three years younger than me but I think we had a few things in common. Roger my playing partner had won back-to-back titles in his very first year on the US Tour. In the second of them, he left his $40,000 winner's cheque behind him in the bar. There was also a strange coincidence involving another 'stake' with regard to him.

When Roger won his biggest tournament – the Memorial in Ohio – he beat Hale Irwin after a Play-Off. But he got lucky when his ball, which was heading deep into galleries, ricocheted back off a stake and onto the putting surface. With my new and more aggressive playing partner, I too knew that I had to try and do something. I had to show more aggression and wage an all-out war of attrition on the course. It was the total wrong approach and it lead to ultimate disaster.

Whereas I had started my Masters experience in very bright fashion the previous day, I had a woeful start to the second round. It was well and truly over for me when I actually made bogey on four of the first six with the only birdie coming on the Par 5 eighth hole.

Out of the ashes of a debut debacle and missed cut, I can always look back on certain aspects of it with great pride. The previous day I had made three consecutive pars at three of the toughest holes on the course including two at Amen Corner.

In the second round, after my bogey at the sixth hole which put me at +9, I made two birdies and five pars in seven consecutive holes from the 7th to the 13th. In true 'Fighting Irish' spirit, I retrieved the situation somewhat to get back to +7. I also conquered the deadly trio. I am very proud of that even if I did go on and double bogey the 14th as well as bogey three of the last four holes. That is because silly mistakes cost me in my first round and pushing the boat out to make things happen cost me in my second round as well.

My official US Masters Scorecard in Augusta (courtesy of US Masters Committee): 78 79 157

My round with Roger was a shot worse than it had been the day before. A 79 meant that I would not be able to play the weekend. I picked up a cheque for $1500 which converted to around £800 in old Irish punts. That would certainly not be enough to tempt my uncle.

But nobody can ever take away from me the fact that after my battles and skirmishes, I beat Amen Corner. I will always be able to boast that there are not too many golfers who can say they have a one hundred per cent record on the 10th, 11th and 12th at Augusta. On those three holes, in both rounds, I made par on all of them. In the first round I bogeyed the infamous 13th known as 'Azalea' but in my last round ever to be played at that beautiful setting in Georgia, I rectified that wrong and made birdie there.

Some people may say that I am picking at straws here but I would say go and examine the statistics of the greatest golfers who have played that 'turn' at Augusta. On some of the easier holes I made errors and I felt it was a pity I had not played the course before.

A twist of fate also dealt me a bad hand when the Masters Committee decided in 1977 not to automatically invite players back the following year. Up until that year, players who were invited and played at Augusta were automatically sent their annual invitation.

Ten years after we played that second round, Roger would go on to lead and finish fourth in the Masters. He has since gone on to say that it was the single biggest regret of his career.

In 1987 Roger shot the best round of the week which was a -6 under 66 in his second round.

Going into the final day's play he was a shot in front of Langer, Crenshaw and Norman but a +2 round ruined his chance. He missed out by one shot on entering a three-way Play-Off and one of the most dramatic sudden-death Play-Offs in US Masters history. Who can ever forget Larry Mize holing an outrageous chip down and across a lengthy and hugely undulating green to break the heart of a luckless Greg Norman, with Seve, 10 years on from his debut, the third-man in the play-off. The Aussie also lost a Masters to Nick Faldo when he threw away a six-shot lead.

****

I put my Masters misfortune down to pure and total inexperience of the course. Seve and Peter Oosterhuis made the cut without doing anything spectacular over the weekend. Tommy Horton missed the cut with me but many more would follow us down the years. In 2010, an amazing 18 European players missed the cut. They included Rory McIlroy, Luke Donald, Paul Casey, Padraig Harrington, Graeme McDowell, Ross Fisher, Martin Kaymer and Edoardo Molinari. Rory shot a 77 in his second round for 151.

So I was in good company in joining that club. With regard to Rory, I had very old clubs and it was just silly errors that cost me when I ran up all those bogeys. Yet on 157 he only bettered me by six shots with his modern weapons.

I might add that a year later in his infamous 'Masters Meltdown', Rory went through the four-hole turn at Augusta in his final round in 7,5,5,5 which is +6 for those dreaded holes. In saying that, I do feel that Rory can definitely win the US Masters in the near future.

In many respects and aspects of the Masters I was never alone. There have been many more great golfers who missed the cut. Like a fine wine Augusta takes a lot of patience to master and even then, just a single mistake can ruin your entire round. Not alone did I stay around for the weekend and watch Tom Watson win by two shots from Nicklaus, but I remained on for a few extra days with the priests. I regret that I would never get the chance to play Augusta again and correct the errors of my two rounds.

Perhaps as the world is so ever changing, the powers that be in Augusta should move with the times. They ought to make it more open so that more people can get to see and experience what I saw. I have a book which is all about Augusta and in particular the relationship between Bobby Jones and Cliff Roberts. Roberts was not a very well liked man for a whole host of reasons.

Many believe that he took advantage of the terminally-ill Jones to further his own rags-to-riches rise which ultimately led to his taking over the running of Augusta. Others believe he kept in place the 'elitism' that Augusta is known for and branded him a racist. Augusta still retains an elitist attitude today and it is largely off-limits to the public.

A few days later I returned to Europe. I was armed with so much more to add to my game from my time spent there.

Watching Jack Nicklaus play was fascinating. To see how he went around that difficult golf course was a real privilege. Sometimes he deliberately missed greens on the correct side so that he left himself an uphill shot rather than a tricky and dangerous one downhill. This was the sort of play you have to see rather than read about. It was this experience that I so lacked on my debut.

Nicklaus was sheer experience as was Tom Watson. I admired Tom's magnificent iron play and his short game. His brilliant use of the putter on slippery and undulating greens was a sight to behold.

Later that year, and three days before my 29th Birthday, Elvis Presley died at the age of 42. His death would be mourned by the entire world and it was one of those occasions, like the death of JFK, which will be forever remembered. In stark contrast and just a month later at the end of September, Clifford Roberts committed suicide by shooting himself on the banks of the lake at the Par 3 course. That very course which hosts the famous Par 3 event on the eve of every US Masters.

CHAPTER 9

Drinking & Golf Don't MIx

*9th Hole: 'The Postage Stamp' 126 yards, Par 3 Royal Troon
1989 The shortest of all British Open holes which I birdied in
my 1st & 4th Rounds*

I flew straight from Augusta to Spain for the Spanish Open
at La Manga. I finished 25th and picked up a cheque that
barely covered the flights. Nevertheless, I was hoping that
result might be a springboard to a good '77 season. It got
worse. The next few events indicated that I would have to
endure more of the same of my previous season's poor form.
The following week I missed the cut in the Madrid Open with
a miserable +11 and rounds of 77, 78.

At the French Open in May I suffered another MC with
two rounds of 76. It now appeared as if my rounds of 78, 79
at the Masters were probably no reflection on the perceived
difficulty of Augusta at all. In all likelihood it was more to do
with my woeful form. I got a brief boost when I finished third
behind Liam Higgins in the last ever Kerrygold International
in Waterville. This would prove to be the highlight of what
would eventually turn out to be another poor year.

Everything else would fall into the 'also ran' bracket. I ended
up down the scrapheap searching for a few hundred quid in

the lower leagues of Top 30s, Top 40s and Top 50s. That year I finished 52nd at the Open in Turnberry and tied 50th at the Irish Open, which netted just 50 quid.

I then took off for an unbelievable schedule of events. I played four tournaments in three weeks from Scandinavia on 21st July, into Germany, on to Newcastle and ending in Holland on the 11th August.

In that period I missed the cut at a brand new tour event back in my old haunting ground of Newcastle. But I finished down the field for a few quid in the other three continental events. The total earnings from those tournaments amounted to around £800 which, with hotels, travel and a wife and kid to support, was barely enough. But at least there was money coming in. It was better than nothing and even fifty quid from the Irish Open was a help.

Of more importance was that the money earned also provided me with the means to another event. It was my ticket in, with a chance to win. All the time I was hoping to hit the jackpot and get back to winning ways. That is where I knew my potential belonged. The importance of collecting a few small cheques was crucial — as it is today. It is sheer and utter survival. The alternative of giving up or having to qualify is not worth thinking about for all of us who love the game dearly.

I was feeling so frustrated as I had been a winner with my graph continually rising from '72 to '75. Now I was struggling big time and to make matters worse, from my position at the rear of the field, I had to watch the arses of those up ahead plunder everything.

After returning from the Masters, Seve won three more titles – the French Open, the Uniroyal and the Swiss Open. Other Spaniards from the Armada were arriving in stunning force behind him with Ramos, Gallardo, Garrido (twice) and Pinero all winning.

What has largely been forgotten from that '77 season is that another hungry golfer appeared on Tour. Greg Norman was to make a massive impact on world golf similar to Seve and his contribution has been under-stated. When he captured the very Martini International that my uncle and I had both won, he scorched the course. The Shark's style of golf, brought fresh from the infested pools of talent in Australia, was awesome. His new brand of aggressive golf and monster big-hitting, combined with Seve's silky skills and determination, brought world golf to a whole new level. There is absolutely no doubt that they made golf it what it is today.

All I had to show for my year was a trip to America for one of their majors and a third place finish in Kerry. But 1977 did end on a high note for me. I seemed to be only happy and content back among friends and I was smiling again towards the end of the season.

In the Irish Matchplay which was held at Galway Golf Club, I enjoyed a thrilling semi-final win over Peter Townsend. In making it to a third final in five years, I had beaten Peter in all three. But this match went all the way to the 21st before I finally beat him.

A very funny incident happened in the final. I faced John McGuirk who was an older brother of Paddy McGuirk. We were having a tremendous tussle when all of a sudden a cattle truck pulled up just opposite a green where John was practising before the final.

Out popped Martin Thornton (pronounced Morch-een) and he made straight over to John on the green. Now Martin was one of Galway's greatest characters and I will give him a good mention here as he deserves it. As John was lining up his putt, Martin bellowed out: "You're wasting your time son as he'll beat you anyway!"

I had never witnessed the like of it before. Everyone was

115

amazed. But John and nobody else was going to complain or utter a word against big Martin. At the time Martin was a farmer and publican but he was famously known as the 'Connemara Crusher'. He boxed professionally in the ring as a heavyweight and there were rumours that he fought for the World Heavyweight title but that is not true. He did fight 24 times in England and Ireland just before World War II and he did get the slightest possibility of a crack at a big fight. That was when he fought the legendary Bruce Woodcock for the British Heavyweight title in August 1944.

Up to that point, Martin fought 24 times winning 16 with eight of those wins coming by way of knockout. But he also lost eight fights and was stopped in four of them. In 1937 he suffered a third round knockout at the hands of Butcher Howell in Milltown, Dublin. This title fight with Woodcock took place at Dublin's Theatre Royal and it was reputed to be worth £1,000 to the winner. That was an absolute fortune back then. Rumours also circulated that this would be a stepping stone to fighting the great Joe Louis in America.

Woodcock, from Doncaster, entered the ring with a record of having won all of his 11 fights. He had also stopped Martin a year earlier after two rounds in Manchester. This was seen as a re-match with the winner taking all. It would end abruptly after the third round. Poor Martin took a right pummelling and his corner threw in the towel. He would never scale such lofty heights again. In contrast, Woodcock sold out everywhere. He was British and European champion from 1945-50 during which he won all 21 fights by stoppage.

Martin may have also helped me win my third Irish Matchplay title. His intervention stopped McGuirk in his tracks. Up until then it had been a close battle between us but I managed to win it on the last few holes 3&2. The celebrations started and the drinks began to flow again. It was great to win once more in front of family and friends. We could have all gone to Martin's bar which was situated slap bang in the middle of Spiddal if only it had been big enough.

That little pub was tiny. You could hardly swing a cat in it but it was so popular. It was a little bit of Connemara right in the heart of the city. Martin was always behind the bar telling tales about his fights and the four walls were adorned with framed boxing photos.

Even that little example showed where the root of my problems stemmed from. Rather than concentrate on knuckling down and practising hard for the tour, I was mad keen for the craic and the celebration. Drink, laughter, banter and sing-songs. That is what I lived for. All my life I have loved meeting people and having fun. I am a typical Galwegian in that regard. I was even in 'Tigh Martin' and I would say I even sang along to traditional music in there many times.

The evidence from my professional golf results pointed this out. In other countries I was finishing down the field. When I came back to home events I was finishing high and winning.

Four, five, six and seven years of severe European drought followed on from my great year in '75 without even a hint of a tour win in sight. It would be even longer until I would eventually win again.

During that long barren period it was so hard. I think the toughest thing to stomach was not so much the younger guys coming through but it was seeing some of my closest Irish buddies carrying off big wins.

Darcy and I did win a Better Ball Championship in Bournemouth down south in England. We actually teamed up to win it for a second time in '78. I also won the Irish Matchplay but what I really yearned for was another big European win to my name.

Eddie Polland was doing extremely well and John O'Leary

was starting to make huge noises. He took that title in Manchester very impressively and he would go on to become the second Irishman to win the Irish Open in 1982. They deserved it because they knew where to draw the line. They were disciplined and they had to make sacrifices. I did not want to sacrifice the social scene and so it was entirely my own fault.

Basically I had become selfish and I was just too full of myself to realise it. Then again I probably did understand it all but again selfishness took over and I became ignorant of the situation. I even made excuses for myself until a good man pointed all this out to me.

One day back in Shannon, a club member named Larry Walsh said to me: "Your game is not what it used to be. Are you not working at it?"

Some may have viewed this as very brazen. But he was straight up and honest and I said:

"Larry, the biggest problem I have here in Shannon is that I have nowhere to practise. When I practise on the golf course my balls are getting mixed up with those of the other players. I need to practise in a more private environment."

This was typical of my attitude. It was a pathetic, silly and selfish excuse. Larry replied:

"Is that so Christy? Well you know, each time I pass the golf course at 7am on my way to work, I never see you out there practising when there would be no members about."

I will never forget those words from Larry. They hit home hard like a kick up the arse from a wild Connemara donkey. I went home later and sitting down with Ann I told her:

"I am giving up drink and socialising to work hard on my game. Please get me up early."

You could see her eyes widen with the pleasant surprise she got. It was also the sort of look you get from a loving family member that is saying to you, "Well, it's about time. I thought you would never cop on."

I spent years running around the roads of Shannon and practising several hours a day from early morning. All the time I
was crying tears in sheer frustration. Sometimes real tears but
mostly pent up emotions that were ready to burst forth into
tears. They were cold lonely days and it gives me creepy shiv-
ers when I think back to them now. The frustration and even
depression were caused by my worrying day in and day out if I
would ever get back to the top of my game again.

There were many days when I literally saw my uncle in my
front vision as I daydreamed. His words warning me about
moving to Clare echoed over and over in my head. That had
nothing at all to do with the wonderful people of Shannon. I
had made my own bed.

I know it has often been said before but it is so true that if it
was not for my wonderful wife, I do not know what I would
have done. Ann has always been a quiet and reserved lady. But
she is so strong and sensible and so she has always been my
firm rock. In Carlow when she was finished nursing at 6pm
each evening she helped me on the practise grounds. Even
with a baby, and listening to my moaning and groaning in
Shannon, she picked me up and got me going again.

She called me each morning. To get rid of the monotony
and the local temptations we then practised even harder.
We would drive to the plains next to Connemara Golf Club
where we would stay for hours on end. I would hit golf balls
in all sorts of weather until my hands were sore from all the
hitting. Day in, week out and month over she would be there
with me collecting the balls and bringing them back for me to
hit again. Never once did she complain.

By the early 1980s I had two more mouths to feed. Ann gave
birth to Nigel and Darren. Two boys that filled me with great
pride but at the same time put so much more pressure on my

shoulders.

Deep inside I saw my role as the bread-winner but the little money that came in from golf vanished just as quick. The Clubhouse was a welcome distraction after practising while the tour then became like a sort of factory job. You jumped on a flight abroad to join up with your fellow workers. All of us clocked our cards and set off for our week's work. We worked hard and then hoped that there would be bonus money for performance. Those who worked hardest were rewarded best.

After stamping our cards and having them verified by the boss in the office, wages were issued. Satisfied with another pound after another round, it was off to the bar to chat over a beer. Then we went our separate ways until returning to work the following week. The routine led to a rut. But you constantly convinced yourself that you were trying your best. You were not alone. A lot of your buddies were in the same boat. You accepted the situation.

A lucky break is needed. Sometimes that lucky moment will arrive for a golfer totally out of the blue. He or she might win a big event after five or six years which will solve a crisis. However much I hoped for this, it was not happening.

What did I expect? For those golfers who do rediscover the winning touch after time in the doldrums, they obviously work so hard. They find an extra 10 per cent from somewhere. I was down the field in the Top 50 doing the same things week in week out.

The worried frowns caused by the pressures of golf were easily replaced by the smiles and laughs in a bar somewhere — anywhere. A bar with a piano and music was even better. A funny incident springs to mind regarding an old Double Diamond team event which was held in Gleneagles, Scotland. Even the title of that event brought alcohol into the reckoning as it was sponsored by a drinks company.

Christy Senior was the team captain. One night Eamonn Darcy and I stayed out. We thought we had got away without having been seen as we tip-toed back to our hotel. In the grounds of Hotel Gleneagles as we approached the back entrance at around 6am, we saw someone in the early morning mist approaching us. Quickly realising that it was my uncle, we looked at each other in horror as we tried to think of an excuse.

Senior was astonished to see the pair of us and he asked:

"Good morning guys – where have the two of you been?"

I do not know which of us answered but all I know is that we came up with the following:

"We got caught out by tricky pin positions so we decided to walk the course early to get a good feel for it."

As he continued on walking, he replied with a wry smile:

"Fair play to you lads!"

All the time though I knew that things could only get better. Something deep within kept whispering that I would be fine. In the bunkers I kept plugging away. Out of the rough I found fairways and from the water I could get a drop. The signs were everywhere.

One day it happened. At the time I could not see it and I did not know where it would lead. Like love being blind, this future was blurred because it happened off course away from golf. Looking back now, I can see clearly that the turning point in my whole life was provided by a God-send. Into my path one day, the angels sent forth another Salthill man. When John Mulholland spoke to me he changed everything.

From choppy seas and lost in a storm, John helped me to steady myself. When he suggested that I go to meet a friend of his involved in the insurance business, my course was about to be chartered correctly. Out of the blue one day he said to me:

"Would you like to return home to Galway? John Burke and

his wife Peggy are very good friends of mine. They run a very successful insurance business in the city. I was talking to them and they said they would be interested in sponsoring you on tour."

I had no hesitation in asking John to set up a meeting with the Burkes. In my heart and soul I just knew this was what I was looking for. Sponsorship represented a certain financial stability. I also knew that I was ready to leave Shannon. The meeting went very well. John and Peggy saw me as an ideal vehicle for their Pan Atlantic Insurance business and I was more than happy to help. Later they changed to Celtic Insurance and they sponsored an international golf event in Galway.

There was huge sadness in leaving Clare but I knew it had to be done. The people were so good to my family and I enjoyed some of the best times of my life there. I would never forget that. So much so that just recently I purchased a beautiful property in Killaloe.

However, leaving was not just about me. Galway meant extended family and so Clare was just a little too rural. I wanted my kids to have the upbringing that I had experienced. It was essential that they would have the best of everything and Galway fitted perfectly. So Ann and I sold our home in Shannon for a good price. In moving to Galway in 1981, we purposely decided against moving to the bright lights and the buzzing nightlife of Galway city. That would just mean more of the same old routine and bad habits.

Gort, outside Galway, was to be our new home for the next decade. We purchased a beautiful bungalow there and it was idyllic. It was just like getting rid of the old habits in Shannon and at the same time having everything else in Gort just as we had before. In other words the quality of life was first class. Our new neighbours and friends were simply wonderful people. Like the people in Clare they were so friendly and so straight up and genuine. We never ever wanted for anything and we were finally home.

My children Ann, Nigel and Darren had the ideal schooling. The little country school was only fifty metres or so from our new house. It was so beautiful and it was situated on a little bi-road. The kids were taught by two fantastic teachers and they could not have wished for better conditions. When other kids had to be up an hour early for school, mine were so lucky in that they could get up 10 minutes before classes began – not that I recommended that!

One of the best things about it was when their lunch break arrived. The three of them could pop across for lunch and then still get back to the schoolyard in time before afternoon classes began.

Everything about this new move was so refreshing even to the point of my new practise regime. A farmer by the name of Mr. Nolan owned the field next door to our bungalow. He very kindly agreed that I could have the use of it for practising. Nor did I have to ask him or anybody else to cut the field for me. Sheep grazed on it so unlike cattle, this meant the grass was shaved almost to the soil. Mind you, they did have to contend with golf balls flying about and they did not understand the word 'Fore'!

There was never a dull moment for the family in Gort. A local river also came up from an underground spring and then disappeared back underground about 200 metres away. It was stocked full of trout and I caught so many of them during relaxing days of fishing.

The kids enjoyed many summer days swimming in that river. My new home was also very close to my favourite golf course at Lahinch. I played two or three times a week with dear friends Dr. Paddy Joyce, Tommy Lambert and the late Sean Murphy.

Some years later, Lahinch Golf Club bestowed on me the title of 'Honorary Member' and it was a very proud day for me. Particularly because Gort and Lahinch were so close to my heart and together these places helped to improve my game drastically.

After a 'seven-year itch' from 1976-1982, my game was about to take off again. I would peak to such a point that I would play the greatest golf of my entire career during the next decade. It all began with the British Open in 1983. How appropriate that it was in the Open. The last time I made a real and notable impact where the public and golf world stood up and took notice of me was when I led the '76 Open at Royal Birkdale.

In '83 I returned to those Southport sand dunes once more. On the beach running alongside the course, the great racehorse Red Rum limbered up for his assaults on the Aintree Grand National which he won three times in the '70s. Typical of the so-called 'horses-for-courses' theory, I began that season poorly but then hit form at the old Martini International won by Nick Faldo. In a tournament that will always hold special memories for me, I finished 11th.

Incidentally, that success was the second of five wins for Sir Nick that year with Seve winning four. Bernhard Langer won three. The Irish were not to be outdone with Eamonn Darcy winning the Spanish Open and Des Smyth taking the Sanyo Open.

Only a week after my 11th place finish I came eighth in a tour event in Leeds winning another £1500. That event in Yorkshire brought up three wins in-a-row for Faldo. I had not put in back-to-back performances like that for some considerable time and it got even better. Some indifferent performances followed where I fell into that old habit of finishing down with the 'also-rans'. I am not trying to make excuses here but there are many times when golfers become ill as well. Many are struck down with common flu's and viruses. You simply cannot keep up the same good level of consistency every time. You become run down and fatigued. I returned to form at the Glasgow Classic in Haggs Castle exactly a month after finishing in the Top 10 in Leeds when finishing seventh after a second round -6, 66.

I earned over £2000 for my efforts in that event won by Bernhard Langer and just a week on from that I earned almost £2500 from another seventh place finish. That was at the Scandinavian Masters won by Sam Torrance. Having secured four Top 10 finishes or thereabouts in just a few months, and over £7000, I was in fine form going into Birkdale. With that kind of form, and the fact that I had proven course form at the course, I told Ann that I was beginning to get that feeling again.

After all the years of being somewhat in the doldrums, life was now feeling so good. I now had stability. I had good money coming in, good sponsors and good new friends. Also the kids were happy at school in Gort while Ann was happy that we were all happy.

Whereas on my previous trip to Royal Birkdale I made world headlines to be joint leader, I got off to a bad start in the first round in '83. Only for that +1, 72 who knows – I could have been a contender to win it because I gathered up a head of steam and finished like a train.

A good solid second round of -2, 69 put me up into the Top 20 and at the same time it took pressure off knowing I had made the cut. In the third round I was disappointed with my level par 71 as it gave me just too much to do being seven shots adrift of Tom Watson.

With nothing to lose in the last round, I gave it my best shot. It proved to be my best round of the week but my 68 left me five shots behind Watson who won it. But it lifted me up into a share of eighth place alongside Faldo, Denis Durnian and Bill Rogers.

Rogers actually scored an 'albatross' that day when he holed his second shot with a 1-iron to a Par 5! It had been some 12 years since a similar feat had been accomplished. However the day belonged to Tom Watson who hoisted the Claret Jug for the fifth time.

I earned almost £12,500 for my Top 10 finish and I had to be very happy with my game that year. I felt the opening round cost me dearly as I was in such fine form coming into the event.

At the end of that year and being positive, I acknowledged that '83 had been a fine year with another great British Open. I had a string of Top 10s and 20s to my name and I accumulated nearly £30,000 in money. Significantly, and even allowing for the increase in prize-money, this was the most money I had ever won for an entire season. With my new found happiness and lifestyle, I was hoping that it would continue in that rich vein.

By 1984 a need breed of Irish player rose to the fore on tour. The likes of Des Smyth, Ronan Rafferty, David Feherty and Philip Walton began to make an impact even though there was not a single Irish winner that season. It was very much the same pattern for me. I began slowly but in May I finished just outside the Top 20 in the Italian Open and finished ninth in my next event, the Car Care Plan tournament in Leeds.

After the first round I was lying in second after shooting 69. I played consistently but never threatened the winner Nick Faldo, eventually finishing seven shots behind. It was the second year in a row I did well in this event and I picked up another £2000. The consistency of Top 20 finishes continued right the way through to August and the cheques all mounted up. In that month I played my best Irish Open since my win in 1975 and but for a poor opening round, I would definitely have finished in the Top 10.

Having started with a +2 round of 74, I shot sub-70 in each of the final three rounds. 67, 69, 69 lifted me up into joint 17th. Bernhard Langer won the event and in doing so he equalled my winning total of -21 under par. I won on that mark at Woodbrook in 1975 and we still share that joint record today.

A week later at the Benson & Hedges International at Fulford outside York, I won my biggest cheque of the year but I felt I should have gone close to winning.

Sam Torrance was on fire in that first round recording a 63! But I was in second place in a group four shots behind after shooting 67. After the second round I was still very much in the hunt and I was still only four off Sam's lead.

Two steady if unspectacular weekend rounds of 70, 72 ended any hope I had and I finished seven adrift. The wily Scot with the famous black moustache went on to win the Sanyo Open in Spain beating Des Smyth in a Play-Off. In that penultimate event of the season played outside Barcelona, I held another great chance of winning. A third round 75 put paid to my chances but I secured my highest position of the year in 7th. It was yet another big cheque and another Top 10.

At the end of what turned out to be another very good season, I ended up with total earnings of almost £25,000. The game was still holding up. The consistency was very good.

The only thing missing and what I was crying out for was another tour win.

CHAPTER 10

Sweet And Sour

10th Hole: 399yards, Par 4 Royal St George's, Sandwich 1985.
Incredibly I made my 7th birdie in a row at 10 (from the 4th)
to shatter a few records

Tunisia in north Africa was where I began the 1985 season. Typical of my starts in the previous years, I finished way down the field for a few hundred quid. But it was very much a warm-up for the season and a chance to get some warm African sun.

Des Smyth and Eamonn Darcy, who had both finished in the Top 10 there, flew straight to Madrid in Spain for the next event along with Philip Walton. I decided to take a break for a month as I had a plan for a plan!

The Car Care Plan event in Leeds was now a tournament I felt I could win having finished in the top dozen there in my previous two starts. After rounds of 69, 70, 69 everything was going as expected and I was in third place going into the final round. There was a huge prize on offer with £26,000 for the winner and even the second took home £17,000. David J Russell led by a shot from Sandy Lyle who was a shot in front of me and I was also a shot clear of David Feherty. It was very close.

On the final day I hit one of the worst rounds of anybody in the Top 50 when posting a poor 75. I ended up in a tie for 10th with Tony Johnstone of Zimbabwe and Des Smyth, and I felt very angry with myself.

This was now becoming a bad habit and it was something that needed serious addressing. It had to be eradicated from my game. On quite a few occasions in the previous years I had put myself in a good position to win only to blow it all with a bad final round. It was very important to work on this aspect of my game for an essential reason. The implications of my last round were enormous. 1985 was the first year where it became quite noticeable that money on the European Tour was increasing like never before.

Events with a normal prize pool of around £100,000 in previous years, which had jumped from around £25,000 in the 1970s, were now reaching huge pools of over £250,000. Three events in particular were the British PGA, Dunhill Masters and European Open. Golfers were now feeling pressure like never before. As we all witnessed these huge increases in money, so too did the public and the press and they would jump on it. From then on, if a putt was missed or a position or two was dropped, it could cost thousands.

My determination not to let this happen again seemed to pay dividends at the Irish Open in mid-June. An excellent last round of 67 at Royal Dublin was never going to be enough to trouble Ballesteros and Langer but it lifted me up into eighth place for a nice pay day.

I finished five shots behind Seve, who beat Langer in a memorable Play-Off. My own performance showed that my game was still solid and just a week before the British Open I finished in the Top 20 at the Laurence Batley International at The Belfry.

Although I completed the event in +6 with rounds of 72, 72, 75 and 75 those scores are a little misleading as the last three rounds were played in very difficult conditions. I was still feeling very good ahead of the biggest event of the year at Royal St George's in Kent. Better known as Sandwich, the Open now had a whopping prize fund of nearly £600,000.

There were feel-good-factors everywhere and together they all helped to spur me on to what would become one of the most memorable events of my entire career.

How in the name of God they made Sandwich a Par 70 I will never know. Everyone knows that it is one of the most difficult golf courses of any major. Someone once described it as 'like playing golf on the moon'. A cruel statement perhaps but not one golfer finished that 1985 Open under par or even level par. That was a measure of its extreme difficulty. There are just two Par 5s; two of the 12 Par 4s are 490 yards and two Par 3s are nearly 250 yards.

In those circumstances it was not surprising I got off to a bad start. I took three putts for bogey at the first hole but I got back level at the second with a 12ft birdie. I bogeyed again when three-putting the third. It seemed as if it was going to be another bad day at the office.

I repaired that damage with another 12ft birdie at the fourth. That was followed by a slightly shorter one from some 10ft at the fifth. At the Par 3 sixth I rammed in a monster 25ft birdie to be -2 for my round. The holes were suddenly looking like buckets to me. At the Par 5 seventh hole I hit a perfect drive down the middle and followed that with a 3-iron to the green. I rolled the putt up just short of the pin and then tapped in for a simple birdie. That was my fifth birdie which moved me to -3.

After making another long 20ft birdie on the eighth, I just looked up to the heavens. I was wondering what was going on. It was at that point I became aware of the enormity of what I was doing. Then all sorts of record thoughts began to enter my mind.

When I struck a 6-iron to within just a couple of feet of the flag at the Par 4 ninth I was -5 and there were still nine holes left. It was crazy stuff. Then the negative thoughts start to battle your positive ones and you begin to wonder when the bogey will come.

I left myself with just an 8-iron into the 10th where I made my seventh birdie in a row to go -6. At this stage I did not know about the sequence of birdies or its consequences.

All I was thinking about was the course record and whisperings of a £50,000 cheque.

Tom Watson knew what I was doing and mentioned this figure to me. Word spread fast and wide around Sandwich. The crowds began to swell. I was now on for a score of 64 which I knew would at least put me very near the overnight lead. That was top priority.

Had I not three-putted two of the opening holes I would have been at least -8 and with eight more holes to go I would have been in firm control of the all-time British Open record. Nevertheless I still had those eight holes in which to try break the Open record of 63.

The birdie blitz ended at the 11th when I just missed. I tapped in for par but then birdied the 12th with a 15ft putt for -7. Now I was back on course for 63 held jointly by Mark Hayes (1977) and Isao Aoki (1980) but a 62 would put me down in Open history forever.

I knew the Royal St George's course record was surely mine. It stood at 65 and I was two shots to the better of that if I made pars all the way home. I was firmly fixed on one target of one more birdie. One in six holes with a Par 5 among them. My heart started to race.

It was thumping in my ears and I went a little weak when I realised the position I was in. Tom Morris Senior and Junior; Vardon; Jones; Cotton; my uncle; Palmer; Nicklaus; Player; Watson etc – none of them had been in a position like this. Immortality beckoned.

Not one player, from the thousands of golfers who have played, has ever scored 62 or better in a British Open. Here I was, Christy O'Connor from Knocknacarra in Galway, on the verge of not just beating 63 or the course record 65 but shattering them.

Standing on the 13th tee I was a little nervous. It seemed as if Watson up ahead was thinking of me. All eyes on the course were firmly fixed on my next move. The media and photographers had swarmed in a circle and I knew the world was watching.

The 13th was a Par 4 and I knew from looking at my scorecard that the 14th was a Par 5. If I could get through this 13th, the

Par 5 14th looked a certain birdie. It is always dangerous to look ahead but the Par 5 was in my head. As I teed up the ball, all the murmuring suddenly died down. People started to hush each other. Stewards held up long rectangular objects that looked like cricket bats which proclaimed for everyone who looked up at them 'QUIET PLEASE'.

Quiet. Peace. Tranquility. It can be a terror. You can hear your heart beating harder and faster. You can almost 'hear' the sensation of the sweat oozing out of your arms, your hands, your legs and your brow. Almost hearing it makes you feel every drop. The smallest little things begin to niggle leading to annoyance and irritation. In my shoes Seve would have asked a photographer to stop clicking or zooming or many other golfers would have asked the crowds to move back. This is what the tension does to you.

For me I had to cope with it in my own relaxed manner. A case of my calm battling against hyper-tension which when it is combined equals shaking or small tremors. It was all very uncomfortable. I was hoping a seagull or a passing train or anything noisy would come and give me some help. I was alone with my thoughts of glory and I needed some relief. My body was firming up and my mind was muddled. I needed to concentrate on the swing.

All I got was silence. The only object that moved was not even in my vision. It was one of those big red and white passenger ferries which was behind me out in the bay. The wires of the world were awaiting my next move.

Whack! Looking at my ball in the air I just knew it was wrong. It turned wickedly and ended up in the rough. All day I had played majestic golf and now, as my body tightened up, my swing did not forgive my limbs for deserting it in its moment of urgent need. A bogey five on that Par 4 was the punishment. Slipping back to -6 actually proved to be the perfect tonic and the antidote to my inner turmoil. It spurred me on to repair the damage and to get on for that record. I was determined again on the 14th tee.

The ship was steadied and all negative thoughts and all nerves had left my body. With the demons gone I could concentrate on birdieing this Par 5. Despite my best intentions I found trouble again and I ended up with par. Akin to a bogey, a great chance went awry.

Time was running out. There were just four holes left. On the 15th with the driver out, I found myself making sure everything was correct. Like a pilot checking all his switches, I was making sure I was holding correctly, standing correctly and head straight. After hitting a perfect drive I was in good shape in the middle of the fairway. But my 3-iron shot missed the green and I ended up taking my fourth bogey of the day. It was a moment of pure frustration. The wheels were coming off. All records looked vanquished.

Back to -5 after two bogeys in three holes along with the spurned chance on the Par 5, I had only three holes left. The only requirement now was one birdie to beat the course record and receive all the accolades from the media as well as a big fat cheque.

After landing safely on the putting surface at the Par 3 16th I missed the birdie. It never looked like going in and so a safe par ensued. The situation had boiled down to just two stabs at the record. The law of averages roared in my head that I would fall short again.

For the most part my hitting off the tee had stood up magnificently all day. On 17 it did so again and I hit a peach as straight as a gun barrel. A short iron into the heart of the green set up a 20ft birdie. I nailed it! With just the 18th left I needed a par to record a 64.

After a day of high drama the situation was simple. A par would enable me to break the record at Royal St George's; a birdie would give me a share of the British Open record and if I holed my second shot I would enter the annals of Open history forever more.

Holing for an eagle was not at all impossible. On the day I was peppering the flag on almost every hole. Furthermore, I had holed for an eagle not once but twice in British Open qualifying in

Scotland some years before.

Making a disastrous bogey was not an option at all. A great round was not going to be ruined and so negative thoughts never came into my mind at all. I was not going to push the situation and do anything stupid. I was relaxed and relieved with just one hole left.

Another perfect drive set up the chance. I followed that by hitting a 2-iron to within eight feet of the flag but I missed yet another birdie chance. I nevertheless tapped in for par and I had beaten the course like it had never been beaten before.

I was on fire that July day. I shot a -6, 64 for my opening round. It was only one shot outside of the British Open record held jointly at 63. In reality though, I should really be holding the outright British Open record today as three times in that round I three-putted. My round consisted of 10 birdies, four pars and four bogeys. I just really went for it and I threw everything at the pin. I kept going at it for the whole round and I never once played safe.

I also had my uncle Christy to thank for doing that.

When I sought out his advice on how to win the Open, he told me the following:

"You must be brave enough to attack the course; brave enough to be positive and not negative and brave enough to play each hole and each shot at a time."

The back-slapping and congratulations showered on me after that round is something to be treasured. The day will always remain with me as one of the highlights of my career. I had broken the course record of the great Sir Henry Cotton who had held it for 51 years.

Indeed, 78-year old Sir Henry, who set his record in 1934, was there to meet me at the 18th. Clapping me off the green and with a big beaming smile on his face, he asked me tongue-in-cheek: "Well done lad! Are you sure you have played all 18 holes?"

"Henry, it felt like 27!" I replied.

An evening of some contention and confusion then ensued. To

this day I am still a little in the dark over it so perhaps the R&A or someone might fill me in on the missing links.

Tom Watson, who was playing in front of me, mentioned that there was £50,000 on offer for a new CR (course record). He actually kept referring to it during the round when he bumped into me on the course or when I would arrive on the same tee as him. He was not the only one. Word went round the entire course that Christy O'Connor was about to break the CR and that I was in line for £50,000. I queried this with the R&A afterwards but they told me this was a false rumour.

I can only take them at their word but it does seem strange. A 51-year-old record had been broken and a figure of £50,000 was bandied about so I would love to know how that sum of money arose. Someone did not dream up that figure and just put it around. Money is one thing but a piece of history is quiet another. I had to be very proud of my round that day and I did create four new records. After 27 years, one still stands to this day and I certainly think a second one remains as well and it will take some beating.

Along with breaking the course record, I also became only the second man in history to shoot 64 in a British Open first round. This was first achieved by American Craig Stadler two years earlier and would later be equalled by Rodger Davis, Ray Floyd and Steve Pate.

Present record books will show that I hold the accolade of the lowest opening round in an Open along with those four greats. The third record I created that day was the fact that my four-shot overnight lead was, up until then, the biggest opening round lead in Open history. There is however one record I created that day which I think I still hold until someone corrects me otherwise. I birdied seven consecutive holes from the fourth to the 10th.

When I think about that now, and looking at Sandwich today, I cannot believe it. I know that Mark Calcavecchia holds the record in the States with nine. There are also a good few who have eight birdies in a row. But I do not think anyone has ever managed, in a single round, seven in a row in the Open or any of the majors. I stand corrected.

At the next Open in Sandwich in 1993, Nick Faldo would break my record with a 63 which puts him up there as a joint holder of the British Open record round. Only seven other 63s have been recorded in British Open history. Greg Norman also shot 63. Norman also equalled my 64 in his final round of the '93 Open. But very few others have come anywhere near it. When Darren Clarke won there in 2011 and even allowing for all the new technology, the best round was 65 shared by Thomas Bjorn and Tom Lewis.

The last thing I will say about that great round is that all the 'ifs', 'buts' and 'maybes' can be dispensed with. For years I stated that three-putting on three occasions cost me British Open immortality. I had a 61 or 62 there for the taking but I blew it.

But to be honest, those three-putts were at the very start of my round and I still had eight holes to smash records. I could also say that the turning point was not birdieing the Par 5 14th. Being greeted by Sir Henry and taking his great 51-year record is all that matters.

Next day my record was all over the newspapers. Most carried a photograph of me wearing my trademark white cap and with a mop of much-needed hair underneath covering each ear!

I was holding up both my hands with five fingers showing on one hand and one finger on the other signalling 6. I was -6 under par and four shots clear of the field after that extraordinary opening round.

It was not just the newspapers in England and Ireland which carried that photo and story. News spread all over the world. Amid baseball, hockey and American football reports in the sports section of Florida's 'Boca Raton News', a banner headline proclaimed:

BRAVE ADVICE HELPS IRISHMAN BREAK RECORD IN OPEN

The euphoria and celebrations that evening, as well as the confusion over the money, had an undoubted and adverse affect on my game next day. Everything seemed to be unravelling after a miserable +6, 76.

I was level par, back to where I began and back down to earth with a huge bump. All my great work was undone and it seemed as if I had thrown it all away. How misleading the score of 76 can look to the press and public without giving an explanation for it.

The thing is I played better in that round than I did in my opening record-breaking round. I played some of the best ever wind shots that day. Also, I can remember playing as my cap struggled to stay on my head and blew off several times. As bad as the round appeared to me, almost everyone else struggled. While it may have looked like the game was up for me, I lay only one shot behind Australian David Graham and Sandy Lyle going into the third round.

Only two players who made the cut that day managed to break par. Bernhard Langer shot 69 while Eamonn Darcy coped best with the winds to shoot a fantastic 68. Only a shot behind, I was still in with a great chance of winning the British Open.

After the penultimate round it was still all to play for and only two men were in front of me. Langer added a 68 to his 69 to take a share of the lead with David Graham at -1. Lyle and I were joined by American Mark O'Meara on +2 and we were three off the lead.

In the final round of that 1985 British Open I was paired with Lyle in the second last group. On tour I'd met Sandy a few times before. He was quiet enough and so I always found him to be an absolute gentleman. Teeing off just behind us were Langer and Graham. I limbered up with a few swings and looked down the fairway. Most of us golfers do this to keep the nerves away. We know that the eyes of millions as well as the crowd are on us. It is nerve-wracking.

The announcer Ivor Robson, who has being doing it for 38 years, took the microphone:

"Ladies and Gents this is Game 29 and on the tee from Ireland — Christy O'Connor Jr."

There was applause accompanied by a good few Irish roars and I was away.

After my first round and the way I played the second round in the wind, I was so determined. Even my penultimate round of 72 showed that I was still handling the course and the wind pretty well. I treated this round as if it was my last ever chance to win the Open. You can only give your best and that I did. I was proud of the way I played — so proud. I felt I outplayed Sandy all day. The pressure was gradually telling and my experience over Sandy was coming into play.

I know there were two guys behind who had a three-shot lead over us but when Sandy lost his ball on the 14th, I felt that was one opponent I had taken care of and beaten. He was one less rival to worry about and I just had to keep it up and hope that it would be enough. Then there was a delay while we all searched in the thick grass for Sandy's ball. It brought me back to the Martini International of all those years ago and I was just hoping that this was not going to be a bad omen.

Would you believe that with the five minutes almost running out, and Sandy ready to take his penalty, someone roared "OVER HERE!" At that 'Martini' my ball was declared 'lost' and I ended up losing the tournament by a shot. But now, after having a huge advantage over Sandy, he got a huge break. His ball was wedged so deep in the thick, wiry and long grass that he had to aim over towards neighbouring Princes Golf Club. That was the extremes of the situation he found himself in.

When I was looking over at him I remember thinking that when he connected with the ball — if he connected with it — he would have to hope and pray that the ball would not flash out of there too quickly or he could find himself in worse trouble. As it happened he could not have wished for the script to be written any better. He popped it out onto the fairway and left himself a

1-iron of around 250 yards to the back of the green. Then he proceeded to sink the putt. It was a bizarre and most unlikely birdie.

Those sort of things can leave you feeling deflated. I had to get on with it under a certain amount of pressure and I did well to make par. I was still in contention but then came more twists which ultimately sealed my fate.

Lyle made another birdie on the 15th whereas I took three putts from the front of the green. On the 16th I dropped another shot. I knew my ball had finished in the bunker to the front right but when I walked up there I just had to shake my head and frown. The ball was plugged and it was 'unplayable'. I managed to make par at the last two holes but it was all over for me. When I looked up at the scoreboard after the round I literally felt like getting sick.

I came so close to winning. The scores revealed that Sandy became Open champion with a final round of level par 70 to finish +2. I was only two shots behind him after a 72.

Everything went against me in that last round and everything went Sandy's way.

That is not to take anything away from his great win and I applaud him for his tenacity in beating a tough course and conditions. It is the fates and the rub of the green that I blame.

I have no doubt that bad luck cost me a British Open and my first major that day. For three quarters of my round I felt in great shape and in complete control against Sandy. The outrageous incident on the 14th was the turning point. That played on my mind going to the 15th and then the ball plugging in the 16th bunker ended my hopes.

With just a few holes to play I have no doubt I would have beaten Sandy were it not for those incidents. In beating him I would have won the British Open. As it happened I took several putts too many and I tied with O'Meara, Graham, Langer and Jose Rivero for third. Each of us took home a cheque for around £27,000 but that was cold comfort to me.

Statistics will show that I finished tied for third and I created enviable records. But I will always view it as the major that eluded me.

Peter Alliss, who was commentating for the BBC, said that I had been fantastic from tee to green all week but my putting let me down. Peter, who has always been a great admirer of my uncle, may have been right. In the first round the holes looked like buckets as the ball went in from all over the place. Perhaps I did not putt well after that. I walked off the green to my wife Ann who said:

"Do you realise that you made 37 putts today. That is six to seven putts too many."

We then found a quiet corner and the two of us just cried our eyes out. I knew that was my moment. We both knew that in all probability I would never again get such a glorious chance. The 1985 British Open should have been mine. It was the one that got away.

CHAPTER 11

An Irish Jersey

11th Hole: 1st part of 'Amen Corner' – 505yards, Par 4 at Augusta 1977. Ranked as the Masters' third hardest hole of all-time, I made par in both my rounds

I played some of the best golf of my career in 1985. All through the season I played event after event with the intention of making my second Ryder Cup appearance foremost in my mind. Tony Jacklin was the European Captain again after leading the side in 1983.

Another consolation from the Open was the prize-money which helped me up to 11th in the final standings. With the consistency I showed on tour, and after finishing so close in the tour's main event at Sandwich, I felt that I had done enough to make the team.

When it came to the two 'Captain's Picks' from those who had finished outside of the Top 10 in the money, I held two distinct advantages. I was the one very much in form and I was the hard luck story in 11th.

But Tony chose not to pick me.

I was horrified and angry to the point that I did not speak to him for a long time after. I did not speak to him because I had tried my heart out all year and I felt that, as Captain, he should not have been swayed.

I always felt that Tony had been influenced and that the man largely responsible for my omission was Seve. Between them, Tony and Seve decided to pick Jose Rivero. This was my over-riding feeling, especially with an unprecedented four Spaniards in the team.

To say that I was stunned by the decision is an understatement. In actual fact it caused uproar in Ireland and I see that I am still listed as one of the 10 best players from a particular Ryder Cup year to have been left out. What made the whole sad episode even more poignant was the sudden deterioration of my father's health. The furore in Ireland, as well as his witnessing my own sadness, anger and disappointment, had a profound effect on him.

He was so proud of the way I had knuckled down and got my life and career back on track. He saw how close I came in the Open and he was delighted with all the media reports concerning my efforts there. But he was never the same man after the Ryder Cup team was announced. Less than two months after Sam Tor-rance helped Europe to their first win over the United States in almost 30 years, my father passed away on November 4.

That entire episode, which was both sad and infuriating, is long gone now and confined to history but I still hold the same opin-ions. To me there was simply no explaining why a Captain would pick Jose Rivero over me as I had finished much higher than him in 11th.

Long after Tony Jacklin's decision I heard and read all sorts of accounts. The main one being that Jose was chosen as he had won at the Belfry the year before the Ryder Cup. What had that got to do with 1985 I had often asked myself?

So he won at The Belfry in 1984 and the Ryder Cup was to be played there. But, like me, he was winless in 1985. Crucially, he did not play the very last event in Portugal where I was just out-side the Top 10.

In repeating what I said earlier, I tried my heart out in 1985 and I played right through the year from start to finish. I finished 11th with 12 men to be selected and I was in form. I felt that on current form — and nothing to do with the previous year — I should be picked.

If people wanted to talk about the penultimate event, the Spanish Open, then I thought 'bring it on'. Rivero finished ninth on the strength of a third round 65 — one of his two rounds in the 60s. But I was on fire with opening rounds of 69, 68 and 69. A 71 then dropped me to 18th. That was the very Spanish Open where I was paired with Seve and he said those insulting words to me. Some people might see no harm in what he said but I sensed they were also apologetic words for me not being picked as the team was known by that stage.

I met Jacklin at a later match between GB & Ireland and Europe. He was Captain of the GB & Ireland team as well and I was playing under him. It was staged at the Aloha Golf Club in Spain and for the entire time I just ignored him and refused to talk.

His late wife Vivienne was a lovely lady. She sensed what was going on. When I came off the 18th after a match, she made her way over to me. I will never forget her words to me: "You know Christy it wasn't all Tony's fault."

To make matters even more confusing, Seve stated in his best-selling autobiography:

"I was very surprised and disappointed that Christy O'Connor Junior was not selected on the team."

As I read those words I thought 'how could he have been disappointed when everything was to his liking?' His quote made no sense whatsoever. He boasts continually in his book about putting European golf on the map so surely four Spaniards was a dream for him.

Seve even talks about all the Ryder Cups at length but in a later Ryder Cup which I was to play an integral part in, he did not mention me at all nor did he give that 1989 event many paragraphs. I was also very disappointed with that.

I must be honest to myself here and say that I did not believe Seve. It pains me to say that particularly as the great man is no longer with us. I actually believed the words of the late Vivienne

Jacklin. She intimated very strongly that her husband had been influenced.

My great golfing buddy Eamonn Darcy also suffered appallingly at the hands of a Ryder Cup Captain. His omission was even more of a shock than my own. In fact, I will go so far as to say that Eamonn's rejection was an absolute disgrace. I think you may agree. Eamonn finished in the Top 10 would you believe. Going into the final week he was seventh in the standings for the 1991 Ryder Cup to be played at Kiawah Island. But he was shafted in favour of England's Mark James who finished way down in 27th position! Bernard Gallacher was Europe's Ryder Cup Captain at the time. It is common knowledge that when Bernard visited Eamonn, who was in his London home at the time, the latter told him that he was not going to play the final event in Germany.

He did his calculations and probably saw that he could not finish outside the Top 10.

So preferring to rest and get prepared for the Ryder Cup, he informed Bernard of his decision. Apparently Bernard agreed and reassured him that everything was fine.

If Bernard was not happy about it, then he should have asked Eamonn to play. As events transpired, results in Germany pushed Eamonn down from seventh to 10th but he was still in the Top 10. Notwithstanding that, Gallacher rejected him in favour of Mark James. I do not know if it was as a direct result of that controversial decision but from then on the Top 10 became sacrosanct. That is how it should have been all along. As regards my own 'rejection', I decided when writing this book that I would finally have my say.

After all the years of keeping it welled up inside me, and after all the years of having my own opinions on it, Tony Jacklin's have been well documented. Now 27 years on, and with so much water under the bridge, it is high time to lay my cards on the table.

So am I happy all these years later with Tony Jacklin's version of events? Tony maintains that he was not influenced in the choice of Spain's Jose Rivero. He has stated that he picked him purely because Rivero held course winning form at The Belfry.

My answer is an overwhelming NO. I should have been picked ahead of Rivero. The whole of Ireland knew it and my father knew it. I have no doubts whatsoever that Tony Jacklin was influenced.

I believe that Tony can never and will never own up to it because as a Ryder Cup Captain that would be hugely embarrassing for him. No Captain could ever admit it. His wife as much as admitted to me that it was not 'all' Tony's 'fault'. His constant denials over the years have to be continually dished out. There is no way that a Ryder Cup Captain can ever admit to being told or advised by someone to drop a player. But one would have to be very naïve to believe that they do not listen to others.

On that subject there is another thing that I would like to say about the disgraceful omission of Irish players from past Ryder Cup teams. Certain elements within the British and European PGA are anti-Irish.

I have no doubts about that either. Tony Jacklin was influenced full stop. If it was not Seve who wanted another Spaniard in the team then it could certainly have been some members of the 'old establishment' within the PGA who were, after all, his bosses.

It is an even bigger national and international disgrace that there has never been an Irish Ryder Cup Captain in its long history. Beginning with Ted Ray in 1927, there have been 39 European Captains up to Jose Maria Olazabal in 2012.

Besides the majority of English, as well as Welsh and Scots that have lead the side, Ollie is the third continental European to captain Europe following on from Seve and Bernhard Langer. But there has not been a single Irishman despite our illustrious achievements.

To me it is doubtless very political bordering on an overwhelming sense of anti-Irishness. How else can one explain it? Just take a look at the list of great Irish Ryder Cup players and heroes down the years.

Christy O'Connor Senior, Fred Daly, Harry Bradshaw, Jimmy

Martin and right up to Eamonn Darcy, Philip Walton and Paul McGinley. It is downright shameful that there has never been an Irish Captain. Just look no further than my uncle as a prime example. Right up to the modern era when Nick Faldo surpassed the 50 points mark, Christy Senior held the points record for a European player with 36. He enjoyed such an illustrious Ryder Cup career. The BBC golf commentator Peter Alliss is forever talking about him in glowing terms as one of the best golfers of all time. Senior also held the European appearances record of 10 which was eventually surpassed by Nick Faldo reaching 11 in 1997.

Why have all the various Ryder Cup Committees down through the years not made at least one of these great Irishmen the Ryder Cup Captain? That is a very serious question that needs to be asked. It is high time we ask it and get answers because it cannot go on like that.

The 2006 event in Ireland was the perfect opportunity to appoint an Irish Captain. It would have been almost like a 13th man on the team. That was an opportunity shamefully missed. Many years ago there was another Irish venue shortlisted for the hosting of a Ryder Cup. The final decision came down to Lord Derby who had the casting vote. It was no surprise that Ireland lost it.

A long line of disgraceful wrongs can now be finally put right. I am sure that I am not alone in asking and appealing to the current Ryder Cup Committee to select Paul McGinley as the next Ryder Cup Captain for 2014.

Everyone saw how hugely popular Paul was when his teammates flung him into the lake complete with tricolour after he holed the winning putt at the K Club. He was overlooked for the Captaincy before when he was made 2010 Vice Captain instead.

After he assists Ollie again in 2012, if Paul is not made Captain and this injustice continues then we know without any shadow of doubt that the selection committee are anti-Irish. Some of their reasoning just does not make sense either.

When I was bidding for it in 2004 — and I campaigned very

hard with Sean Quinn — they turned me down on the grounds that a major winner should Captain the side. I have never heard such rubbish.

Sam Torrance never won a major and Mark James made one of the biggest balls-ups when he lost a huge lead to the Americans. I am absolutely disgusted with the attitudes and I have continually watched this go on ever since my uncle was snubbed. He was never asked once to be Captain. This was despite the fact that both Dai Rees and Bernard Hunt went on to lead the side on several occasions. With respect to those two great players they were nowhere near the level of my uncle.

The last word on the subject must concern the huge bands of loyal Irish golf followers.

It is a huge miscarriage of justice on them. They have supported the Ryder Cup in every corner of the globe with the tricolour everywhere to be seen. It's a disgrace.

****

For the 1987 Ryder Cup I was even more determined to make the team. I wanted to prove a lot of people wrong. More than anything I wanted to do it for my late dad. I was feeling his loss terribly. It took its toll and I did not make it. The grieving over my father's passing away became far too much to handle. As hard as I tried at golf, there was something inside which was gnawing away at me. There were so many memories of my father — good and bad — and they would not leave my mind.

The grief was like a constant pain but without any pain – just a numb feeling. Sometimes the sadness became overbearing to the point I felt like bursting into tears. There were also many regrets. If only I had made the Ryder Cup for his sake; if only he had been with me for some of my great moments; if only he had spent more time with me on tour. All this meant that my game suffered.

In the later part of his life my father and I became so close that we were like best friends. We were like brothers. Actually my brothers and I called him John all the time — not dad. We had great times in his last years and I am so happy about that. He was never a drinker. Occasionally he would take a drink and I suppose the term for it today is a 'social drinker'. But when he came out with me he just loved his hot whiskeys and he lived for music. Many a great night was spent in Gort. I would bring him into Tom Lambert's pub and we would enjoy the great music and join in with the songs. But away from the merriment he had problems with his heart and so it was a very sad and worrying time for all of us.

For the last two years of his life he moved into our home in Gort where he was very lovingly looked after by Ann. I was away playing golf most of the time but when I came back I would value the times we spent in the house or in Lambert's.

My dad John became a great companion. He helped enormously and was a huge influence on my children's young lives. Often I would hear him telling or reading stories to them. Sometimes I would feel a lump in my throat seeing him with my own children. I would find myself thinking back to my own childhood days in Knocknacarra listening with my mouth open wide to stories told by my own parents and grandparents. On so many occasions we all packed up the car and went off for the day. We went to the Burren in Clare or we fished off Black Head. When we landed a catch everyone became excited. Ann, together with the kids, rushed over to see what I was reeling in and their grandfather then got himself ready for his favourite task. On a long line of lures and feathers, the dark blue and shiny grey wriggling bodies of some six or seven mackerel were brought ashore.

While dad quickly freed the slippery fish from the hooks, Ann then prepared a fire on a bed of rocks. As all cooks know, fish is very easy and quick to serve up. There is nothing quite like the taste of beautiful freshly cooked fish eaten there and then on the spot.

Dad was also very cute. On the way home I would look at him in the back seat from my rear-view mirror as I drove. He would bounce the kids up and down on his knees singing and telling them stories but all the time he was trying to keep them awake. He knew that if they fell asleep I would have to keep driving and so bypass one of his favourite music pubs near home. If he managed to keep them awake however, I would pull in and we would listen to music for an hour or so. Ann would then drive us home!

Those were the days of such blissful happiness which are rapidly disappearing now and that is so sad. No amount of glory at golf or brilliant business deals can compensate for such family days out. They were magnificent memories. Suddenly I would snap out of it after making a bogey on a green in England's Moor Park. A double-bogey would follow the screams of a fish eagle high in the skies amid the haunting ice peaks of the Crans Montana mountain range in Switzerland.

Then thoughts of making the Ryder Cup would spur me on to achieve a good Top 10 finish but I would miss a cut the following week. So much baggage in my head was far too much to handle on my own until one day I was cleansed of it all.

It all came pouring out one day. It spewed forth and it kept on coming for days on end and by the time it was all over I was cleaned inside. Worse than any cold turkey syndrome, this was the hardest tonic I could ever have received.

I was golfing in Spain with Eamonn Darcy and some friends from Gort. We were all smiling and joking and having a great relaxing time when suddenly, out of the blue, I heard my name called at the reception. A bit surprised I made my way over to the receptionist. He spoke in very poor broken English. I told him I was Christy O'Connor and I asked what the matter was. He said that he was sorry to tell me that my father had died.

My world collapsed around me. I fell to the floor and was out cold for a few seconds. I do not have to go on and tell you that the tears flowed out of me. I was distraught. My best friend; my brother; my singing buddy; my companion was gone. The one person who forced my hand and made me determined to make my own name at golf was now gone from this world. He was gone from my life and I was so gutted that we would not share important moments that I was determined he would see in future. Dad was not there for a lot of my success in '75 and after that in various other events like the British Open. He shared my anger and disappointment at not making the '85 Ryder Cup.

In my mind I had always told myself I was going to make up for it all. In the early years he was largely missing from my life but in his later years we became close. I was going to win and I was going to make that Ryder Cup and I was going to make sure he saw it.

Then in an instant he died. I will never forget that moment in a faraway Spanish golf course. When I composed myself I rang Ann. She was so upset as well and the two of us were crying our eyes out. I wanted him back. I had always hoped he would get well so that when he was fit and able, he would one day see me play my best golf again; he would see me do well in another British Open; another Irish Open — but above all that damned Ryder Cup.

How could he leave at that particular time? I had so many plans prepared in my head and I wanted to pay him back. I desperately wanted to give him back something for all he did for me, especially as we had become such great friends much later in our lives. That bereft feeling enveloped me. I would never get a chance to do the same as Rory McIlroy at the US Open and just say 'thank you dad' as I made a Ryder Cup team or won another tournament. It was harsh. It was cruel. But there was one small comfort.

He died out in the fresh air and on Irish soil he loved so dear. On one of his daily walks in Galway's Coole Park, he just collapsed and passed away. It surely was a great blessing that he went out of this world on green grass that had been a part of him all his life.

****

Gradually we picked up the pieces and life went on. We gathered up dad's personal belongings and we made new changes in and around the house. Then one day we decided to make a new addition to the family. My father always loved animals and to this day I love to walk in woods and fields with my own pet Labrador. We decided to keep my father's dog Coco. Dad walked him daily and Coco stayed beside his body in Coole Park for seven hours until he was found.

In my own life and pastimes I also made sweeping changes. A year after my father died I joined Gort Gun Club. In winter I would walk with friends for miles shooting pheasant and duck. Thinking back to the days of Peg and Silver, I purchased some horses which I kept in the field beside us. In his horse-trailer, Eamonn Darcy would bring his horses with him from his Wicklow home and we would ride out in the fields with the local hunt.

Life was good again and my golf was getting better. In line with that there was a brilliant buzz beginning to sweep across the entire country as something happened in 1986 which was to totally transform Irish sport.

In February 1986 Jack Charlton was appointed Republic of Ireland soccer manager. In 1988 he qualified them for the European Championships in Germany and in Italia 1990 he brought them to their first World Cup finals in history. Who will ever forget those hazy summer days when Irish soccer reached unprecedented heights? Ireland beat the old enemy England in Stuttgart and of course then went on to reach the last eight in the World Cup two years later.

It all helped to spur me on to better things as well. Back on tour and in the first event of the 1989 season, which began in February, Jose Maria Olazabal won the Tenerife Open with Philip Walton fourth. I was back in 40th and my form was still not great. I missed one cut in the first half dozen or so events and I finished down the field in the others. But on April Fools' Day, my game seemed to come together at last.

After shooting a third round 69 following opening rounds of 70 and 72 I found myself in a tie for third place going into the final day's play at the Volvo Open in Italy. I was lying on five under par and just three shots behind the leader Vijay Singh. The old habit of a bad last round haunted me again as I shot 73. In all honesty it mattered little anyway as I would have had to shoot 64 to beat Vijay. The great Fijian won by three shots. I was delighted with my form and finished fifth to receive a nice cheque for £9,000.

Jersey in the Channel Islands was our port of call the very next week. It was always very high on the tour agenda of golfers. It had a real summer holiday feel similar to Butlins or Pontins and we stayed with Carol Upton and her husband who were so hospitable to us. I got off to a very bad start with a +2, 73. In a strange sort of way, and in keeping with the jovial and warm holiday atmosphere, I just decided to loosen my elbow after that opening round. I had nothing to lose and I felt I might as well enjoy the last few days.

Next day I put together 70 but then on so-called 'moving day' I shot straight up with the leaders after a magnificent five under 66. That left me on a total of 209 meaning that only Denis Durnian was in front of me by a single shot.

Playing with Denis in the last group was a great privilege. Not only was he a fantastic golfer but he was also a sound character. I knew him very well and we got on great together. His talents were such that he shot a mind-boggling 28 on the front nine holes of a British Open. That record still stands today and I would not be surprised if it is the record for all the majors. It is also incredible that he never played in a Ryder Cup.

I can remember that there was not much between us for the entire day. Both of us played fairly good golf. All the real drama came at the very end by which time I had managed to turn a one-shot deficit into a one-shot lead.

Taking a 5-iron for my second shot to the 18th green, I found the bunker. But I made a lovely connection with my sand wedge as I got the ball fairly close to the hole. Denis made two putts for par and I looked over to see an expression of resignation on his face. His body language suggested he expected me to knock in the par putt to win. However, my ball was just a little bit further away from the hole for comfort. I faced a putt of around eight feet but it was very tricky. It was downhill on a fairly fast surface.

It had seemed like an eternity since my last win and now, less than three years after my dad had passed away, I had another tour win less than three yards away. I missed. Denis and I would have to go back to play the 17th Hole in the ensuing Play-Off. I never felt comfortable over the putt. That was ironic as for the previous three rounds I had found a new putting technique which was fabulous. It was strange and weird. I never had such a putting style before. The technique involved drawing the putter back very slow. It was almost like slow motion. Then I would follow through in exactly the same slow format. The feel was beautiful and smooth and it worked like a dream. The first play-off hole was like a role reversal of my debacle on the final green. This time it was Denis who made the telling error. He ended up taking a bogey five whereas I knocked my second shot on the green.

I had two putts to win and that feeling is always so sweet. Any golfer in that position knows that it is almost impossible to lose. Bubba Watson was in a similar position in the 2012 US Masters. I never had any cause for concern and I won.

Being crowned Jersey European Airways Open champion felt great.

I took off my cap and shook the hand of Denis. I looked up to the heavens and said a silent word of thanks to my maker and to my father.

The feeling was fantastic as I walked off the green and into the arms of my wife Ann. It had taken 14 long years to win on the European Tour again. The victory was all the sweeter precisely because of that huge timespan.

It was such a relief. There was also immense satisfaction in having so much faith in my own abilities. In the end it may not have been pretty but I was a winner again. I knew it was a matter of time. I had been knocking on the door and now it had finally opened.

In holding aloft the trophy I wished that all the knocking on Heaven's door would yield some sort of miracle and that I would be able to see my dad smiling and applauding. Alas I could not see in but I know he savoured every second of it.

That victory was dedicated to his memory. When the celebrations died down and I came back down to earth, I had time to digest the win in more detail. The £30,000 first prize put me right up into the Ryder Cup picture but there was still a long way to go. Press, television and radio all carried the story of my win at La Moye in Jersey. Next morning I read the sports pages and I basked in the newspaper reports and the glory of a 40-year old veteran who had won again after 14 years.

Across the globe the news travelled fast. Some of the biggest newspapers in the world gave my win several paragraphs and more. Among them were well-known papers like the Los Angeles Times while the Houston Chronicle described my win as 'nervous'.

I was back among the elite again. I had the taste of a modern victory and I wanted more of it. It was just a pity that my dearly departed dad never got to see. In the meantime, I had some very important and unfinished business.

CHAPTER 12

Under Pressure

12th Hole: Second part of 'Amen Corner' – 155yards, Par 3 at Augusta 1977. Ranked as the Masters' second hardest hole — with Rae's Creek in front and bunkers at the front and back of a hugely sloping green — I made par in both my rounds

Ann and I had a blazing stand-up argument — in public and in a restaurant — after my third round in the 1989 German Open. It was a week after my 41st birthday and after the final round the next day, the European team for that year's Ryder Cup would be announced. The row began after I told her that I lost the putting technique which helped me to win the Jersey Open. But my wife was not having any of it. She felt that there was a lot more to what I had said and that suddenly losing my putting stroke was only an excuse.

She let me know about it in no uncertain terms and she did not care if the whole world heard her views. Looking around rather sheepishly I hoped that nobody I knew was watching. That did not matter to Ann and there was no stopping her. She tore into me with her basic argument being that I was looking for a bit of a secure cushion and an excuse if I did not make the Ryder Cup team.

There was one round left to play before the European team would be revealed. I understood what she was saying. Ann had pushed me all year and now she felt that I had become complacent. Just because I won the Jersey Open did not mean I was in the team. She saw a false sense of security coming over me — a certain willingness to just bask in what had been a great season and just take that. Perhaps I could coast home and if that was not enough then I could always say that my putting stroke deserted me.

It was lazy-minded. Ann was right to be furious. She knew my personality better than anyone and she could see the warning signs setting in. In effect, she was nipping my defeatist thoughts in the bud before they had time to settle and grow. I promised her with reassurances that I would knuckle down and work hard to cement my place in the European team for the remaining round. After that penultimate round I was lying in the Top 20 on -5 following rounds of 70, 70 and 68.

In reality I was looking at all the other golfers ahead of me who were firing in birdies and their rounds were in the 60s. My putting touch did not seem to be working as it had done on tour for the previous few months. But I had to knuckle down and work harder.

A last round 67 meant that I finished in the Top 30. On the whole I was quite pleased with my performance as the pressures were so huge. Besides Ann pushing me I saw Tony Jacklin peeping out from behind trees — literally.

The last round was also a further improvement on the previous one so I was fairly happy.

It was another high enough finish and above all it was showing that I was maintaining the high level of consistency that I had shown from the start of the season.

My putter had been on fire all through the year since my win in Jersey. After a Top 30 in Madrid, a Top 20 in Spain and making the last 16 of the World Matchplay in St Pierre, Wales my game really took off.

At the Volvo PGA I shot a last round 65 to finish joint fourth with Seve and Mark McNulty.

That round tied the best of the week with Gordon Brand and

Seve and I picked up a cheque for £18,000. A couple of weeks later I went one better and finished tied for third in the Dunhill Masters at Woburn behind Nick Faldo. That earned me another £20,000. I was seventh at the English Open, which ironically was at The Belfry, and just outside the Top 10 in the Irish Open.

The money was all adding up and moving me fairly comfortably into the automatic Top 10 for Ryder Cup selection. There were plenty of other Top 20 and Top 30 finishes as well. I was playing my top game with all the big boys like Seve, Nick and Bernhard.

Inside my mind I suppose I had been a bit cocky. I had a feeling that there was no way Tony was going to overlook me this time. The accumulation of money was also cementing that feeling but I needed a good kick up the arse from Ann to keep those thoughts away.

Thankfully I came up trumps in that last round with a 67. But from feeling fairly comfortable about making the team after my good win in Jersey, it was now squeaky bum time because I was almost certain to finish outside of the automatic places.

In fairness to all the great golfers involved at the end, it was testament to how everyone knuckled down and fought tooth and nail for a treasured Ryder Cup place. People like Gordon Brand, Sam Torrance and Ronan Rafferty were playing their best golf ever. A blanket photo finish was the outcome with so many of us clustered together just outside of the Top 10. Because of this I felt I could miss out again and I was feeling worried sick. Once more it would all come down to Tony's choices. I did not know how it would go. After losing out in 1985 it was easy to understand my worry and torment. If I was rejected again — after a very good and very consistent year — it would have been a most severe and painful blow and one I might never recover from.

More than that, it would be hugely embarrassing. My family and friends were excited; fellow Irish golfers were rooting for me and Ireland was ready to forgive the 1985 exclusion fully expecting that I had delivered and deserved it this time around.

Then a funny thing happened in the locker-room afterwards

which puzzled me. Bernhard Langer, with that devious, quiet smile of his which is set deep into his pale stone-faced features, winked at me.

I was wondering why he winked at me and looking back now I should have asked him what he was winking for. Maybe when I bump into him again we will have a laugh and he will tell me what that was all about. It was certainly not a 'howya Christy' wink or a wink of smug satisfaction after his Top 10 finish which cemented his own place in the team. I could not pick up his vibes at the time but I was soon to find out.

Ann and I took a flight to Heathrow Airport and then got a connecting flight to Dublin. One of the top Aer Lingus officials approached us while we were in our seats and congratulated me on making the Ryder Cup team.

For a moment I would not believe it. I could not take the word of someone who was not party to Tony Jacklin or the team. But Ann and I were then left in no doubts when we were told that it was all over the Irish news and evening papers. I still did not believe it. At that moment Langer's wink suddenly sprung to mind. It all added up. He knew I was in the team but he was under orders not to let it out. But the team was out and my wife and I were seemingly the very last people to know about it.

We embraced and screamed with delight. There were smiles all round. Champagne was delivered to our seats courtesy of Aer Lingus. The bubbly matched the effervescent mood now on board. When we toasted our success we glanced at each other for a few seconds in a combined and almost intertwined look of relief. You could almost see our lips blowing out an elongated version of the word 'phewwwwwww'.

Disembarking at Dublin Airport, and making our way into the Terminal building, airport workers and passengers burst into applause. The hair and goosebumps stood up all over my body. We were so proud.

Before making our way home Ann insisted that we go to a little church and say prayers of thanks to the Almighty. At home the phone was hopping and locals popped in to congratulate us. A little while later Tony Jacklin rang to congratulate me.

The Ryder race was over and yet it was only starting.

****

The pressure was off and it was ready to run riot. It gathered up momentum. In a totally ironic way the applause and the congratulations only served to entice the pressure back in a way that was worse than ever.

I would get up out of bed in the mornings after that great night and 'whooosh' — it would come gushing into your system like a burst water pipe. The veins in my body seemed to tighten each time I thought about it.

It was constantly simmering under the surface of my skin. The long, lonely weeks and months leading into two years of prior build-up can never prepare you for this. As you read this you can only get a superficial understanding of my situation from these words.

Every single thing starts to annoy you. You feel on edge. Because sometime, somewhere, somehow, someone placed on my shoulders the responsibility of an entire continent. Is it their fault? Oh really — then why did I accept it?

Your body feels an onset of panic. You cannot sleep properly. You want to go to the pub. You get scared. You get frightened. You wonder if you really deserve to be in the team. You think negatively, about the poor performances and missing a cut in the penultimate event.

That last point eats away at you. You tell yourself that the other players were so much better over the season and the year before. In turn that drills deeper into you and instills an almost sure fact that you are the weak link in a strong European chain. Goodbye.

I was always desperate to be a part of this but now I am not so sure anymore. What if my putting deserts me and I miss the final putt to hand the USA victory? What if I do not get so much as half a point for my colleagues? It all adds up to you asking your-self:

"DO I REALLY WANT TO BE ON THE EUROPEAN RYDER CUP TEAM?"

All those terrible ingredients and those unwelcome impos-tors together make up PRESSURE. 'Pressure' is a word that was formed in the womb of etymology and then conceived in the Oxford dictionary. Its very structure can weigh you down.

The first half is 'press'. Will the PRESS slam you Christy? How are you going to cope with the huge expectation from everyone which will constantly press down on you? The second half is 'sure'. Are you SURE you want this Christy?

All of this was on my shoulders and the competition had not even begun. It was horrible. Even worse was the fact that I was not an individual operating alone in a singular event where it was just about me and how I performed and where I would end up. You can get over dropping a shot; missing a putt and losing a tournament because that is personal and it is for you. The Ryder Cup is for your teammates, for your country and for Europe. You know that if you make a costly error you take them all down with you.

Certain joyous moments briefly take the intense pressure away from your aching head and shoulders. But even then those very occasions can actually heap it all back on top of you again like the day when my Ryder Cup gear arrived in Gort. I organised a special fitting session for my family and friends. I felt like a male model strutting my stuff up and down the room in my various Ryder Cup uniforms. That was a lovely, special day.

The golf bag was emblazoned with the Europe logo but we could still put our own personal merchandise in it. I was contracted to North Western Golf Clubs at the time but I cleaned and polished some of my favourite clubs to put in the bag, including a Ping 2-iron.

We all flew to The Belfry for a team meeting on a Monday morning. How strange it was to see us all together. The most famous names in European golf and there we all were sitting down together and chatting.

It was a funny situation to me. Week in and week out we were all in competition. We were trying to outdo one another and win as individuals. Now here we all were mingling as one big team. Some guys who we thought did not get on were now the best of friends.

Nick Faldo came over to me and said:

"Christy, you have been playing brilliantly all year. Just keep doing what you are doing because you are doing great."

The famous winker Bernhard Langer said the same but the best advice of all came from Seve. Whether he was serious or he was just trying to gee me up I do not know. He said:

"I wish my game was as good as yours."

Practise rounds then followed soon after. Jacklin would form various pairings and then change them around again for the afternoon session. This was all designed to see who the Captain viewed as the golfers who got on best and who played well together as a pair.

On the Thursday — which was the day before the Ryder Cup teed off — I was paired with Spaniard Jose Maria Canizares. We were scribbled down on the sheet to face the awesome duo of Seve and Jose Maria Olazabal.

We beat them 3&2 so I suppose Seve was right after all! But there was a huge surprise and even a shock in store. I felt that we got on great and we thoroughly enjoyed ourselves beating the formidable Spanish best friends. But Tony Jacklin split us up. Instead he put me with Ronan Rafferty when it came to the actual competition.

Although Ronan was from Warrenpoint and he was a very talented golfer with a great future, I found it very difficult to gel with him. Generally I would be a laidback and easygoing character. When you do not know someone particularly well it is difficult to make a judgement but I found with Ronan that I always needed to please him. That is the best way I can explain our not gelling.

Tony did not play me on the opening day of Friday Foursomes and Fourballs but he played Ronan in the morning Foursomes with Bernhard Langer. Their match was actually the turning point in the morning play.

After the first three games we trailed the Americans 2-1 with Ronan and Bernhard the last match on course. If they won then it would be all level going into the afternoon play. But they lost 2&1 to Mark Calcavecchia and Ken Green. Europe trailed 3-1. However, the Americans were in for quite a shock later in the day. They lost all four games to trail 5-3 overnight. The highlight of that afternoon was the outstanding display of Ballesteros and Olazabal, who thumped Tom Watson and Mark O'Meara 6&5.

I was up early on Saturday morning as together with Ronan we faced Calcavecchia and Green. I knew 'Calc' fairly well from playing events like the British Open. He was always known as a very sociable guy. I did not know very much about Ken Green. Poor Ken has had an absolutely horrendous time in the years since and I will not, out of respect for him, go into any of that. On the golf course he was known as a bit 'flighty' and he always played with his traditional green glove.

On paper and even teeing up that morning I always felt we had the beating of them. Even when the game warmed up I felt we would always beat them but it then turned into a bit of a nightmare to be honest. Ronan and I just did not gel. We were looking out for each other too much. In fairness to us both I think we were very nervous. When Ronan missed a short enough putt from around eight feet on the 16th it was curtains. We lost 3&2 and I felt that was very harsh.

Despite the fact that we were always looking out for each other and in hindsight probably too much, we should have beaten them. Do not take my word for it. A policeman walked with me to the clubhouse. He smiled at me and said: "Christy I don't know how you boys lost. You never looked second best to them."

164

All smiles during a photo shoot for the book with the big dog!

Spending time with my wife Ann and our grandchild Ava and (below, from left) myself, Ann and Nigel with daughter Ann and Mark Belton on their wedding day

Sharing the limelight with Telly Savalas and Greg Norman after another hard-fought battle

A very proud moment for me as I receive the Freedom of Galway City back in 2000 and (below) dotting the Is and crossing the Ts on the honour

Accepting my Hall of Fame award from three-time Major winner Padraig Harrington at the Sports Personality of the Year awards in 2002; (below) getting set for the 2006 Ryder Cup at the K Club with AIB's Billy Andrews

With Christy Senior at our conferral in NUIG and (below) observing the form with my son Nigel at Leopardstown racecourse

With Ann following my triumph at the British Masters in 1992

My beloved little granddaughter Ava is my biggest fan

All pics courtesy of: Gary Ashe, Thomas Sunderland, Getty Images, Sportsfile, INPHO and Mac Innes

Earlier Nick Faldo and Woosie beat Lanny Wadkins and Payne Stewart 3&2 to increase our lead to 6-3. But up ahead of my match, Sam Torrance and Gordon Brand lost heavily to Chip Beck and Paul Azinger.

Together with our loss it meant that the score was now 6-5 and we all went to shout on Seve and Ollie in the last of the morning games. Our rocks and our flagship came up trumps again. In a thriller they edged Tom Kite and Curtis Strange 1up. We led 7-5.

In the afternoon Jacklin sent out his big guns. America actually squared the match after winning the first two games. But after Howard Clark and Mark James unexpectedly beat Payne Stewart and Curtis Strange, it was all down to Seve and Ollie again. Once more they came to our rescue with a 4&2 hammering of Calc and Green. Europe led 9-7 overnight and the match was very finely balanced going into the final day. The win by Seve and Ollie was of huge importance.

If they had lost then the scores would have been level overnight at 8-8. That would have put huge pressure on all of us. Now the pressure had eased significantly. I felt good and I now thrived on our overnight lead. I could not wait to do battle in the final day Singles.

CHAPTER 13

One Shot

13th Hole: Par 5 at Queens Park Club, Bournemouth 14th May, 1972. '13' is unlucky. My ball was pilfered by a kid in the Penfold Tournament. I was a shot ahead but after taking a penalty for a 'lost' ball Peter Oosterhuis beat me in a Play-Off

Going into the final day's 12 Singles matches in the 1989 Ryder Cup, we were 9-7 in front of USA. Jacklin put Seve, Bernhard and Ollie out as the first three. The thinking was that if they could get off to a solid start, Europe would be almost home and hosed. However, if things did not go to plan then he put Ian Woosnam, Nick Faldo and Sam Torrance as anchors in the last three. I was due out in the seventh match against the then World No.1 Fred Couples.

Amazingly Seve and Bernhard were beaten. Paul Azinger beat Ballesteros on the last hole and Chip Beck had a surprisingly comfortable 3&2 win over Langer. The sides were level again at 9-9. Olazabal steadied the ship once more by beating Payne Stewart on the final hole and we went two points clear again after Ronan Rafferty won. Ronan took out a great scalp in Mark Calcavecchia after 'Calc' drove into water on the last hole.

When I walked to the first tee for my own match with Couples, I could scarcely believe the atmosphere. It was such that you could almost reach out and touch the tension. I will never forget seeing Tom Watson's face. Tom was getting ready to play Sam

Torrance three games behind me. He was so quiet and he was ashen-faced. Here was a man who had won everything in the game and he looked like a quivering ghost.

It was strange because after the fiercely pressurised build-up, now I did not feel half as bad. Going into the Foursomes with Ronan the previous morning helped. Once the action got underway I felt much better.

When I saw that expression on Tom's face I almost felt like saying to him:

"Hey Tom, I am feeling the pressure for sure but I don't think I'm feeling it half as bad as you are!"

The atmosphere generated by the crowds was incredible. As I left the practise ground for my game with Fred the cheers were deafening. They thought they were helping – and they were – but that is also when my insides felt like falling out.

In that practise session I was probably a little less nervous than most because I got great confidence from the presence of my uncle Christy. He was there scrutinising everything I did and I also got great advice and encouragement from my brother Eugene.

I had never met Couples before. But he was officially the best player in the world and I was a huge admirer of not just his play but his laidback attitude. However, in order to do my game justice for the cause of Europe, I immediately blotted all that from my mind.

The cheers of the crowd roared out again as I made my way from the putting green to the first tee. As I stood there with Fred Couples, our caddies and the referee, it felt like two gladiators were about to enter the arena for the Romans' pleasure. I took a deep breath and I felt like all the eyes of the world were focussed on me. I knew how the Christians felt as they were about to be thrown into the cauldron of the Colosseum in Rome. Little did I know then what lay in store as Fred and I shook hands.

He seemed like the real gentleman I had always admired but I was surprised we were similar in height. From seeing him on television I always felt he was a lot taller. He was also one of golf's big hitters as he could hit a ball out of sight with wooden-headed clubs.

My late brother Sean and my brother Albert were there in the crowd as were half of Galway, Clare and the west of Ireland who turned up to support me. That made me feel a lot better and in a way I felt I was in a home away from home.

One of the best bits of advice that I received came from my uncle Christy. I will always remember his very prophetic words to me just before I began my round:

"You are here today because of your swing. Don't forget to concentrate fully on that."

Fred unleashed one of his trademark boomers from the first tee. I stood there watching the flight of his ball. I was willing it to come down as it seemed as if it would never come out of the air.

It was an ideal start from him but it did not rattle me. My uncle's words came to mind and I knew I just had to remember them and also play my percentages. I was not the longest or shortest hitter but I knew I could more than match his taking two shots to reach the green.

We both made par. At the second hole I made a nice birdie to go 1up and Fred squared the match with his own birdie at the third. Any nerves were now well and truly shaken off and we were really warming up.

He unsettled me at the fourth which was a Par 5 over water perilously close to the green. In all my years playing The Belfry I had never seen anyone go for the green with the second shot but Fred pulled out his 4-wood.

Not alone did he make the green but he carried on through it to the second fairway behind it.

In my entire career to that point, and having played alongside countless numbers of golfers, I had never seen anyone hit a first and second shot so far.

He was constantly out-driving me by almost 50 yards. But I still played my own game, concentrated on my swing and calculated percentages to halve the hole. Fred then went 1up at the fifth with a birdie and I squared the match yet again with birdie on the very next.

I can remember around that stage looking up at the scoreboard and seeing the amount of 'red' that had already won or was leading. The Yanks were battling real hard with the likes of Azinger, Beck, Stewart and Calcavecchia all putting it up to us. In fact by the time the match two holes ahead of me came to a premature end, the USA were 10-9 in front. That is because Tom Kite served up a real roasting to Howard Clark, hammering him 8&7. Seeing all the red in the ascendancy had an effect on me. I felt we were getting hammered and as I did not want to be a victim I told myself:

"I can't win the games for the other guys but I can certainly beat Fred in this one."

Exactly at the halfway stage I stepped up a gear. I secured one of my best birdies at the ninth. Both of us were on the putting surface in two. With a putt from around 30ft I canned it to go 1up (remember those old tin cans from Galway Bay!)

The adrenaline within my body was in overdrive after that birdie. It welled up and forced me to clench my fist and punch the air. Previously I felt as if I had been hanging on to Fred's coattail but now I was bubbling as I stood on the 10th tee to survey the situation.

In normal circumstances I would never go for it or even do what Seve did. Many years before, he drove the green and a commemorative plaque was recently laid there on the side of that green to recognise his daring feat. But I just knew that Fred, in the form he was in, would go for it. My caddy Matthew Byrne looked at me and thank God he agreed with me when I said:

"We're going to have a go."

With slight left to right fade, I watched my drive turn in the air. Like a laser-guided missile it threaded its way through the tree-guided green left and right. It passed through but it also carried the green and into a bunker at the back.

Fred then stepped up and with no fuss he found the green. He made two putts for birdie and levelled the match again. An over-exuberant moment of pumped-up adrenaline had cost me but I was determined to show Couples that I was not intimidated by his play.

We remained level until a big turning point at the 13th. It is one of the shortest of the Par 4 holes on the course, measuring just over 380 yards, and so it represents a very good chance of a birdie.

He went 1up after making a good birdie there and I felt this was a huge slip on my part. I thought I had lost my chance at that point because there were only five holes left to play and both 15 and 17 would be hugely advantageous to him as they were Par 5s.

The 15th really showed that the pressure was beginning to affect us both. It can only be described as a comedy of errors. Both of us had birdie putts from around seven feet but we both missed. The half meant that he was still 1up with just three left to play.

It was a case of 'now or never'. I gritted my teeth and firmly told myself that if I did not birdie the 16th, then the match was as good as over. A half was really no good with the big-hitting Couples looking forward to the 17th. The percentages told me that a birdie or par at the 17th would mean that my chances of beating Fred Couples would be over. He would most likely reach that green with a putt for an eagle but an almost certain birdie as well.

Of course I was still very much alive in the contest for an all important half point but to beat Couples I simply had to birdie the 16th. I gave myself a great chance when striking a beautiful second shot to just over three feet. Deep down I was not overly happy when approaching the green to wild applause. Little did the crowd know but my ball was facing a very nasty left to right fall. It was such a tricky green.

Fred missed his birdie chance so I was faced with a slippery putt to win the hole. The speed and line are all important. Too little pace and the ball can curve wickedly and miss the hole. Too much pace and if it clips the cup, the ball could end up even further away.

In such circumstances you have so much else to deal with. Fred did not give it to me. He knew it was by no means easy. The crowd were hushed. The eyes of the world were on me. I could hear my heart thud in my ears.

I made it! We were all square with two left.

On the 17th I hit my drive as far as Fred's. I was playing so well and he knew I just would not go away. I started to wonder why the pressure had not affected him as he just kept on playing the way he had been. At no point was there any sign of him breaking.

This was the last Par 5 and it represented a great opportunity for one of us to grab the game by the scruff of the neck. I was so pumped up. My drive demonstrated this and I wanted to keep up the pressure. Surely he must crack soon as I had kept apace with him.

I asked Matthew for the 2-iron as I was going to try to chase it up onto the green for the chance of an eagle but certainly a birdie. I did not want to give Couples any sniff of a chance or show him any sign of easing up.

There was no way after levelling the game through sheer will-power at 16 that I was now going to allow him the chance to win this hole and go to the last 1up. We were all square and I was determined and very focussed at such a crucial time.

It struck the ball well, but again there was just a bit too much adrenaline in the strike. The ball raced through the green. When I reached my ball I was somewhat despondent to see that it was nestled in a horrible spot. But Couples was in a bit of bother of his own.

His second shot came to rest under the lip of the bunker on the right. There was little chance of an eagle from either of us to go down the last with a cushion of being 1up.

In fact it was hard to know just who was in the better position.

Golfers instinctively know the situation is bad when the full white of their ball is not showing. When a ball sits up like normal, you can do so much with it. You can get the club right under it, you can pitch and run or you can even try a 'Mickleson flop'.

I could not do any of that. In order to make sure that I actually connected with the ball properly I would have to hit it firmly. I would have to make sure that I wrapped the club right around it rather than topping it, slicing it, fluffing it or duffing it.

This meant a firm punched shot and in such circumstance you never know how the ball is going to come out. You know one thing for sure. It is going to fly out at pace and so you just hope it will not run through the green.

It positively flew out and my heart was in my mouth. The ball was flying towards the pin and for a second I was begging it to slow down or even hit the pin to halt its pace. I got an even bigger bonus. It lipped the cup and came to a halt just eight feet away.

The pressure must have been monumental on Couples. He saw my ball close to the pin for a birdie. He had to match or better that in order not to fall behind going down the last hole.

He played an exquisite shot from the sand to leave himself an even shorter birdie chance than my own. As this topsy-turvy match was reaching its conclusion, there would be even more drama.

Eight feet and a chance to go 1up but excruciatingly I missed. It looked like it was certain to drop but it stayed out. I was gutted. I had blown it. Couples had a putt from about six feet to go 1up with just one hole left. It was curtains for my hopes of beating him.

Jacklin was squatting by the side of the green. I shook my head, grimaced and looked away almost apologetically. It was a signal to our magnificent support that I was so unhappy at missing. Inside I felt empty. At best, I felt that all I could hope for now was to win the 18th for a half. I leaned on my putter and watched Fred Couples survey his short putt to go 1up.

It looked an easy putt but then I noticed that perhaps all was not lost. Fred looked troubled. I watched his hands and his cross-handed stroke. Something seemed not right about it. All of a sudden he seemed unhappy with this putt; not sure about its line or even his whole putting technique. He seemed uncomfortable. My senses were suddenly sharpened as my eyes focussed in on him. In an instant he seemed to lose all of his previous faith and trust in his putting. He moved the putter back to strike the ball home for the win and a most alarming thing happened.

His hands made an involuntary move. He missed. I could not believe what I had just seen. Of course in golf anything can happen and there are really no surprises but he seemed so solid all through our match.

Was he finally cracking under pressure?

We remained all square playing the very last hole. I had one chance left. Despite the miss Fred seemed cool and unfazed. He was showing no outward signs of pressure. Like a dog that would not let go, I constantly snapped and bit his heels but he still seemed strong. Keeping my advantage from the win on the 16th, I stood on the very last hole with the honour of driving. 'Honour' seems like a strange word given what lay in front of me. It was akin to a condemned man being given the 'treat' of his last meal.

The 18th at The Belfry is one of the most feared holes in golf. To make it even harder I had to deal with crowds alongside me; the world's media; huge congregations up around the green and Fred reeling and raging inside. There are generally two ways to play this daunting last hole and I consulted with Matthew for a few moments. You can play a right to left fade to avoid the water but as you avoid that hazard, every yard means an extra 10 yards' distance or carry to the green.

We made up our minds that we would take the easier option of hitting a shot with slight fade. This was my favourite left to right draw shot. The big disadvantage with this shot was that it would inevitably leave me with a much longer second shot to the green.

When I unleashed my drive I was in a blind spot to see where it came to rest. It looked like I had executed the drive to as near perfect as I could but I was hoping that it finished up alright. A simultaneous cheer and applause rang out from the crowds up ahead so I knew my ball had found the fairway. That was huge relief but I knew the hardest part was to come because I was now left with a very long second shot.

Couples seized on my playing safe to launch one of his boomers. He took the other route and did the exact opposite of me hitting a massive right to left drive. It worked like a dream for him. He was left with a mere 7-iron to the green. Inside I just had to admire him. He never flinched all day. I was playing my best golf in years. I was driving and hitting like I had never done before because of the class of opponent I was facing.

Most of the crowd were on my side but from start to finish he was as cool as a cucumber playing his golf. He looked so relaxed as he moseyed around the course but inside I knew because of how I felt, that he must surely have been feeling the heat too. We were opponents but it was a great match and a real battle between two gladiators from very different parts of the world. When I reached my ball I could not believe what I saw. It lay in a bare spot with no grass underneath.

I do not know how you would feel playing your second shot from there. Perhaps you would like to be on lush green grass. Maybe the very best golfers in the world would also have preferred something a little softer underneath.

I felt excited. It had been a long time since I had seen a ball lying like this. I relished such a shot as it was similar to all those shots I played in Salthill and in Lahinch as a young boy and teenager. To me it was like playing a shot on a weather-beaten links course.

Perhaps the fates were helping me with what was going to be a very daunting second shot. If I was to survive this monumental tussle with Fred Couples then this was going to have to be the shot of my life. I had come this far and I had one fairway shot left.

I could almost sense Fred feeling smug as he glanced back at me from his lofty position up ahead waiting for me to hit. I had to dig deep down and gee myself into a state of real focused determination.

Just when I was telling myself this, and sizing it up with Matthew, I got a bit of a fright. There was my Captain Tony Jacklin beside me again with Bernard Gallacher and I remember wishing they were not there. I did not want them watching me. I wished that they would disappear and I certainly did not want any communication from them. I was trying hard to concentrate only to hear Tony say under his breath:

"Just one more swing for Ireland. Anywhere on the green will put huge pressure on him."

One more shot. Suddenly Tony's presence did not seem so bad. Actually standing there and hearing his words reassured me. It was so ironic that he, of all people, should be standing there shouting me on. It seemed totally inappropriate.

This is what it had all boiled down to. The last hole; the last day; the last fairway shot I would play. Perhaps even the chance to prove you so wrong Mr Jacklin for rejecting me in 1985.

I was going to give this last shot everything. The hot adrenaline pumping in my veins all day was now sizzling. The drama; the roller coaster of emotions; the advice from a man who was all of a sudden taking a huge and exciting interest in my game was stirring me.

All sportsmen and women know this feeling. You have one chance left. You have one moment in time. The last 15 minutes and one last gasp effort. This was it. It was now or it would be never.

The rush is on. Legs scurry to my left and right along the fairway as people search for prime position. Up ahead the galleries increase. Couples looks back at me waiting. Golf buggies move into position. Your concentration, your senses are so sharp and prickly.

Camera lenses are pointing in my direction. All eyes are on me. European eyes are depending on me. Americans are praying in unison with Couples that my shot does not make an impact. I am primetime viewing.

Matthew was in that same place as me. We were both figures of concentration. He advised me the following:

"Take the 2-iron. You played a great shot with it at the last hole and you can do it again."

He opened the bag wider for me to take out that club. I went over to line up my shot. I feel so proud of him. I feel so proud of Ireland and I am so determined that I will put my very best effort into this shot. My last shot.

Another great wave of emotions suddenly envelopes my entire body and the most acute sharpness and alertness is cemented by ingredients of pride, excitement, eagerness and now, above them all, sheer bloody confidence.

The very peak of adrenaline had now placed me 'IN THE ZONE'. Where have you been all my life baby? What a time to arrive! Now that I feel you here caressing my arms, head and shoulders I am not going to let you go until we sing together for the fat lady.

Together we are going to play this shot. We are going to do it for Ireland, for Europe, for Matthew, for my uncle, for Ann — FOR ME. More words from Senior echo in my head:

"If you come down the stretch with a chance, don't forget a full turn on the backswing."

There I was recalling those very helpful words in the middle of a fairway with the eyes of the world on me. Most professional golfers hit quick and sudden and I would make sure to make a natural and full swing.

So here goes baby. I am so full of confidence now. I stand and pick my line for the ball straight to the pin. I swing back with head rigid and eyes firmly on the ball. At the top of my full backswing I remember not to rush down.

Steady, steady, steady — then release. My swing falls back down naturally and in a calm, assured motion and then 'whoosh'. It was perfect. I felt the sweet spot as my ball soared through the air like a small, white fireball.

My head rises up naturally from the follow-through. My eyes roll up and down surveying the ball's speed, direction and line. Quickly they send messages to my brain. They gather information from all sources available. Some are most unlikely.

I look at the ducks on the lake in front of the green. The birds are going about their relaxed business undisturbed so I know that my ball is a real beauty. She has passed silently and high above the birds burning out her noisy 'fizz' into a graceful finesse.

That means only one thing. She is heading for the green and for my Captain at least, that is good news. I watch her slowly swoop in to land. She seems to be right on line. My mind screams forth the golfer's plea 'be good'. I delight in seeing it make the green.

From over 200 yards back she looks like she is going to home in fairly close to the pin. But I am too far back to tell. The galleries will tell me. Then an almighty clap of thunder is accompanied by the vision of a Mexican wave-like ripple of applause and cheering.

Over 50,000 people crammed 12-deep around that 18th have just roared their approval. My God she is a beauty! I can see her elegant poise and from the scale on my map she seems a foot from the pin but I know in reality it is more likely six feet or so.

The crowds are still roaring but we must pause and wait for Fred's riposte. In the meantime I just cannot resist stretching my head up and standing up on my tip-toes to get another glimpse of my baby. Stay there and do not move until I reach you.

As the crescendo of noise decreases to a murmur, Couples gets ready to strike a simple shot to the green. I know for sure that he must feel under pressure by now. I will know just how much he is feeling it after his shot.

If he leaves it close then he will have done what he did all day — remaining defiant to the last and treating pressure like water off a duck's back. If not, then after his blip and yip on 17, he has finally cracked.

An orthodox simple shot from Fred turns into his dreaded nightmare. He hits his worst shot of the day. Instead of pitching it straight into the green he hits it way wide. Jacklin was right — he seems to have 'gone'. His ball misses the putting surface and ends up almost 15ft off the green on the right. At that moment I felt an enormous sense of relief. I knew that I had a much better chance than Fred of winning but I would only know for sure once I got to see my ball.

As I strode closer and closer to the hole, the cheers from the crowd got louder and louder.

I took off my cap and waved to acknowledge and thank them. Then I saw what all the fuss was about and I was overcome with emotion. My ball lay just over 3ft from the pin.

At that precise moment I felt so much more than a brick wall pulled off my back. I cast my eyes to Heaven. I blessed myself and then I just burst into tears. Martin's shoulder was a relieving place to bury my head for a few moments and sob.

I could not control my new gush of emotions. Everything in my head just forced the tears out. The years of toiling had finally achieved recognition. I was now doing it on the biggest stage but it had not always been like that.

The tournaments lost; the poor form; the incidents; the accidents; the drink; the hard times hit home. But most of all were the thoughts and images of the many friends who stood by me and helped me through to this moment on the very last hole at The Belfry.

Above everything in my head was the over-riding image of my father. I so wished that along with my uncle and my brothers that he could have been there to see a moment well and truly replace all the heartbreak. All of this forced the tears out but I had to compose myself as there was still the matter of a match to be won. Putts of even shorter than mine have been missed. I had to keep my concentration. I had to show courtesy and respect to my opponent.

Freddie had an extremely difficult pitch. The green would run away from him as it fell hugely from back to front. In the circumstances he did magnificently to chip his ball to just eight feet. As he was furthest away he was first to putt.

However, with a six-inch break, he overdid it and missed. My moment had arrived to take centre stage. My heart pounded. When Fred missed I watched him anxiously. I wondered if he would make me putt. Of course he would I thought as this was no 'gimme'. Even though I had two putts from just over 3ft to win, it was a great release and a fantastic realisation to know that

I had finally won our match when Fred walked up to me and conceded.

I stooped down to pick up my marker and as I did so I murmured the words of 'Our Father'. I blessed myself again and looking up to Heaven I thanked God for the most wonderful day of my life.

The crowds rushed the green to congratulate me. My wife Ann was one of the first. It was without doubt the proudest day of my life. I was so proud of myself after all the years of playing with patience and persistence.

It seemed like it took an hour to leave that green. There were literally thousands of well-wishers and I shook so many hands. There is one particular person I remember above all the happy faces.

The 6'6" tall Policeman who walked with me after my match with Ronan Rafferty the previous day, came through the crowd. In the most adorable Cockney accent he said:

"Well done Christy! You have done us all so proud."

I would have liked to join Tony Jacklin back out on the course to support some of the players finishing their matches but it was impossible. I was literally swamped by people and I could not get away.

The Press were also there and suddenly they all loved me. They were all looking for quotes. I can recall looking and listening to some of them and who they represented. I was careful not to cooperate with some who were most undignified to me before. In fact, I could not wait to get away from many of them and just join my friends in celebration. One journalist actually accompanied me all the way to the nearest bar for a quote. Needless to say he was followed by others.

We all congregated in the team room. I used my six 'Guest Passes' to get somewhere approaching 100 people in there! The evening and the celebrations were only just beginning and there were so many Irish people around including Minister Frank Fahy.

My good friend Chris De Burgh was there but I will always

remember the late great US golfer, Payne Stewart. Payne, who was tragically killed in a plane crash, was playing the harmonica and among many songs I lashed out a good few bars of 'Galway Bay'.

Also playing in our own special band was former British Prime Minister Margaret Thatcher's husband, Denis Thatcher. He loved every minute of it and as I played the spoons I told him: "It's very hard to get a pair in England in the right key!"

We partied all night with my brothers. Nobody slept and there were a lot of blurry eyes at 9am next morning. My journalist friends had their say with The Guardian proclaiming:

'O'CONNOR LEADS THE GREAT ESCAPE'

It is scarcely believable that the last three Europeans – Torrance, Faldo and Woosnam – were all beaten. Gordon Brand Junior lost as well so it was left to Jose Maria Canizares and I to bring Europe home. We lost the singles 7-5 but tied 14-14 to retain the Cup.

Freddie had to take a flight home a few hours after the match but he said goodbye before he left. There were still plenty of Americans around that morning and the Europeans were still full of energy for partying. Payne Stewart was absolutely fantastic. He was mighty craic and it is just so sad to think of what a huge waste of talent his sudden death brought. I thank you Payne for those marvellous memories and may God be good to you.

The party continued on to Ireland later that evening. We were met at Shannon Airport by thousands more well-wishers and so many of us travelled in a convoy through Shannon and on to Gort. It was like a scene from a successful Irish soccer team returning home. Car horns were blaring and people stood by the sides of roads waving and cheering. I can even remember a Travelling family waving golf clubs up at me.

My brother Eugene, who played the accordion, organised a big session and we carried it on the whole night in as many places as we could. I cannot remember where it began or ended but I know we visited Galway Bay Golf Club and many bars in Eyre Square.

Even then it did not end for days and weeks after. That is because phone calls and letters arrived for me from all over the world. I actually received five refuse sacks full of post with one particular letter addressed to:

Christy O'Connor Junior,
2-iron,
Ireland.

Prince Andrew sent me a telegram of congratulations. He is a great golf fan and a few years later I opened a new part of The Belfry with him. I cannot thank everyone enough for their messages of support.

One of the greatest honours bestowed on me was when I was made a 'Freeman of Galway'. I felt so proud that day. I followed the likes of President John F Kennedy, Cardinal Cushing and my uncle Christy, who were also recipients of that title. The only thing missing from that wonderful time was my mother and father.

They may have been absent in person but in spirit they were very much with me — and that one shot.

CHAPTER 14

Leaving My Pitch Mark

*14th Hole: 555 yards, Par 5 Galway Bay Golf & Country Club.
Teeing off along the Bay you can cut as much off the shoreline
as you dare. This can leave a second shot to the green but I advise
playing the fairway for an easy par*

On the 27th January 1990 I teed off in the Kenya Open at
Muthaiga Golf Club in Nairobi. It was first staged in 1967 and
some very illustrious names have won it including Seve, Ken
Brown, Maurice Bembridge, Trevor Immelman and Edoardo
Molinari.

Buoyed up by the wonderful experiences off course on Safari
with my family, as well as the huge confidence taken from my performance at the Ryder Cup the previous September at The Belfry,
I took the first round lead after shooting a -5, 66. I followed that
with a -4, 67 in the next round and after another 67 pushed me
to -13, I held a two-shot lead going into the final round. It was
probably the best tournament golf I had played up to this point
particularly hitting three rounds in mid-60s.

In the final round I became a bit jittery. It is rare enough to win
'wire-to-wire' as they call it and you are also there to be shot at.
After three-putting two Par 3 holes and finding trouble off the
tee, things looked bad. But I managed to hang on. In the end a
late birdie helped me to fend off the challenge of Englishman
Chris Platts by a couple of shots. He was the son of Lionel Platts

from Harrogate and I have a very funny story to relate about Lionel.

Many years ago we were playing a tournament at Wentworth, which is affectionately known to us all as 'Burmah Road'. Lionel's caddy was still 'under the influence' from the night before and everything was fine until Lionel barked out an order to him.

On a huge two-tiered green he asked his caddy to stand next to the pin. But his caddy did not hear him properly and so he removed the pin and walked 30 yards to the right where he stood leaning on it and waiting for Lionel to play the shot.

From a low level below the surface of the green, Lionel putted up to where his caddy was standing. He seemed very happy with his effort but as he walked up to green only to find his ball 30 yards to the right, he was dismayed. I will leave the rest to your imagination.

My level par round which comprised of three bogeys and three birdies won the Kenyan Open for me on a score of -13, 271. In the 45 years of that event, I became only the fourth man from the Republic of Ireland to win it. Ernie Jones, Liam Higgins and Eamonn Darcy preceded me. No Irish golfer has managed to triumph in Kenya since. In 1991, the year after my win, the Kenya Open became part of the European Challenge Tour.

In 1990 I also represented Ireland in the Dunhill Cup at St Andrews. We faced the Americans and I will give you one guess as to which Yank I was paired against — Freddie Couples yet again. Before the match I remember thinking that if Fred beat me, everyone would say that my win against him at The Belfry was a fluke. So from the start I was really fired up to prove that my famous victory was not a one-off.

It was a tit-for-tat battle throughout. At the 15th I sank a 15ft putt to go 1up. The next was halved and then I was faced with a dilemma when looking at how to approach the penultimate hole. That 17th is another one of golf's most feared holes with its famous 'Road Hole Bunker' and the pin set just six paces in from that trap. I told Matthew my caddy that I was going to attack the hole. In going for it I remember saying to him:

"I have to go at it and get at least a half. If I don't, and Fred wins the hole to level it up, then with his length he could drive the 18th hole and perhaps have an eagle or birdie to win the match."

I hit what I still believe today was the finest shot of my career. It was even better than my 2-iron to the last hole at The Belfry. With a 4-iron I hit a magnificent fading shot high in the air and it settled like a dog with sore feet just four feet from the pin. Freddie walked up that 17th fairway with his white handkerchief tied to his club and the crowds cheering wildly. It was televised live on BBC and fair play to Fred. I gained tremendous admiration for the man over the course of two epic matches with him.

An even louder cheer ensued when he walked over to my ball and picked it up. He handed me the ball for a 2&1 victory and taking off his cap, said these words to me:

"Christy that shot was even better than your 2-iron at The Belfry."

We walked off that green together accompanied by fans and plenty of Irish roars to a great little pub called 'The Jigger' which is near the 17th hole. It was time to celebrate another great win over my famous adversary but by now, a firm friend.

A member of the Tour Committee then came in to find us. He asked who had won. As the winner is supposed to report the outcome I suddenly feared being disqualified. But thanks to Fred and all the good humour, they let it go and took it all in good heart.

****

It was around about this time that I began to get seriously involved in Golf Course Design. I had dipped my feet in it in 1987 when I was involved in the extension to Rosslare links but in the meantime I really got stuck in to learning all about it. Although I still had a huge appetite for playing as a professional on tour, I envisaged a much more lucrative career elsewhere. There was huge money to be earned from designing golf courses worldwide. No amount of money the top professionals in golf earned could ever amount to what one could earn as a course designer. There were huge opportunities everywhere with China and South Korea having massive potential.

As well as that it was all relatively new back in those days so I got into it ahead of a huge posse that'd follow later. I had a great verve for design and I had studied many aspects of it at great length.

I particularly liked learning about the great designers and architects. I really became fascinated by all aspects of it. People like Tom Doak, who worked with Ben Crenshaw, as well as Tom Fazio, who redesigned Waterville in County Kerry. I studied the McKenzie Courses around the world, which included my beloved Lahinch. So although I had not given up on tour golf by any means I was getting the bug for course design in a huge way. Grass, soils, trees — I studied all of these at great length. They are an integral part of designing golf courses and I left no stone unturned in finding out everything possible. The more I delved into it the more I wanted to know.

In 1992 I was visiting City West in Dublin which was one of my courses under construction. I boarded a helicopter to fly to another project and when we were airborne at around 200ft, it decided to stop. I can still remember the female pilot screaming: "Oh Jesus!"

I can recall the ground coming up to meet us at a ferocious speed. I was absolutely terrified. The chopper came down and hit the roof of a house named 'Teach Saggart' which belonged to Jim Mansfield. When it hit that roof it swept over onto the roof of a barn in the backyard of that house. It then smashed into the ground and lay on its side. To this day I can still smell the kerosene and as I lay there I wondered when the thing was going to catch fire.

Both of us scrambled around in our seatbelts little realising that we could not undo them no matter how much we tried. With the overpowering smell of fuel in the air I thought we were going to die. I feared that we were going to burn to death. It was quite a terrifying ordeal. We were helpless and then I could see Jim Mansfield and his son Jim screaming at us through the broken windows to 'get out'. They soon realised we could do nothing.

Young Jim then jumped through the broken window with his father screaming at him to keep back for fear of an explosion. He opened my buckle and then after he took me out he went back in for the pilot. For the rest of our lives we will always be indebted to him for his bravery. Perhaps the chopper may not have caught fire but he did not know that at the time. He was a real hero and it was a nightmare which I wish to forget. A scan revealed that I only received cuts and bruises but the aftershock only hit home a fortnight later. I was playing in the PGA at Wentworth in Surrey when I started to tremble. I had to be escorted from the course.

After resting up for a couple of days, I drove to Woburn, just an hour from north London. When I was driving up there I remember thinking to myself that I was crazy to be going to play in the British Masters. I should have been at home in Ireland resting.

One of the first people I met in Woburn was Seve. I told him what had happened to me and he could not believe it. He had a painful and squeamish look on his face and when I finished the story he told me he would never travel in another helicopter. The funny thing is that he missed the cut at Wentworth so he felt as miserable as I had felt in the days before. So as the two of us arrived at Woburn with plenty of time to spare, I introduced him to a few beers and that certainly brought the smiles and laughs back.

We talked about old times and it was as if we had been buddies for years. He invited me to practise with him and his caddy Billy Foster next day. That was a great day. As well as being alive and healthy we seemed to settle old scores and get things off our chest.

Approaching the end of our round Seve invited Billy to play the 18th with us. I had not realised up until then what a fine player Billy was — so good in fact that he was the only one of us to birdie that hole.

My late friend Barry Willet, who was the head man in the club construction department of Mizuno, bumped into me. He took me over to their on-course trailer which travelled around to events on tour throughout Europe at that time.

Barry presented me with a brand new driver which had a gold coloured head. I fell in love with it immediately. I found that I was very comfortable with it in my hands. I drove the ball so straight and long as well as fading and drawing with it at will.

I began with a steady enough -1, 71 which left me five shots adrift of leader Ove Sellberg of Sweden. In the second round I improved with a nice round of -5, 67 but on a day of very low scoring that left me some six shots adrift of Bernhard Langer who shot 65.

The third round was washed out so this meant we would have to play 36 holes on the final Sunday. At 44 years of age and after my accident just a few short weeks before, everything was against me.

In the morning I shot 66 which moved me up into the thick of things and I just had enough time to grab an egg sandwich before going out for the final round. I was well and truly out of it after the front nine holes but then I hit a purple patch.

I went on what can only be described as an unbelievable birdie blitz which was bizarre. Birdies on 10, 13 and 14 were followed by miraculous birdies on the final three holes as well. My new driver was a God-send but the old trusty 2-iron also came up trumps. With a 2-iron on the 16th, I managed to thread the ball through a very tight gap in trees to 10ft where I sank it. I followed that by drawing a ball around trees with a 9-iron to make a birdie on the 18th.

When I finished and looked up at the scoreboard I saw that I was the leader in the clubhouse. However, Nick Faldo, Tony Johnstone, Glenn Day, Stephen Richardson and Bernhard Langer were all still out on the course.

In any case I knew that at the very least I would secure a top-five finish. But by the time they completed their rounds only Tony Johnstone of Zimbabwe had matched my score. Richardson was third with Nick Faldo fourth.

On a -18 score of 270, Johnstone and I had to Play-Off. I could not believe the rich vein of form I had hit. To score successive rounds of 66 twice on the final day was beyond my wildest dreams. Suddenly I was in with a chance of another tour win.

I found myself in this miraculous position after some of the most incredible of circumstances. A few weeks previously I felt I would die and now I was in a head-to-head with Tony Johnstone for the British Masters title at Woburn.

Everything was so strange beginning with the drive to Woburn and thinking that I should turn around and go home to rest; the goodwill with Seve; the new driver from Barry and then the 36 holes on the Sunday. This was indeed a very peculiar case of aftershock. This was nothing compared to the pressure of Ryder Cup and the near-death experience so I was revelling in the spotlight again. I had nothing to lose and I played the First Tie hole in a very relaxed and almost enjoyable manner. At worst I would earn a cheque for second.

After another great drive straight down the middle, I hit an 8-iron to just two feet to win the Play-Off. I was 1992 British Masters champion and with it I earned a huge cheque for almost £125,000.

If ever you needed proof of miracles then that win was another example. At my age and on what is known as a difficult golf course I hit birdie after birdie after birdie to record my fourth win on the European Tour. I was over the moon and still in shock.

****

For the next few years I soldiered on and although I did not win anything major I was very happy with my consistency. In fact I created another milestone when I finished in the Top 100 of the European Order of Merit for 20 consecutive years from 1972-1992. Many European legends cannot boast of a record like that. The years of plugging away from event to event and picking up £200 here and there paid off. One only has to look at what befell

Lee Westwood and David Howell to see how hard it is to remain consistent.

It was becoming harder and harder to combine my new found interest in course design with my playing career. So on my 50th birthday in 1998, I joined the Seniors Tour. This allowed me a lot more time and space to develop new careers on two fronts. The Senior Tour could be quite lucrative especially in the States and after my earlier work on Rosslare and Galway Bay golf courses, I could devote much more time to designing golf courses.

Tom and Breda Reid invited me over to their home in Glasson, County Westmeath sometime in 1994. They were fabulous people from a farming background and they asked me to work on a beautiful site surrounded by lakes.

Not for nothing is Westmeath known as 'The Lake County' and my work on their course in Glasson reminded me so much of Killarney. City West Golf Club followed in 1995. That beautiful course was one of three I designed for Jim Mansfield. However, everything does not always work out as sweet as planned. Inevitably there will be problems and unfortunately another project that Jim and I got involved in came unstuck.

The PGA National in Naas, County Kildare was so exciting. It was to become the home of the Irish and European PGAs complete with administrative offices. But then came the recession and as a result of that NAMA moved in.

I built Mount Wolsey in County Carlow for Donal Morrissey in 1996. This was yet another very happy experience in my life as a long lasting friendship was formed with the Morrisseys. This course was unique in that you could be playing a round of golf and yet you could walk off the course and into the town of Tullow in five minutes. It was the original home of the Wolsey family that owned the famous car company.

Esker Hills Golf Course in Tullamore, County Offaly was my next project. I incorporated the natural landscape of the Esker Riada valley and the contours created by the ice-age glaciers into its design. It has been described as a 'mini Ballybunion'. Donal

Molloy, who was involved in the concrete business, asked me to construct that course for him and I will always be so proud of it. A daughter of Donal's later went out with Shane Lowry, who honed all of his skills from playing that course. A funny thing springs to mind in the building of this course. I always tried to arrive early on site as Donal's father was a real character. If he saw me he would invite me in for a chat over a glass of whiskey.

The Committee of Headford Golf Club in Kells asked me to add a second golf course to their existing course in 1997. Whereas some of the courses I had designed were brand new and cut out of farmland and Lakeland, Headford had golfing tradition.

In the early 1970s the course held the Irish Dunlop Masters with all the top professionals of the day like Darcy, Polland and Peter Townsend taking part. It was a fabulous inland course full of giant trees of all varieties, some of which were centuries old.

That was built on the famous Headford Estate owned by Lord Headford. The whole area is massive and with that in mind their Committee requested that I build a brand new golf course out of wild and overgrown lands by the Blackwater River. Of all the courses I have designed, the 'New Course' at Headford is without doubt one of my proudest works. At the outset it represented a fantastic opportunity for me and when it was completed I think I presented them with a truly magnificent, challenging golf course. In fact I will never forget the facial expressions of the Committee when I showed them the layout and the plans. They nearly fell off their chairs and they were as excited as I was.

Two islands were used which brought in holes 8, 9 and 11. In the construction of this course I was also dealing with so much history. There was an old burial ground situated there as well as old out buildings with murals. It was all so stunning and beautiful. When I began my work the area was so overgrown. It was like a jungle. There were brambles so thick that I had to wear special thick clothes and gloves so as not to receive deep cuts and gashes. On occasions it could be quite frightening as well.

Late in the evening when I was looking to get home, I could get lost. In order to get out of the deep undergrowth, I would listen out for the traffic on the road in the distance as a guide. But with the noise of the Blackwater, I became disorientated in among the scrub.

When it was all cleared and we came up with the finished article it took my breath away. The Headford New Course will always be one of my proudest achievements. It is a truly magnificent course where Brendan McGovern is club professional.

Ian McLoughlin started the ball rolling on my development of Roganstown Hotel and Golf Course, which is a 36-hole course at the back of Dublin Airport. It was unique in that it had a river running from one side of the course to the other. When I looked into the planning and layout of certain holes I incorporated the river into several of them. Jack Nicklaus played a few practise rounds there as he used to stay in Roganstown during his own design of Killeen Castle.

John and Marie Cusack of the famous Cusack Homes Group entrusted me with the job of designing Knightsbrook Golf Club in Trim, County Meath. I will never forget meeting John for the first time. He showed me the boundaries of the course from which to start and after that he never bothered me once. He just put the money in the bank and let me get on with my job. It showed great trust and there is nothing I like more than to work without interference. I think John was thrilled with the end product. Knightsbrook Hotel and Golf Course is now one of the nicest destinations in Ireland. Golfers and visitors can fish the Boyne and view the splendour of the old Abbey and Trim Castle situated on the banks of the river.

Shortly after that Nick Faldo and I were commissioned by Oceanico to construct a 36-hole course in Portugal together. Although I had played alongside Nick on tour several times, this was the first time I got to really know him and in a totally different way. As a golfer on tour he was a very tough competitor who was totally focussed on his own game. He had a hard outer shield which was almost impossible to penetrate or break down and that is why he only ever had two words to say.

If I said "Good shot Nick", he would reply "Ah Ha."

If I said "Good putt Nick", he would answer "Um Hum".

So it was never enjoyable to be drawn with Nick for four and a half hours of golf.

Course design to Nick would become exactly the same as his golf career. With all his success in golf throughout the world, Nick was knighted by Her Majesty the Queen. He is now known as Sir Nick Faldo to give him his proper and correct title.

In his new capacity as a course designer and a person of immense standing within the game, he saw his new career exactly as he did his golf. He treated all other course designers as if they were his competitors on the golf circuit. He almost played them. In other words a 'Faldo Course' was not just a course designed by Sir Nick Faldo — it was better than a Nicklaus, Norman or Palmer course. I knew I had a job on my hands to construct my 18 holes better than the 18 holes which Nick was assigned.

The two areas of land that we were both given to work on could not have been more different. One could be forgiven for thinking that these two courses almost mirrored our very own characters. Nick's course was undulating while mine was flat and low-lying. I decided to excavate several lakes and I also used the extracted land-fill to contour my course. I do not know how Nick felt at his end but I was very happy with my finished product.

Thank God my course turned out to be much more amateur-friendly than Nick's. I made sure to have much bigger and wider landing areas as well as having plenty of necessary bail-out areas around the greens.

John Daly has also dabbled in course design and in total contrast to Faldo, I have found John to be a breath of fresh air. I met him several times when he was over here designing one of his courses in Blarney, County Cork. Despite his many altercations with authority, John is one of the friendliest guys you could wish to meet. He is also one of the most beautiful golfers to watch. Of course he can hit huge distances but he has a sublime putting stroke which won him two majors. It is so sad to see him carry around all those gremlins on his shoulders which have been well documented. I only have good wishes for him and I dearly hope we see his great game come to the fore again.

Tiger Woods seems destined for golf course design in a big way. He has already had a start in Dubai and it is so impressive. I paid a visit there and I could not believe the amount of sand he moved and the thousands of gallons of water he used each day. Oceanico actually asked Tiger to build a third course along with mine and Faldo's in Portugal. Alas, his fees could not be matched. What a pity as I would love to have played his course.

****

I have met Tiger several times and I must relate a funny thing that happened while he was playing in the 2006 Ryder Cup here in Ireland. It involved the golfer's toilets which were in a 'Portaloo' close to the first tee at the K Club. Caddy Billy Foster went to use the toilet. When he went in he found no loo paper so he went into the one next to it. As he was leaving that toilet he saw Tiger rushing quickly into the toilet which had no paper. After Tiger had completed his business, Billy heard him roar out in his American accent:

"Oh shit there's no fucking toilet paper!" to which quick-witted Billy shouted back:

"1up for Europe!"

As regards the costs concerning exactly how much golfers are paid to design courses, I know there are all sorts of figures bandied about. The public are under the impression that golfers are paid 'a million' to construct a course. That is not true. Firstly and most importantly, it all depends on the scale of the course that is going to be constructed. If it is a small, modest course then it will have much smaller costs than a large-scale development.

When the money-men then decide who is going to design the course that will also vary greatly. What I charge will go hand-in-hand with the size of the project and my fees would be a far cry from what Jack Nicklaus or Tiger Woods would charge.

A new course can run between €4 million — €30 million. The larger cost would include waterfalls, fully grown mature trees, lined lakes, bridges and surrounding stonework. It all depends on what is required and it all adds up but aesthetically the course benefits. Our fees range between €300,000 up to €2 million with only the very top designers coming anywhere near the larger figure. Some of those top earners would also require expenses for things like fuel for their private jets but I have not reached that level yet!

I love design and I love talking about it. It is a revealing insight into not just playing golf but also seeing the golf shots and getting a feel for it. You must have at the forefront of your mind that you want to design something for both low and high handicap golfers. Ever since I was a young child I also had an in-bred appreciation of land from the very acres of farm I grew up on. Therefore I feel very strongly that a beautiful piece of land is almost sacrosanct and it should be looked after. Many beautiful areas have been absolutely ruined by too much man-made design. When you first survey a piece of land you must look as far as the eye can see so as to incorporate everything in the environment into your work.

My next piece of heaven to work on was Concra Wood in Castleblayney, County Monaghan in 2006. It was most beautiful and because of its massive lakes I planned several holes along lake edges and across them.

Christy Senior also gave a helping hand on this course. I used to love when he arrived and I would explain the direction and layout. He has a very keen eye for strategically placed bunkers and curves to holes. This was one of my biggest earth-moving jobs. We moved well over a million cubic metres of soil to make the course accessible. I firmly believe that a course should be walked rather than taking the lazy and unhealthy option of using golf buggies. Concra Wood fills me with pride. They hosted their first big tournament in 2012 and the fundraising efforts from the members of the old nine-hole course were awe-inspiring. It just goes to show what a small golf club can achieve even with a massive outlay.

Apart from Portugal, there were two other European courses I was proud of. In 1992, Mamers in Holland was reclaimed from the waters of the old World War II shipping docks. I had to work to their strict environmental laws which forbade digging.

Budapest-Gate International Golf and Country Club was a most magnificent course which I built around a natural fish lake in 2007. It is situated in Bicske which is 20 minutes' drive from the capital. Budapest is one of the world's most beautiful cities. It is divided by the famous 'Blue' Danube river and it is only a little over two hours flying time from Ireland. So it is very accessible for golfers and shoppers and there are plenty of Irish Pubs as well.

Working conditions in Hungary are so much different to our own. Similar to Holland, they work to very strict environmental laws. After every single metre of soil was removed, I had to ask the Environmental Officer to come and inspect. The work was constantly interrupted as he investigated the situation so not surprisingly the course is still under construction. But it is turning out to be fabulous. I was also very honoured to be made President of the Hungarian Golfers' Association.

My newest projects are just getting underway. I will be working on one course next to Lisbon Airport in Portugal. I am also very excited at the prospect of working on a course near the Croatian border in Slovenia.

Aside from winning tournaments and also representing Ireland and Europe, there is something much more profound in golf course design. I feel I have given something back to golf through time, effort and all the knowledge gained through my experience. Therefore I will always feel a great sense of fulfilment with regard to all the courses I have designed. This is where I have really left a legacy. It is my very own pitch mark that will really benefit golfers for many generations to come.

CHAPTER 15

Darren

15th Hole: 414yards, Par 4 at St Andrews in Dunhill Cup v USA 1990. A 15ft birdie to go 1up was the turning point in my match v Fred Couples and two holes later, after an even better shot than my 2-iron v Fred in the Ryder Cup a year previously, he attached a white hankie to his club and waved it in surrender

My second child Nigel was born on 12th December 1978 in Limerick. Quite obviously, like most fathers, I had high hopes for my first son. From a very early age, there must also have been a lot of pressure on his shoulders with regard to becoming a golfer.

After Christy Senior and myself I suppose it was no surprise that people, including some of his own immediate and extended family, felt that he would duly follow in our footsteps. I really wanted him to golf but if he did not so be it. It would be his choice.

One of the earliest memories I hold of my infant son Nigel still makes me laugh. When we were living in Shannon he loved this little pair of brown boots that we purchased for him. In fact he became a right little showman when he wore them in public.

When we went to the local Point to Point horse races, he would dance the leather off them. In front of horsey people he would put on a real exhibition and the more people gathered around and laughed, the more he danced. It was hilarious I can tell you.

I was delighted when he took to golf as well. It seemed very much like there would be no worries concerning a new generation of golfer about to arrive in the O'Connor clan. He was full of enthusiasm as he came with me to the golf course.

On days when I was practising I would empty a dozen or so balls out on the grass beside where I put him sitting. Looking down at his little face I would instruct him to roll a ball over to me and as he did so, I would hit it a few hundred yards down the fairway.

As I came up off my swing I would see his eyes staring down the course trying eagerly to follow where the ball was going. He was only three years old and I think that he really enjoyed those days to the point of developing his own love for golf.

Seeing that he was developing a real taste for the game I then kitted him out and had some clubs cut down to size for him. He would practise all day long in the back garden where I also carved out two small golf holes for him.

In actual fact when it started to rain he would refuse to come in. My wife would be so worried that he would catch a cold or something but she had a real fight on her hands to get him away from his play.

The older he got the better he became and the more it rained the more he stayed out in it. Ann was forever calling for him to come in but he would often say to her:

"Mam I have to learn to play in rain because so many competitions are held in the rain."

He certainly had a point there. When he started in the small two-teacher school down the road, he even played when he came home during lunch hour. He seemed to do nothing else and he was growing to love it more and more.

There was no doubt in my mind that he seemed destined to follow Christy Senior and I into golf as a career. He had all the makings of a champion. It was not just me who felt that way. The lady golfers in Gort could not get enough of his talents.

When he was 10-12 years old, and as there was no Professional based at the club, they would often ring the house looking for Nigel. Ann would then ask him to go up to the golf course because a certain lady was looking for a lesson. Then he started to teach my wife how to play. Can you believe that! In all the time I had been playing and practising it was my son Nigel who taught Ann how to play golf. He taught her very well too.

Not alone was he good in the physical and visual aspects of the game but he was also a very good instructor. He had fantastic patience. Whenever she hit a bad shot he just said:

"Great shot Mum."

Nigel quickly progressed to a 4-Handicapper. By the time he was 14 he started to represent the Galway Bay club in Junior and Senior Cups. He had a voracious appetite and when I came home from playing in Europe he would ask me all about the tour.

In fact ever since he was a young boy I could see from the way he practised that he would make up into a very good golfer. I could see him playing the fairways like myself and winning trophies.

Nigel had very different views. He preferred not living on the road or in the air as I did. He chose his very own path in life which was to study law which he now practises for a living. The brutal reality of having to beat other men to earn a living was not for him. There could never ever be a situation where a prisoner might be taken. He had to be merciless. He had to be ruthless. Every other professional golfer was the same. Smiles beforehand and smiles after but out on the course in competition it was all-out war.

All over the world it is dog-eat-dog in golf. Seve literally exposed his fury to opponents and officials; 'Shark' Norman intimidated everyone with his awesome power while later, the cold assassin's stare of a Tiger prowling for prey struck fear into golfers everywhere. Of course I was a little disappointed as I felt he had most shots and was therefore well equipped to deal with tour play. In some ways it all worked out for the best and today there is nothing like enjoying a social round of golf and a drink afterwards with your son.

On that subject, I have never seen anyone who can lay off golf for two to three weeks or even longer and then step up on the tee and strike the ball so well. Nigel is a very good golfer and oh how I envy him sometimes.

However the best compliment I can pay my son Nigel is nothing to do with golf. Put simply and plainly, he is one of my very best friends. You know you have a true friend when you can have a heart to heart chat anytime about anything.

My other son Darren was a completely different character. He was two years younger than Nigel and he had a real sense of devilment in him. He was not wild but he possessed a willingness to take risks.

If Nigel was perhaps a little more laid back and relaxed, Darren was very much the opposite. He could be all-out 'gung-ho'. In fact he often got his older brother into trouble. If clubs were broken, damaged or mislaid it was Nigel who was very often blamed.

Similar to Nigel, his game progressed rapidly. He also represented Galway Bay in Junior and Senior Cup and he became a 2-Handicapper. I liked what I saw in him but I must also admit that I became more and more envious of him — even jealous.

He was going through the ranks like a Trojan. He had real raw fight. He had guts and determination. Above all, his character brought out in him on the golf course a real willingness to deflect nerves, tension, pressure and the whole occasion in order to WIN.

It all combined to make him a natural. He had the ingredients to make it on the tour. But to get there he had to do what all the greats have done. He had to display all those qualities against the best in under-age competition. This was something that I never had the benefit of. I had to learn my trade by putting together makeshift clubs and then looking for a job as a club professional before going straight into golf on tour. That was the old days which are well and truly obsolete today.

Darren had at his feet all the mod cons of today's youngsters in all aspects of life. In golf he had good quality equipment and in various competitions he could pit himself against others of the same ability and generation. But he still had to go out and prove that he could do it. His chance came in 1998 when he travelled to Youghal in County Cork for the All Ireland Boys U-21 Championships. He won the U-17 event. Ann and I were so gutted to miss out on seeing his first major victory.

We had travelled all over Ireland to see both he and Nigel play. Ann had travelled literally thousands of miles with the boys as I was often away on tour. Both of us could not hide our disappointment at missing Darren's big moment.

There were however double celebrations when he arrived with his trophy. I was getting ready to celebrate my 50th birthday in City West and he joined in the celebrations. There was a moment during that night when he presented the trophy to us which was so special.

He loved functions, parties and celebrations as much as I did. Senior reminded us of a time when he took Darren and Nigel to play a Junior event in Westport. He chaperoned them and gave them advice on their putting and golf swings on a lovely weekend away.

On one of those evenings, he called the waiter for the bill as they had finished up their evening meal. Casting his eagle eye over the receipt, he called back the waiter saying:

"There seems to be a mistake as you never added the wine to the bill?"

At that moment, a rather sheepish and slightly embarrassed Darren interjected to say:

"Sorry Christy that is my fault. I already paid for the wine but I did not have enough to pay for the dinner. Would you mind paying it and I will get you back?"

My uncle laughed so much and he could not stop teasing Darren about it afterwards. When he told me the story several times after the event, he laughed so loudly. That was Darren for you.

In winning that All-Ireland U-17 category, Darren only lost the main U-21 event by just a shot. This was just the beginning of his building up a reputation and a standing in the game. Along the way he beat some notable names.

Personally I think that one of his best victories was when he and Nigel played in a Senior Cup in Tramore, County Waterford. They both played very well but Darren was only 14 and he beat Ronan Flood. Flood later became better known as Padraig Harrington's caddy and both of them come from the Stackstown club in County Dublin. My good friend and former caddy Tom O'Connor also hails from that club and some time later he related a funny incident to me.

Tom was Captaining Stackstown that day in Tramore and because he used to carry the bag for me he would have been very well known to my family. When my sons saw the Stackstown crest on his jumper they started teasing him. This went on for some few minutes but Tom had a trick up his sleeve that the boys were totally unaware of. Without warning he took off his jumper to expose a shirt with the Galway Bay crest. Darren and Nigel were gob-smacked and all three fell about laughing.

As the eldest of my three children, it must not be forgotten in talking about my sons, that my daughter Ann was also a very good golfer. At that time she was in college in Dublin.

When she was 12, Ann could hit a 3-iron 150 yards. I recall the days as I practised in Gort and how she would be hitting her 3-iron and then running up ahead to the ball so as not to slow me down.

She studied to a very high standard and also graduated from the Smurfit School of Business. I believe that only for her commitments in Dublin, and UCD in particular, she would have been an excellent low grade handicap golfer or even higher.

After celebrating my 50th birthday I became eligible to play the Senior tour. I had always wanted to play on the treasured US Senior tour as I had also planned to take Darren over with me and search for a golf scholarship for him.

From what I had seen of my son, and from my experience, I knew he had what it took to become a great golfer. I was very confident that in getting him on a scholarship to one of the top US Colleges he would become a serious challenger on the US

Collegiate tour. He had huge potential. Similar to Rory McIlroy today, Darren could hit the ball huge distances. He was hitting the ball so far that he would often out-hit both Nigel and I with drivers and irons.

Boy did he know it. I was very jealous as was poor Nigel. He would often try to tame him or even distract him from hitting mid-wedges 150 yards. A Christmas golf excursion in Portugal was a case in point.

Darren developed a new technique to his game which was termed a 'sling hook'. The opposite of driving straight down the middle of the fairway or left to right, this involved hitting it right to left. Darren found that he hit the ball much further this way.

Envy or jealousy or whatever you want to call it forced the both of us to keep saying: "Darren, you can't play golf constantly using a hook." But he would just shrug our comments off with a wry smile knowing that he had out-hit us again by 20 yards or so.

****

On the 7th September 1998, my wife and I were in Dublin sorting out accommodation for our daughter Ann who was about to begin her studies. We were just about to go out for dinner when the phone rang.

Do not ask me how I knew but I had this dreadful sense that something had happened to Darren. When my wife Ann picked up the phone it was poor Nigel on the other end and when she fell quiet my heart fell to the floor.

I just knew. I had a 'sixth sense'.

As she went to pick up the phone I remember saying to her: "This is trouble."

My poor son Nigel — my heart went out to him as it still does today. He had to break the news of Darren's car crash to us. He was at home on his own and in his state of shock there must have been so much going through his mind.

How he managed to have the courage to take on this huge

responsibility and ring us is something I will never forget. Rather than a doctor or a Garda, he broke the dreadful news to us that Darren was gravely ill and unconscious in Galway University Hospital.

They say in desperate times and situations that is when family rally around. If Nigel was so brave then my daughter Ann was also so strong. She got this sudden surge of strength which briefly comforted my wife and I.

I can still hear her calm words of fortitude. As she handed us both a hot beverage, she said:

"Mam and Dad, Darren is not gone yet. Where there is life there is hope."

Her words poured over and over in my mind but I felt that I needed them backed up by more. I did not know who to turn to. In the end I rang Jim Mansfield Junior who had pulled me from the wreckage of a helicopter some years before.

Jim was fantastic. We were all in such trauma that none of us were fit to drive. He and his wife jumped straight in their car and came to pick us up and they drove us to Galway. All I could think about the whole way — apart from my poor son Darren — was Nigel.

By now he was accompanied at our home in Galway by my late brother Sean as well as my other brothers Eugene and Pascal. For the entire three-hour journey we all prayed together in the car. We begged the good Lord not to let him die so young. All of us were staying strong for Darren. Our great faith in God kicked into auto mode and this was such a huge sense of comfort. All of us were so strong and I was so proud of my wife, my daughter Ann and my son Nigel.

Even stronger was Darren. He fought like a tiger for his life. He clung on for as long as he could from an almost impossible situation which claimed the other two lives at the scene of the accident. Unfortunately Darren passed away before we reached Galway. As we drove into the Hospital grounds I knew from the crowds of people gathered around the entrance that we were too late. Our immeasurable grief poured out. 17-year old Darren O'Connor had passed away.

We cried our eyes out. We hugged each other tightly and sobbed against any comforting shoulder that presented itself.

It was so sad. To my dying days I will see Darren's almost transparent fingers crossed on his chest as he lay in repose in the hospital. It would have been so comforting to have been able to say a last goodbye to him while he was still alive.

Nothing could stop Darren from that dreadful date with destiny. Against the wishes and demands of Nigel, he took his mother's BMW to Killarney to meet a girlfriend whom we did not know. Travelling with him to Kerry was his friend David Quinn from Rahoon. David himself was only 18 years old and a year older than Darren. He died at the scene as did the driver of the other vehicle which hit them.

Michael Hynes was in his early 40s. He was the proprietor of a Londis shop in Miltown Malbay, County Clare. After collecting supplies for his shop from a wholesaler in Galway, he drove back home to Clare towards Ennis.

After an almost complete round trip of over 200 miles, Darren was just a quarter of a mile from home when tragedy struck. He was hoping to make it home before Ann and I returned from Dublin. Nobody knows what actually happened. This was despite a driver travelling directly behind Darren for some considerable distance. The driver gave this evidence as well as the fact that he was travelling at 50mph which meant Darren drove at the same speed.

There were no witnesses to the precise moment of impact which occurred on a straight stretch of road 300 yards outside the Galway village of Kilcolgan on the Limerick side. Driving conditions were reported as very poor after a day of heavy and persistent rain.

With all this evidence the Gardai still ruled that the crash was Darren's fault. I was stunned and to this day I simply cannot understand how this can be. With no witnesses and no firm evidence — even from the driver behind — I believe this is a very unfair ruling.

It seemed as if the fates were loaded against Darren. Even the ambulance was delayed getting to and from the scene because of the crowds and traffic at the September running of Galway Races. We asked so many people what happened. We have searched our souls to find an answer as to why and how this tragedy occurred. But we struggle on with our thoughts right up to the present. It has left a huge hole in our lives.

During Darren's wake at our house in Galway I stood almost mummified as literally thousands of people passed through the door to pay their respects. I can recall thinking that it was still just an horrific nightmare. As the crowds eventually subsided and moved outside, we were left alone with our son and brother to say a last goodbye. In my life, and in the lives of my wife and my daughter and son Nigel, it is something that will remain with us and we will never ever forget it.

At the funeral mass in Salthill, the church was packed out. I do not know how we got through it with the media and the eyes of the entire congregation upon us. The Taoiseach even sent a representative.

But somehow we did and next day the Irish Independent picked up on something I said. Reflecting on it now, the words I uttered were in golf parlance. They were very thought provoking and entirely appropriate:

"Darren had just reached the 17th and if he had not seen the rough he would have strolled home."

There are a few people that I would like to single out for their tremendous help at that time. Before that I would like to pay tribute to all our neighbours and to the people of Galway who were magnificent. I would also like to pay my sincere thanks to my brothers. They rallied around and they tried to comfort us with their unwavering support and great unconditional love. I will never forget it. Not for the first time, Christy Senior was a giant. Once again he used his amazing psychology to try to ease our pain. He always seemed to say the right things at the right time.

During the funeral procession to the cemetery in Rahoon, he walked alongside my brothers and I. Every step of the way he managed to keep me going by recounting details and experiences throughout his own life. He was just trying to numb my mind. But I will always owe Christy Senior a huge debt of gratitude. It must also have been so difficult for him. Inside he was no doubt hurting as much as the rest of the family. He thought the world of Darren — and he paying for his own wine in Westport!

How ironic that Christy Senior and I were at the head of a cortege on the way to bury the newest generation of golfer to the family. Who knows — Darren could have gone on to become the most talented of us all. There is no doubt that he would have turned professional and he would have followed me on to the European Tour. Perhaps he may even have joined the US Tour if my plans for College in America worked out for him.

I will never know just how good a golfer he might have become. But a professional golfer he would have been. He had everything. He had poise, balance, long-hitting, a beautiful swing, good putting and above all temperament. He had a drive and determination to win but he wore it all with a smile. He was fun and he just loved to bring that into competition. I am so glad he savoured under-age success which is always a great yardstick for a bright future.

Therefore it was entirely appropriate that Darren's 'In Memoriam' card which we had printed showed a full length snap of his golf swing. I think that anyone who looks at that can tell immediately what a wonderful talent he was and his was a huge loss to Irish golf.

The card was put together by my doctor and friend Richard Joyce. He penned a really beautiful poem which is on the reverse side of Darren's golfing photo. I have carried that in my wallet everywhere and everyday of my life since.

The poem reads as follows:

A life so short, so incomplete
so cruelly and abruptly taken
leaves us broken-hearted, shattered
feeling lost and so forsaken

In the seventeenth autumn of his life
he has had to leave us all behind
in the spring time of his manhood
a lovely lad, what a smile – so kind

The sadness, the void that's left
seems endless and never to leave us
we miss him so, young darling boy
can there be any comfort to relieve us

From life to death, from tee to green
you had it all with much more to offer
you coped with all the ups and downs
as a young man – and what a golfer!

Darren, you're not gone – you live on
your presence keeps us all together
we hear your laugh, we see your face
you are with us still – and forever.

Rest in Peace Darren. Until we see you in Heaven again some-day, please know that you are missed terribly by your loving family and friends.

CHAPTER 16

From Junior To Senior

16th hole: 450yards, Par 4 at Duke's Course, Woburn in British Masters 1992. My birdie here started an amazing run of four-in-a-row taking in 17, 18 and the first Play-Off hole where I beat Tony Johnstone. It was my biggest and last European win

Among the many letters and messages of support which were sent to us from people of all walks of life following Darren's death, I personally received very heartening words of advice from Seve, Jack Nicklaus and Prince Andrew.

In particular they implored me to go ahead with my plans to play the Senior Tour.

They drummed into me the fact that it would be my own tribute to Darren and that as he was so competitive, he would have wanted me to play. This forced my decision to do it.

Perhaps I would have gone on to play in the Senior grade anyway. After the initial grieving subsides, time heals all wounds as they say. But without their helpful advice I would definitely not have played so soon after the tragedy.

Many people throw themselves into work to take their mind off things and I could have concentrated on designing a new course or two. Perhaps I could have built a new home or even a driving range or given lessons in golf.

Seven months later I packed my bags to travel over 3,000 miles across the Atlantic. It was a huge decision and a big undertaking.

Of course I questioned myself. Was I doing the right thing? Was I doing it at the right time?

I will never forget my flight to America in April 1999 in pursuit of a precious tour card. For the entire seven-hour journey to New York I cried. Looking constantly out the window, I could see Darren's face in the clouds and I could almost touch him.

Similar to any person travelling to a new and strange destination I became even more apprehensive. What if I broke down with these emotions while playing? What if after losing Darren I suddenly felt I missed the rest of my family terribly?

West Palm Beach in Florida was where I began my quest for a tour ticket. It was no surprise that after the traumatic events back home, together with trying to acclimatise to my new surroundings, I struggled badly in the PGA Seniors at PGA National Golf Club. I finished down the field in a tie for 50th place. But then out of nowhere I developed a will, fight and determination to succeed. I got strength from somewhere. Just a few weeks later at the end of April I put in a sterling performance at the Home Depot Invitational.

Held at Quail Hollow in Charlotte, North Carolina I put together a magnificent round of 65 in the final round which almost won me the title. Eleven years later, Rory McIlroy would shoot 62 there to break the course record when he won the Wells Fargo tournament. I came close but the great Bruce Fleisher held me at bay to win by two shots. I finished tied for fourth place earning a cheque for $59,000. But I was so encouraged in only my second start and I was hungry for more.

Two weeks later I went one place better. I finished in a three-way tie for third at the Nationwide Championship. $92,000 brought my earnings to near $150,000 in just three events.

Following those efforts I received a sponsor's invitation to the State Farm Classic in Hobbits Golf Club, Columbia, outside Baltimore, Maryland. This meant that I was traversing the whole of the United States in my quest for success but it was a very small price to pay for my newly found form.

On American Independence Day in Baltimore there was another huge obstacle I had to negotiate — the heat. In scorching temperatures which we in Europe are simply not used to, you could feel the energy sapping from your body.

The humidity was unbelievable. Sometimes you would feel like lying down or even taking a rest. Not for nothing do the Spaniards have a 'siesta'. Again it was a small price to pay. I now had goals in my mind and I willed myself to keep going at all costs.

At the start of each round I took Darren's memoriam card out of my pocket and I pointed it up ahead of the opening hole. I was showing my late son what lay ahead of me and I was hoping for one of his monster drives. I said a silent prayer to him requesting his help.

After my earlier promise it was hard to know how my game would stand up to the intense heat. I need not have worried as my golf got even better. Opening up with a fantastic -7, 65 I tore the course apart! A second round 66 was just as good and I was on my own in front.

My recollections of the last round are very vivid from the 15th onwards. At that time I held a two-shot lead. It looked every much like I was going to win my first Seniors event in just a handful of efforts. I was sitting pretty with just four holes left to play.

The 15th was very narrow and tree-lined. I looked up to the clouds and implored Darren for one last bit of help to carry me over the winning line. But it was so difficult. Not withstanding the pressure, the temperature was over 100 degrees with 90% humidity.

After managing to negotiate 15, 16 and 17 I reached the 18th but I was saturated in sweat from head to toe. I was also shaking like a leaf but fuelled by determination I had victory in my sights. The last hole was a Par 5 so once again I asked Darren for help with the drive. I clutched his picture in my pocket. He answered my prayers and I just about reached the green in two shots after a very good drive.

My second shot landed left of the green and in a tricky position.

With my third I had to pitch the ball over a greenside bunker and downhill to the flag. Using a wedge I watched as the ball rolled 15 feet past the pin. I thought I had two putts to win. I felt huge relief. Yet again it was between me and Bruce Fleisher only this time he was two shots behind me. He had to hole his third shot for an eagle. My third had rolled five yards past from the wrong side but Bruce was playing his from a good spot at the back of the green.

If he managed to chip it in for an eagle and I missed my birdie putt we would have to have a Play-Off. I leaned on my putter watching him. I said a silent prayer to Darren that I would win. He played the most exquisite chip. His ball was rolling towards the cup. The crowd got excited and started to roar. My heart started to beat wildly and I could not believe what I was seeing. His putt was going in the hole for an eagle! Sweet Jesus No!

Just as his ball was about to drop in the hole its roll and momentum came to an abrupt halt. Bruce had come within a bee's wing of eagling it! I breathed a huge sigh of relief. I now had two putts to win by a shot but I did not want to mess up and take three putts. It looked like I was going to finish in style as my putt headed towards the centre of the cup. But it suddenly swung, caught the edge and lipped out. I was now left with a two-foot putt to win my first Senior event.

With every bone in my body shaking violently, I managed to hole the return putt. So many images — of my family and of Darren — flashed through my mind. Bruce congratulated me and in that moment my emotions poured forth into tears.

****

There had been so many tears in the previous months. Only a few weeks previously I wondered if I was doing the right thing as I cried on board the long-haul flight to these very lands I was now cherishing. Finding sudden strength to win was a gift from Darren. The win was dedicated to my late son. Without him I would not have had the incentive and more to the point the dogged will to win. My constant prayers to him meant that he was with me every step of the way on that scorching State Farm Classic course.

Something else happened. In a personal context I felt that I was born again into golf. I was now in a totally different place to the over-familiarity and monotony of the European Tour. This was a whole new world. The Senior Tour was now a refreshingly new ball game that gave me a new start in life. How ironic that out of the trauma, the grief, the despair and the ashes of my dear son's tragic death, I was reborn.

After adding that $195,000 first prize to my earnings, I had accumulated almost $400,000 in six events. Everything snowballed. Invites came in from all over the world and the biggest prize of all came my way in the immediate aftermath of that first Senior victory. Winning in Baltimore meant that I had just secured my Players Card for the US Senior Tour. This was the ultimate prize. In my predicament prior to the card being allocated to me, no amount of winning cheques could match up to its absence from my wallet.

Put simply, I would not have had too many more opportunities to earn prizemoney without that treasured card. I would have had to rely on invitations to events. If I played badly in an event like my very first one, invites would dry up pretty quickly. If that happened then the likelihood was that I would fail to make it in the States. So to any golfer a Player's Card is like gold bullion. It is a yearly ticket to potential riches and glory with the security of knowing that several bad events will not be detrimental to you.

A few days after finishing just inside the Top 20 in the US Senior Open midway through July, I flew back home to Ireland to play in the British Senior Open on July 22nd. I was buoyed up by my recent purple patch of form in America and I could not wait to play it.

One of the reasons I was eagerly awaiting the British Open was because of the venue. It was held in Ireland at Royal Portrush. I felt like I was now returning to the auld sod as a victorious king.

My head was held high and my chest was out after all the sad times. Suddenly there was so much happiness everywhere and I was not going to let it end. I was in a place that I had not been in for a long time and I wanted to hold on to it firmly for as long as I could.

With me in Portrush were my wife, my daughter Ann and son Nigel. It was a pity Darren was not there physically but no longer did we feel sorry for ourselves. Without any doubt we knew that Darren was with us in spirit.

This also brought to the forefront of my mind a very good omen for this event. The last time I had played a tournament with all my family with me was in Kenya. I went on to win it and I was so glad Darren was there savouring every moment of that safari.

Things did not look very good for me in Portrush when I shot 76 in the opening round. However the conditions were atrocious for all the competitors. I felt I was actually playing very good golf and I was putting together a really good round when disaster struck at the 13th.

My ball skipped through the green and straight under a bush. I should really have taken a penalty drop but I decided to have a go at it without any success. This forced me to take a penalty drop for my next shot and I finished up with a miserable seven shots.

Leaving the green a little crestfallen I caught sight of Nigel who gave me a smile and the thumbs-up sign. That was Nigel for you. The same attitude as when he taught my wife how to play golf and kept telling her "great shot mum" even when it was a bad shot.

He lifted me with his reaction. In the past I might have used this bad hole as an excuse to do all the things which might force me to capitulate. Now I was in a much different place. Taking seven strokes was nothing and Nigel reminded me about that.

I was alive; I was a winner and I had a terrific family who gave me the strength to keep going. And boy did I need it as the next hole was known as a real brute. The 14th is so famous that it is known as 'The Great Calamity Jane' or 'Calamity'.

The ship was steadied back on an even keel as I managed to make par. On the closing holes I even got my round back on track with more pars and a birdie to finish with a 76. Although it was not a great start, the day really made it a level playing field for everyone. There was still three days to go and so there was ample time to turn things around. A 69 in the next round was just the tonic I needed. After a slight improvement in the conditions I felt I had kept things together to get myself right back into contention.

On moving day I made even more progress. I shot 68 and despite the great Bob Charles shooting a brilliant 65, I progressed straight up the scoreboard to find myself just a shot behind him going into the final day. I was drawn with two of the greatest players the game of golf has ever known. What a pleasure it was to play alongside the great South African Gary Player as well as the left-handed New Zealander Charles.

It inspired me as I stood on the first tee with them. I also knew something else for sure. They were going to help me no end. It was a dream draw because they were two men who would simply never give up. That is precisely why they have won so many majors and so many events all over the world. They have always played every shot as if their lives and livelihoods depended on it. So I knew they would keep fighting and keep on going.

They would also try to hurt me as well as each other. They would try to wear me down with every shot and putt until I gave in. But I was now in that same privileged position as them. That place where you never give up.

If the guys did not already know it then my appetite was whetted to the point of showing them that this was not the Christy O'Connor Junior that they had known on the old European Tour. By now I was no easy touch that would just subside and fall away. This was a new, happy and confident Christy — a golfer reborn at 50 and with nothing ever again to lose and so much to treasure and to gain.

We all began very steadily. The first slip came on the tricky and treacherous Par 3 sixth. The error came from both Charles and Player. Perhaps after the first few skirmishes they realised they were playing me on my home turf. They missed the green leaving impossible pitches. I hit a 3-iron to just two feet and made a birdie to Player's bogey and Charles double bogey. Typically they never gave up and the latter reacted like a wounded tiger.

He rallied with great aplomb as he hit three birdies in a row to the ninth with Player grabbing two! It was proving to be a fantastic match for the crowds and it was just the sort of stuff I required to keep sharp and focussed.

As Charles fell away somewhat on the back nine, it was Gary Player and I who fought out a real duel. The little South African dynamo birdied hole after hole and suddenly we found ourselves at the top of the scoreboard with Player a single shot behind me.

The 16th proved to be a thriller. It was tit-for-tat as the pair of us slugged it out on the dunes. I hit a good drive and a good iron to the green where I secured par. But Gary hit two magnificent shots to leave a 15ft putt for birdie.

If he knocked it in then we would be all square with two to play. I watched as he took his putting position with that familiar crouch of his. The sight of him almost resembles a small elderly person with a bent back and dressed in black but looks can be so deceiving.

So many majors and tournaments worldwide have been won on the back of that putting style. I watched as he hit it straight. It looked like he read it just about right but at the last moment it lipped out. I was still a shot in front playing the penultimate hole.

This time I hit two great shots to put myself in a great position on the Par 5 17th green. Gary finally came unstuck. He made bogey while I took two putts for birdie. This meant that I had a three-shot cushion playing the very last hole.

I walked up that last hole to spine-tingling applause and in the end I never had any worries. I made an easy par and as Gary took off his cap to shake my hand, I realised I won the British Senior Open. I won by three shots from John Bland with Gary Player slipping to third. My wife Ann, together with Nigel and my daughter Ann ran onto the green. We embraced and cried our eyes out. This time the tears were more of joy than sorrow. Even more, I felt that the well photographed embrace of the four of us actually cemented our family bonding forever more.

Apart from family there is a very special person that I would like to mention in light of that huge win for me. Brian Smallwood formerly caddied for Gary Player and he was by now caddying for me in America and so he was my bagman that day.

More than a caddy, he became a great friend. He helped me through those difficult times and especially when I first arrived in America with a tearful face and heart. Without his help and guidance I would not have hit the ground running in the States.

Brian, you helped me to my first win on the US Senior tour and you helped me with my major win in the British Open. I am so glad you shared it all with me and I will be forever grateful to you. Thank You.

After a few celebratory glasses of champagne with the members in Portrush, we made our way home to Galway. Nigel had us all in fits of laughter in the car as he recounted every shot I played that day and very often he added exaggerated spice to my game. We continued our victory party in Clarinbridge where we were joined by extended family and friends. However the days of celebrating wildly into the late hours and even for several days after were well and truly in the past.

By the standards of past experiences the partying was now much more subdued and for want of a better expression, more 'mature'. In any case, I was already looking forward to jetting back to the US to play my next event which was scheduled for a fortnight later.

The newspapers next day all carried my Senior Open win. Dermot Gilleece in The Irish Times carried my quotes that although I was so impressed by the enthusiasm and great play of Gary Player and Bob Charles, there was no way I would play to their age. In fact, I distinctly recall telling them that ideally I would play about five years on the Senior tour. In my own mind I had always said that I would then like to concentrate on some other area related to golf but my playing career would finish.

One particular paragraph from Gilleece stood out. He wrote:

"examples of superb ball striking were a splendid drive followed by a 3-wood of 250 yards which finished just short of the 528 yard 17th allowing two putts for birdie."

He went on to say:

"But the real revelation was his putting with Gary Player telling him, "Christy, if you continue to putt like that you are going to win a lot of tournaments!"

A little over a week later my next flight to America did not seem anywhere near as tough as the first. But for a long time after I still saw Darren's face in the clouds as I crossed the vast expanse of the Atlantic Ocean. I mean it — I could literally see his smiling face.

On 15th August my return to the US saw me play a course that I love and it is one of my all-time favourites. Egypt Valley Golf Course near Grand Rapids in Michigan was the venue for the Foremost Insurance Championship.

Dick Hurst and his wife were my hosts. They were fantastic and his wife is not only a lovely lady but she is also a first rate cook. Some of the Senior events are played over three rounds. This was one of them and Dick followed me around for all three days.

Another measure of how much I had changed both as a golfer and a human being can be gauged from Dick. When I got near the top of the scoreboard, Dick would often get giddy, nervous and excited. Sorry to relate this to you now Dick but when I saw your reactions, I had to steer well clear of you! The old Christy might have joined in with you but by this stage of my career I was a real hungry hombre deep set on a mission of success — and my tour card.

The course was bloody tough and so I had to have a one-track mind focussed on what was ahead. It was tree-lined and there was water everywhere. Most golfers never admit to it but they secretly fear water. Just look at Sawgrass and its dreaded 17th. At Egypt

Valley there was water all over the place. Not just water — lakes. They were lurking dangerously on and around many of the greens. So if Dick was getting giddy, you can see why I had to steer well clear of him.

It must be stressed that I was not keeping my distance because I was nervous or that by looking at him he would make me edgy. It was quite the opposite in fact. I loved the place and I could not wait to get stuck in and to just get on with it.

Akin to someone intent on doing a job and doing it to the best of their ability, that was the position I was in. I was intent and focussed on the job and I did not want to be deflected from it. It was a major challenge for me. The course reminded me of home in Ireland. It was a real country course. Plenty of water, lots of trees and scatterings of scrub. I could not have felt more at home. Actually, in some ways Michigan probably inspired my design of Kells' New Course.

My game was in fantastic shape and my confidence was sky high. I mowed through the entire field and at no stage did I ever feel like losing. I now know how Tiger Woods felt when I think back to that period of my career. Opening up with a -3, 69, I bettered that with a 68 in the next round. In the final round I held a two-shot lead at the 17th. The last was a very tough Par 5. It contained bunkers along the left and right sides of the fairway which looked to gobble up any wayward drives.

I treaded the ball through those traps leaving 240 yards to the pin. Then with the best 5-wood I ever hit in my life, I found the green which was surrounded by very dangerous and deep bunkers. What a pair of shots. The ball came to rest 15ft from the hole.

After holing the putt for an eagle to give me an almost unassailable four-shot lead, I will never forget John Bland's face. My playing partner had chased me the whole way but after those two shots I had taken him out of the tournament.

John was a great competitor. From South Africa, I had previously beaten him in Royal Portrush to win the British Open and I would have many more battles with him in future Senior events.

Another 68 helped me to become a wire-to-wire winner in that I was leading on each of the three days. It was my third victory of the year and I was in dreamland. I could not quite believe what was happening to me. To use a well-worn cliché — I had to pinch myself.

There was now no doubt in my mind that it was all down to Darren. His face in the clouds and his fantastic long driving intervened in my very being to execute unbelievable shots. Such unbelievable shots gave me — granted me — victory.

A prize of $150,000 was the icing on the cake and a very nice present just two days shy of my 51st birthday. In the remaining eight events I played in America that year I finished in the Top 20 on five occasions. I earned $712,000 for my first year on the US tour.

In that short period I almost became a millionaire in dollar terms when you add my British Open prize to that figure. But it is — and never was — about money. In victory there was another very important thing to address that makes money worthless. My second US win was dedicated to a lifelong friend Miles Murphy who died of cancer.

CHAPTER 17

The Thirteen Pins

17th Hole: 526yards, Par 5 at Royal Birkdale, British Open 1983. A beautiful second shot set up an eagle chance which I holed to finish eighth.

1999 was a great year but it was no more than a tonic for the grief of losing my son in 1998. There remained a great underlying and constant pain that to this day still continues to eat away at me.

After winning my third event of the year at the Foremost Insurance Championship in the fabulous Egypt Valley Golf club in Ada, Michigan, I played two more events in August before flying home after the AT&T Canada Open. I did not play golf again until October.

September would be a time for what matters most — family. On the 7th September we had Darren's Anniversary mass and then just 16 days after that, we all gathered at Portobello College in Dublin for my son Nigel's graduation ceremony.

I was so proud of Nigel that day and I had a real lump in my throat. It was such a big day for all the family after losing Darren and he would have been so proud of his brother watching him being conferred with his Honours Degree in Law.

It was tear-jerking to see him go up to the podium to receive his scroll and we all applauded and cheered so loudly. In that moment I vowed that after I broke his heart somewhat in turning his desires away from a golf career, I would make it up to him.

Nigel was now my only son. He was also my eldest son and where I had previously held ambitions to bring Darren to America, I was determined to do that with Nigel. So I asked him if he would like to caddy for me in the US in Millennium year 2000.

Being well aware that he would be on the look out for a practice in law, I told him that he could come with me whenever the occasion fitted. He did not have to do it full time. To my delight he agreed.

This also gave me another great incentive. I saw 1999 as the year whereby I achieved so much for myself spurred on by Darren. I dedicated some of my wins to Darren and now I would be in a similar position where I was determined to win with Nigel on my bag.

My season began in the Master Card Championship at the end of January where I finished in the Top 20 for a prize of almost $20,000. But right through February, March and April all I had to show for 10 additional events was two more Top-20 finishes.

In my defence of the Home Depot Championship on 7th May, I started off with a promising 69 but faded after rounds of 72, 74. It was to be a similar story through June but then I ran into form just in the nick of time at the US Senior Open.

On the 2nd July I opened up with a 68 and followed it with two rounds of 72. Then after all the American Independence Day celebrations had died down, I produced fireworks with a sparkling last round of 67. I finished tied eighth on -5 under for a $61,000 cheque.

A week later I was to defend my State Farm Classic title and I was delighted that Nigel was on my bag. I was delighted to have him not just because he was my son. He had a real talent for golf in areas other than playing at the highest level.

For a start he was a low handicap golfer so he knew and understood the game very well. Most of all, he knew my game inside out and he knew what made me tick. Nigel also had a very good and keen eye for reading greens. This is an essential part of a caddy's job.

Two heads are better than one as they say. So if a golfer is try-ing to read a putt and if he thinks it breaks from left to right at halfway and his caddy then tells him the same, that is music to his ears. Nigel and I had a very good understanding in that precise way.

Everything was going to plan as we began with a super 66! I felt that nothing was going to stop me and I was going to make it back-to-back wins with Nigel carrying my bag. It was a tough and tricky tree-lined course and I was coping better than all other golfers.

I was still in front at the halfway stage but then the wheels came off. I slumped to a last round 75 and it had nothing to do with Nigel and I but everything to do with the intense heat.

Starting the turn for home on the inward nine, I knew I was in trouble. I felt myself physically draining by the minute. I was wilt-ing and there was nothing I could do about it. It was absolutely scorching.

The temperature was well over 100 degrees with 100% humidity. I was soaking in my own sweat. Nigel did his best to urge me and spur me on but I remember looking at him and he was in an even worse state than I was.

It was not to be but we gave it our best shot. It was disappoint-ing after leading but in the end I still managed to finish in the Top 20 and earn a $21,000 prize. Returning to Ireland for the defence of my Senior British Open, I knew that my golf was in great shape.

Nigel and I played two practise rounds before the British Open with Christy Senior and his son Peter. My uncle gave me some very useful tips. The thing about the Royal County Down course is that you must pick your spots.

It is a blind course in that it is very hilly and you cannot see the fairways or the pins on so many of the holes. So you must pick out a precise spot in front of you which is in the exact direction of the pins you are playing to.

It worked like a dream for the first two rounds. On a Par 71 course I started with a 69 and followed that with a 68. A slightly disappointing third round of 70 left me on -6 and I trailed the leader John Bland by just a shot going into the final day.

The funny thing about it is that I recall a conversation I had with Tiger Woods at the British Open in St Andrews the previous week. I chatted with him in the famous clubhouse there. During our chat he told me that he had just been over to Ireland in the previous few days as he was getting in some vital practise on a links course before the Open. He just happened to pick Royal County Down for his preparations.

When I told him I was going over to County Down after my few days in St Andrews to defend my British Senior Open, we had a right laugh when he shook his head saying:

"Jeez, no senior golfer should ever be asked to compete on that beast of a course!"

Probing him further about this, he revealed to me that although he really enjoyed his time in the north of Ireland, as well as playing such an historic links course, he went around those hilly dunes in 82 shots.

All said and done, Nigel and I had gelled very well together and I felt we had conquered Royal County Down. 69, 68 and 70 were excellent rounds and I just had Bland in front of me by a shot. I felt very confident and I could not wait to tee off in the last round.

We had a good chat the night before. It was important that Nigel knew what iron for me to play. Many of the shots have to be played short of the greens and you let the bouncy links course run the ball on down onto the outing surface.

If you have no experience of playing links courses then you are in for a rude awakening. Golfers who are not in control of their shots will be in trouble. Not picking your spot is one thing but going for greens means that the ball will fly through the back.

I finished our chat by telling Nigel that our plan would be to make the greens and have two putts for par. By doing that we would be patient and our chance of a birdie would inevitably come.

We could not have wished for a better start. It was an early turning point and a dream beginning. With a bumper crowd watching us from an attendance of almost 6,000 I hit a fantastic drive on the Par 5 and followed that with a 6-iron to 40 feet.

Right across the green I watched and watched and watched until my monster putt fell into the cup for an eagle! I had leapfrogged John Bland to become the new leader and when the South African failed with his birdie putt, I was at the top of the scoreboards.

After the ecstasy of an eagle I agonised over the next two holes as Bland hit back to lead again. He made a nice birdie on the second while I made my first big error of the entire week by taking three putts on the third.

Another twist and undoubted turning point came on the fourth. Nigel handed me the 4-iron and I hit a glorious shot with it to 15ft. Up on the green I leaned on the putter and watched as Bland surveyed his putt and then hit a little too far past the hole for comfort.

I knew that I could put him under immense pressure if I holed for birdie. I rammed the putt in and we were level again. Bland knew that he had to save par with his tricky return putt to keep level but he missed and so I was back out in front again.

It stayed that way until the 11th hole when my ball flew through the green and I bogeyed. John made par so we were level once again. For the crowds watching it had become a gripping see-saw match and the title had long since rested between just the pair of us.

The final turning point came on the 14th. After an excellent drive I used a 4-iron for my second but again the ball flew through the green. In fairness to Nigel it had probably nothing to do with club but everything to do with adrenaline, nerves and my tensing up.

When I arrived down at the back of the green I saw that my ball was in a horrible spot. It was lying in a very barren spot with no grass. The situation did not look good. I was scratching my head and between the pair of us we did not know what to do.

In such situations you look for inspiration and a certain reliance on years of experience. Even then everything will be in the lap of the gods. Even more so when I pulled the 5-wood from the bag!

You could just see all the eyes widening and hear all the whispers and murmurs. The sound made by the galleries reverberated into a sort of humming crescendo like a hive of bees as people wondered what on earth I was doing.

I pulled the wood back and released it through the ball. The ball scurried to the green and I hurried after it. Suddenly an almighty roar started. It got louder and louder and louder until it was replaced by 'oohs' and 'aahs' and then huge applause. I could not believe it.

From 90 feet away my all came to rest just a foot from the pin! I looked over in the direction of John Bland to see him looking at me in total disbelief. More so than where my ball finished, he simply could not believe the club I had chosen.

The reason I chose it was because you could actually get some elevation on the ball for the first five or 10 metres and then judging the pace along the green to the pin was all important. In the event I judged it to almost perfection.

Standing on the 17th I was still just a shot in front after both of us made par at 15 and 16. But from all my years and experience of the tour this Par 5 was one of the most daunting that any golfer could wish to face.

From the tee to the green it was littered with gorse and bunkers. The main objective for any golfer playing this particular hole is to just try and keep it on the fairway. John and I both did just that. We hit perfect drives with my ball some 20 yards ahead of his.

I recall John hitting a great second shot. He threaded it through the gap between the bunkers. Although we could not see the green I knew from his shot and his reaction that he was not too far from the front of the green.

He would have two strikes for a birdie so I told Nigel that I simply had to go at the target. In fact I distinctly remember telling him:

"From here on in we're going to play target golf."

There was simply no logic and no point in playing safe and trying to protect my one-shot lead on a Par 5. That thinking would only play into John's hands and give him a birdie chance for a Play-Off.

Taking a 3-iron from Nigel I played into an area the size of a decent green. I could not see it but I knew from the reaction of the crowd and from its direction that I had put it almost exactly where I wanted.

Upon reaching my ball I saw that it could not have been placed in a better position if I had lifted it up and put it there myself. I was left with only 80 yards to the pin. But my third shot also needed a certain amount of precision planning.

With the green facing back to front, I knew not to hit it past the pin as I would only leave myself a very tricky downhill putt. So I hit it around 75 yards distance — in other words five yards short of the pin.

Once again it all worked out brilliantly and I left a putt some 15 feet below the hole. But there is a saying that there is no game that two cannot play and if I was feeling a sort of smug satisfaction with my play, then John was about to take the wind out of my sails.

He pitched his third shot to within one inch! He got his own back on me for what I had done back on the 14th and this time I looked at him in total disbelief! But you had to hand it to him as he was proving his mettle. I said "bad luck John" and I meant it.

His delightful chip meant that he had a tap in for a birdie to draw level with me on the penultimate green. I would have an uphill putt to keep my lead. There was no way I wanted to go up the 18th level and the possibility of entering a Play-Off.

With great calmness, Nigel lined up the putt with me. He told me that in his opinion the putt broke just very slightly from the right edge of the cup. I agreed. Getting down on it I remember telling myself to trust the line but above all to keep my head steady.

I never looked up until I heard the huge roar from the crowd! I nailed it and it was the sweetest feeling. It was to prove decisive and the defining moment as I played the last beautifully. John was dejected but after commiserating I just could not hide my delight.

Nigel and I hugged and we were swamped by family and friends. Winning two British Senior Opens in a row was just the most fantastic feeling. It will always be right up there as one of my finest achievements.

The celebrations went on well into the night and over the next few days and there are a few friends that were with me that I would like to mention. My lifelong friend John Mulholland was present as was Pat O'Grady and his wife Bernie.

Pat and Bernie became great friends of my family particularly since they were of monumental support to us when Darren died. I was just so glad that we were all there to celebrate a brilliant and happy occasion.

Donal Staunton and his lovely wife Raymonde who own the famous 'Staunton's Shop' in Spiddal were also a huge part of the celebrations. All I can say is that we enjoyed the rounds and we all finished under par!

But I had no time to rest on my laurels or keep the celebrations going for a week as I had to fly back to America with my wife and Nigel. That brings to mind a very poignant moment we all experienced at the US Senior Open.

It was held at Saucon Valley in Pennyslvania where my late brother Sean was formerly a teaching professional. It was particularly sad visiting the Pro Shop which Sean had talked so much about and had described to us in great detail and yet he was no longer there.

Very similar to Darren his presence was very much in evidence however and it helped to spur me on. I finished a very creditable eighth in an event which was won by the great Hale Irwin.

In the near dozen or so events I played after successfully defending my British Senior Open, I know that Darren and I, as well as criss-crossing the States, had to deal with the effects of lost sleep, jet lag, fatigue and heat.

Despite all this I saved the best for last. In my 24th and final US Tour event in late October 2000, I put in my best performance of the year in America. At the SBC Senior Classic in Los Angeles I opened with a 68 and ended with a magnificent 66 to finish fifth.

I earned my biggest cheque of the year which amounted to $62,000. LA is the home of Hollywood and all its famous actors and actresses and right slap bang on the very golf course I played, a certain Zsa Zsa Gabor resided.

Her mansion was situated at the back of the ninth green on the Trump National course. I was told that helicopters ferrying guests to her glittering parties came in to land on the ninth fairway. Invitees included well known film actors as well as several US Presidents.

Recently she and her husband Prince Frederic von Anhalt put that house up for sale at a cool $28 million. That brings to mind one of Zsa Zsa's most famous quotes:

"I'm a marvellous housekeeper — every time I leave a man I keep his house!"

Going into that event I knew that I needed to do well. Even though I had won a second consecutive British Open I was under pressure to keep my US Players Card. As I said, this was like gold and I cannot stress enough its importance.

As it turned out my last round 66 in LA which pushed me into fifth was pivotal. I ended up finishing 50th in the US Senior Money List and that was right on the mark as only the Top 50 secured their playing rights for the following season! It was a close-run thing.

In 2001 I began my season in fairly good from. I finished in the Top 10 at the Verizon Classic in Tampa Bay. I also secured a Top-20 finish in the Siebel Classic which was held in another well known area of LA namely Silicon Valley.

From my first four events I finished in the money in all of them, earning $82,000 so there was every reason to expect another very good season. In late March I flew home to Ireland for a few weeks' rest.

****

I was pottering around in the garage doing a few things when I decided to take the bubble cover off my Harley-Davidson motor-bike. It had been parked up through the winter so I decided to see how it was.

After noticing a few spots of rust on it I told myself that I would get rid of them later after I took the bike out for a spin. When I retuned I parked it out in front of the house and after getting a few rags from inside I began giving it a good rigorous cleaning.

Without any warning it suddenly rocked over on top of me! The pain was excruciating and I did not know it at the time but it had shattered my leg in three places. In fact when I looked down at my foot, I saw that it was facing back to front at almost 180* of a turn.

For a brief second I thought that it had been severed and was hanging off. I cannot tell you how bad the pain was. I had been silly to park it on very loose gravel in the yard but all I could think about, apart from the pain, was getting it lifted from my leg. I started roaring for my brother Pascal who was helping me out around the house at the time. When he came running over and saw the state I was in I yelled at him to fetch some sort of strong rope.

At that precise moment my wife Ann drove into the yard. In my stricken state I was situated just around a bend in the driveway leading directly into the front of the house and she was driving in so fast that she almost ran over me! It was one of those days.

She quickly dialled the emergency services and requested an ambulance. Then using a rope she and Pascal managed to lift the bike just high enough off the ground for me to extract myself out from underneath it. But the day was about to turn even more hellish.

It seemed like an eternity before the ambulance arrived. Maybe that was because the pain was throbbing and it seemed to be getting worse. Then when the ambulance eventually arrived, I climbed in to see a heart attack patient who was being urgently attended to!

The poor man was in an awful state in the back of the ambulance as he lay prostrate on one bed and I was on the other bed across from him. As bad as things were for me I was just praying that he would not pass away next to me.

Along the route to the hospital in Galway the ambulance driver must have driven through every pothole on the road. It was such an uncomfortable journey and all I wanted to do was cry out!

Then I started to think about the consequences of my injury and all sorts of thoughts went through my head. Perhaps the biggest worry I now had was for my future. I had a nasty feeling that my golfing career was officially over because of my silly mistake.

Upon admission I was introduced to the Orthopedic surgeon Dr. McCabe. After he had examined the badly injured foot thoroughly he told me that in his considered opinion I had been a very lucky man.

If the accident had occurred 25 years earlier — and in 1976 I was only in the early stages of my golf career — I would probably never have played golf again. Dr. McCabe told me that in my state, one of the options back then would have been to amputate my foot! That was the very depressing news he gave me on what was turning out to be a never-ending nightmarish day. I desperately needed some reassurance for my future. But right then I needed and sort of good news.

Then, looking at my chart and briefly looking at my foot and ankle again, he sat on the end of the bed and told me:

"I'm not making any promises to you regarding your future golf career. But I'm going to try something developed by an eastern European doctor named Petar Zidarov. He is a modern pioneer in putting bones back together."

Following his surgical procedure, Dr. McCabe placed my leg in a

231

very unusual encasement to say the least. The apparatus consisted of three large rings which were placed around my leg and were held there by two vertical and adjoining supports.

Through the middle of the structure, 13 metal pins were inserted through my leg at different points. Each day I was told to turn those pins. On a particular day I had to turn them in a clockwise position and the very next day I would rotate them anti-clockwise.

It was not a very nice position to be in. Actually it could be excruciating at times but I had every faith in my doctor. There were also times when my family and friends had to turn away in disgust as my legged swelled up like a pumpkin.

Upon seeing this sight some believed that my leg was irreparable. However the gross swelling was caused by too much movement during the day. Each evening all the pins and apparatus had to be thoroughly and hygienically cleaned.

The monotony of lying about soon got to me and I insisted on getting out and back on to a golf course. There was no way I could play and in actual fact my future career was in some doubt. But I could now concentrate on my course design projects.

In a previous chapter I mentioned one of my greatest projects when Jim Mansfield asked me to design the PGA National in Naas. It was around this time that my accident occurred and Jim was very worried that I would not be able to do the job.

He was brilliant and so understanding to the point that he built a small stretcher inside a golf buggy for my leg! This meant that I could travel up and down the site all day long to survey my work. But it was not all cushy.

One day I drove through some marshy ground and the buggy got stuck four wheels deep. There was no way it could move and because of the way I was positioned in the buggy I could not move either. Even if I could I did not want to chance getting stuck as well. I had no phone with me. For six long hours I remained there marooned in marshy ground and I was beginning to get worried as darkness was falling. Just as I was giving up hope and feeling desperate a workman came to my rescue.

Even then I was in agony that night. One of the pins burnt my legs as the roasting hot sun was shining on it for hours. Thank God I was able to treat it and I was back to normal in a couple of days. That period during my accident was really so depressing. One of the worst aspects of it was that I was unable to defend my British Senior Open titles in 2001. I was also denied the great chance of creating a piece of very unique history.

No player has ever won the British Senior Open three years in a row. Barring that freak accident with my motorbike I believe that I would definitely have become the first player to do so.

After conquering Royal Portrush in 1999 and Royal County Down the following year I loved the links courses and the atmosphere in the north of Ireland. Over the same Royal County Down links in 2001 I have no doubts I would have gone close again.

My game was also in great shape prior to the accident. All the time I was bursting to get back playing again. After what seemed like an eternity of having shackles around my leg they eventually came off. This was followed by many weeks of massaging the leg to tone up the muscles and I visited various bone setters. I went swimming in the salty waters of Lahinch and this was a cure which my grandparents swore by and which they used for many purposes.

Getting back out on the golf course, I hit thousands and thousands of balls and I felt that I was getting there. But there was one big problem. Coming back of a full swing I was struggling to get my full weight down on the left leg.

If you had any doubts as to my confidence about securing an historic three-in-a-row of British Open titles then I think my performance on my return from injury in 2002 might show why I felt that way.

Only two players finished ahead of me on my return to Royal County Down. Noburu Sugai from Japan won it thanks largely to brilliant opening rounds of 67, 67. I finished five shots behind in third and I collected a cheque for £42,000.

In fact Tom Watson was dumbfounded. He could not believe that I finished the tournament in such a lofty position and virtually on one leg. He also told me that he could not believe I shot a round of 69 in such high winds.

My game was back but there was no doubt that the injury set me back a long way in so many areas. Not least of which was the US Tour. I had to be firing on all cylinders when I returned to America where there was no quarter given there.

Only one hundred per cent fitness and commitment would suffice. Any weakness would be exposed and so I would find myself under huge pressure to deliver. Anything else would spell a disaster of such proportions that it did not bear thinking about.

In one way that crazy accident almost cost me my career in golf. Thanks to the care and expertise of medical personnel I was given a second chance. But the irony was that in another way the setback put me into a position of facing a titanic struggle.

CHAPTER 18

Taking Off My Cap

*18th Hole: 371 yards, Par 4 at Woodbrook in Irish Open 1975.
My second shot ran through into the crowd at the back of the
green but thankfully a tense finish was eased by my receiving a
'free drop'. I pitched to 8ft and holed it to became the first
Irishman and the very first winner of the Irish Open*

When I became eligible to join the Senior events upon reaching
my 50th birthday in 1998, I always had at the back of my mind
that I would probably not be playing it for too long. There were
many other things that I wanted to do apart from playing golf.

After I captured my first British Senior Open at Portrush in
1999, I secured an automatic qualification to the British Open
proper in 2000. How ironic that it was to be held at St Andrews.
There I was at the tail-end of my professional golfing career on
the European Tour and I was returning to the very place where
I made my British Open debut. Little did I know when I first
played at 'the home of golf' in 1970 it would take 30 years for me
to return.

It was my 21st time to play what was the 129th British Open
but only my second time to play that prestigious event at St.
Andrews. Of course I had played in various Dunhill Cups at St
Andrews as a member of the Ireland team but the Open is so
special.

By the time I had finished my first round it was like I had never been away. I hit a -3, 69 and I was in the Top 20 on the first day. I think Tiger Woods led after a 67 with Sergio Garcia just behind him.

Next day I shot 75 to be level par. I was the only 'senior' player to make the cut. That was a huge achievement after being away for so long and over 50 years of age. I was thrilled and I always seemed to perform well on links courses and in the Open.

But nobody could tame the Tiger that week as Woods absolutely trounced the field. He won that Open with a -19 score and was a whopping eight shots clear of Ernie Els and Thomas Bjorn, who tied for second place. I ended the tournament with a penultimate level par 72 and another disappointing last round of 74 to finish up on +2. I tied 60th with Steve Elkington and Americans Jeff Sluman and Kirk Triplett to share a prize worth almost £10,000 each.

When your time is up, your time is up as they say. The future of golf was now in a totally different orbit with the likes of Woods about. He brought golf to a new level and I was just glad that I played well and had a bit of banter with Tiger about Royal County Down.

It was entirely fitting that I ended my professional career in such circumstances and I considered myself very lucky. Many years after I first entered that glorious clubhouse and locker room in such awe, and I stared wide-eyed at its history, I left for the very last time. As I walked up the fairway to the 18th green, the crowd gave me an unbelievable ovation. It almost brought a tear to my eye as I knew I would never experience this feeling again. St Andrews was THE place for any golfer to finish their career but mine was so special.

I could not have wished for a better place to end my professional playing days. A writer could not have come up with such a script. In 1970 I took the wrong route to the place and after walking among giants I had to endure the angst of a growling 'Golden Bear'. Then on the 30th Anniversary of my very first visit I was saying goodbye on a day when Tiger Woods mauled the opposition. From one legend to another and as Jack was irritated by my fluttering around on the first tee, Tiger and I shared a right laugh days earlier.

They call St Andrews the 'Old Lady' and she obviously liked me. But it was not all cosy with her as it rarely is with any woman! In the 1989 Dunhill Cup, Tom Kite beat me in a sudden death Play-Off on the first extra hole between the USA and Ireland in the semi-final when I made an error and hit my second shot into the 'Swilken Burn'. The American team went on to make the final.

But of all the British Open courses, in my heart she is my favourite. In my head however, no course comes close to my favourite Royal St George's, Sandwich. That is where I shot a record 64 in 1985 and the great Sir Henry Cotton greeted me.

In shutting my own locker I knew in my heart that I was not only saying 'goodbye' to the glorious British Open, but also to the European professional circuit. I had nothing to complain about and everything to be grateful for. Two years later at the Murphy's Irish Open held in Fota Island, it was fantastic to see my best golfing buddy Eamonn Darcy finish sixth alongside Padraig Harrington. Des Smyth also finished in the Top 20 and was a couple of shots in front of Clarkey and McDowell.

That event also signalled poor Seve's last ever link with the Irish Open. A few years later he would be diagnosed with a brain tumour and when he passed away after battling it for so long and so courageously, Irish golf fans were deeply saddened by his loss. These were some of the last events that we old dogs played. It is hard to believe that it was only just over 10 years ago. Having travelled along the hardened and long road, it was now time to take life a little easier.

It was time to venture off into the sunset and to rest a while in the shade. Then after being spurred on and inspired by my two sons Nigel and Darren to winning in the scorching heat of American deserts, destiny was to deal me another card. My freak motorbike accident set me back so much. It prevented me from winning the British Senior Open for an unprecedented third year running in 2001 but it also very nearly ended my Senior career which was put on hold for a very short while.

When my leg had healed fully allowing me to rejoin the Senior Tour in 2002, I thought that my third-place finish at the British Senior Open would spur me on. It was as if I was starting back where I had finished off in 2000 but I was in for a sobering wake-up call.

I received a 'Medical Extension' from the US authorities which allowed me to participate again on their tour but under certain criteria. Again I thought I was well on track to recapturing all the glory when I shot a superb 66 in the Bell South Senior Classic. However things did not materialise like I had envisaged. My best performances were 24th in the Royal Caribbean Classic and 25th in the Audi Senior Classic. My earnings totalled $89,000 which was not near good enough and I finished 89th on the Money List.

The repercussions for me were enormous. This meant that I did not win back my treasured playing card by finishing in the Top 50. The net result of that was that I had an almost insurmountable challenge ahead to regain my card. That was a major obstacle which proved to be a bridge too far. The hassle of flying to the US and getting involved in a dog-eat-dog scrap to regain my US playing rights was simply not worth it. But there was one very last option open to me.

The American authorities had been very good to me. I had written to both the USGA (Golf Association) and USPGA (Professional Golfers Association) and they both granted my wishes of an extension. I was delighted. They realised what I had brought to their game in the years before. They also knew how fate had dealt me a bad hand and without any fuss whatsoever they let me play again on medical and compassionate grounds.

Britain and Europe held the exact same criteria by which injured or sick golfers could resume playing. After winning the British Senior Open in successive years and returning after my year out to finish third, there was every chance that I would be treated similarly. I also felt that I had been a good flagship and role model for Europe. I had brought glory home from the US and I was a winner in Europe as well. If I could play on in Europe and win more titles, then certain doors would no doubt open up for me again.

My appetite for Europe had been further whetted by seeing my old Irish Matchplay adversary Peter Townsend winning the very first event of the 2002 European season. Pete captured the Barbados Open. So I wrote a very long and what I thought at the time to be a very good explanatory letter to the Royal & Ancient Golf Association in England. The ironic thing is that they are based in St Andrews — the place I love so dearly.

In the letter I explained that because of my accident in 2001, and the subsequent medical treatment and healing process, I could not play golf that year. I went on to say how gutted I was that I could not defend my British Senior Open and a possible three-in-a-row.

As winner of the British Senior Open in 1999, I gained entry to the 129th British Open in 2000. But after defending and winning the 2000 Senior Open again, I was injured and unable to play in 2001 so I could not use my qualification right for the 130th Open.

Because of that I asked if they would allow me to play the 2002 British Open in place of the one I missed and had been eligible for. I mentioned that the USGA and USPGA had very kindly acceded to my requests to play in the States because of my injury in 2001.

Not only did they not grant my wish, they did not even have the courtesy or manners to reply to my long letter. I felt dejected and disrespected. After all I had done for Europe and for European golf they could at least have had the decency to respond to me. At St Andrews in 2000 I knew deep down that quite possibly it was the end. Then when I successfully defended my Senior Open at Royal County Down a few weeks after St Andrews, I knew I had won an exemption and the chance of playing another Open.

At the back of my mind I was excited at the prospect of playing another British Open but then the injury scuppered my chance of playing. When I did not receive any word back from the R&A concerning my plea to play in it again, it was most definitely over for me.

A little while later, a reporter asked me if I was going to try for the British Open at Royal St George's. I told him that I was tempted. In truth, that was never going to happen as I would have to go through the rigours of having to pre-qualify. Perhaps this is what the R&A wanted me to do. But I felt that in the spirit of 'fair play' as the Americans had showed, that I was 'owed' a place in the Open because of my exemption right from my win in 2000 that I was simply unable to take up.

I also told the reporter that even if I had gained entry to the British Open through the qualifying stages, the Senior Open at Turnberry was just a week later. So it was too close and all things considered there was no way back to play for a Claret Jug.

Meanwhile all avenues to the Senior events in Europe and America also seemed closed — apart from one. Being a Senior Open Champion (twice) gave me exemption to play in the British Senior Open.

In 2003 — after winning in 1999 and 2000; not playing in 2001 and finishing third in 2002 — I turned up at Turnberry. With virtually no competitive golf I came in a little rusty and so it proved when the event got underway.

A third Senior British Open never looked likely as I finished way down the field behind Tom Watson. Fellow Irish players Eamonn Darcy, Des Smyth and Denis O'Sullivan finished in front of me. I picked up €4,000. My golfing career at all levels was over.

Like so many professional sports people, I suppose that I refused to acknowledge my playing days at the very top were at an end. My inner competitive juices compelled me to keep on playing but now with all avenues for a return blocked, the game was finally up.

In the intervening 10 years or so that I have been away, I do of course miss the action. Every summer when the Irish and British Opens and Senior Opens take place, I always feel I should be part of it. Seeing my old adversary Fred Couples winning the Senior Open in 2012 actually reminded me of my own Open wins. More to the point I have been making here, he actually brought me right back to my own experiences when he told reporters:

"I've just found out that after winning here, I've gained an automatic invite to the 2013 British Open at Muirfield. That is a lovely feeling — knowing that I've won a British Senior Open and I'm also in the Open proper next year."

Pangs of nostalgia deepen further when I see how well Tom Watson and Hale Irwin are playing. What a pity Watson made a mistake on the very last green of the 2009 Open at Turnberry which eventually cost him dear as Stewart Cink went on to win the Play-Off.

But in the spirit of looking back on my rounds afterwards — and the good and the bad moments — then in the round of my life that you have shared here with me, I have very few regrets and so much to be thankful for.

Many golfers will not readily admit to it but every professional golfer in the world leads a five-star lifestyle. Whether he or she is carrying a bag of clubs to the airport or ferry-port, the very best places and the very best hotels await your arrival.

Getting there and carrying the luggage is the hardest part of the 'job'. After that you are waited on and pampered every step of the way. Golf courses; hotels; tournament sponsors and the golfer's own personal sponsors look after and cater to your every need.

I am glad to say that in the last few years of my professional career I experienced all this at first hand. Throughout my career I have also stayed in the best hotels in the world; played the top golf courses and visited so many countries on every continent.

However, it was not always like that. I like to think that from my very earliest days in Newcastle when I felt hurt and betrayed and cried all the way to London; then struggling to get a break back home and my struggle continuing in Holland, that I earned it all.

My career was a fairly long apprenticeship which does not seem to happen so much now.

I can recall the days when three or four of us squeezed into a van along with cases and clubs and drove long journeys to England and through mainland Europe.

We were cramped and exhausted and upon reaching our destination, we then went in search of the cheapest B&Bs and small hotels. After Christmas when we ventured to Africa, we stayed with host families.

One thing that saddens me today is that golfers are missing out on all this. The vast majority of them stay in hotels and do not get to see the locals or the history of the place they are visiting. Very few even venture outdoors to mingle with locals.

I do wish the golf clubs hosting tournaments would contact local people and then give golfers the choice and the opportunity of staying with them. It should not always be about commercialism and giving hotels all the business.

Give a slice of the action to local people and afford them 'host family' status. This will give golfers an excellent opportunity of getting out more and not just learning about the locals and the history, but they will no doubt give something back to communities.

As it is, today's professional golfer is surrounded by an entourage. Aside from the agent or manager, golfers now have an array of aides including coaches, fitness instructors, dieticians, physiotherapists, psychologists and advisors.

On many occasions I can remember going to the practise range or green and having to squeeze past four or five 'gurus' who would surround their player. I firmly believe that all of this should happen at home and these people should not be in those areas.

There is a time and place for everything and golfers need the use of the green or the range for their own privacy. Also, a physio's truck is now present at most events on tour so any golfer having problems should be able to go to a private place on the course.

Speaking of the golf range you will see golfers lined up with pyramids of golf balls to shoot. It was not like that in my day. Golf balls were expensive and we also had our caddies down the course collecting them and I can tell you there were many accidents.

Do not get me wrong. In later years I experienced all the latest modern fads as well but I just think that it is a pity that we seem to be abandoning many of the old ways. In terms of being environmentally friendly, as well as in recession, we can learn from the past.

At the end of the day, golf has been extremely good to me. Aside from travelling and staying in places all over the world, meeting people has meant so much more to me. Lifelong friendships have been forged among people from all walks of life.

It is especially nice to be able to say that I have rubbed shoulders with some of the most famous and wealthiest people on earth. Prince Andrew has even become a dear friend but working with under-privileged people has meant so much more to me.

I came from a working class background and I am very proud of that. It is a fact that I have never forgotten where I have come from. Maybe that is all the more reason why I can feel huge pride at some of the lofty company I have kept.

In addition to the President of Zambia and some of the Sheikhs in Dubai, I also played golf with the King of Morocco. Relating to the current climate however, I think meeting Queen Elizabeth II and her husband Prince Philip was very special.

On that occasion it was a huge surprise when the Duke of Edinburgh decided to pay a visit to my table where I was sitting with Ian Woosnam. Woosie kept him up to speed with all the golf jokes on tour and His Highness laughed so much at all of them.

Giving a large slice of something back to golf is imperative upon golfers who have benefited from the game. In respect of my golf course design, I am certainly doing just that but I am also heavily involved in various charities.

Getting involved with various projects involving sick children is especially dear to my heart. To see how brave they are and to know that my doing even the smallest little thing does actually help, is very gratifying.

For instance, autographing a cap or golf ball is such a simple task for any golfer but it can mean the world to any adoring boy or girl. Golfers should think more about that when finishing a round as I have seen the hurt in a child's eyes when a golfer walks on by.

The throngs of young kids holding out caps or balls to be signed is really a beckoning call to any golfer to give a little bit back. After all, the golfer is that child's hero and many a kid has gone on to become a huge golfing sensation in the future.

Hospice Foundation is also very important in my life. In fact it has touched most families in Ireland in one way or another. Over the past number of years and up to the present, I have run many golf events for the benefit of Hospice.

Being on the Board of Special Olympics Ireland is a huge honour. One day Denis O'Brien rang me and he asked me if I would like to join the Board of the organisation. I did not even have to think about it and I jumped at the opportunity. An even bigger privilege is to be able to witness at first hand how those brilliant athletes train and prepare themselves for the biggest competitions of their lives.

At the Special Olympics in Dublin it was fantastic to get to know many of the athletes and to see them win medals. The pride in their faces was something to treasure. It was such a unique and special event and we in Ireland should always be proud of hosting it.

Mary Davis and Denis should also be given great credit for the way they brought it to our shores. I do not think we have acknowledged that fully. We tend to forget those things and quite often we focus on the negative aspects of their politics.

I have never seen anyone work as hard as those two individuals in not just bringing the Special Olympics here, but also in their day-to-day work for the organisation. They should always be remembered for organising a most successful Irish Olympics.

The Opening Ceremony which was attended by Nelson Mandela, Muhammad Ali and Bono, was a fantastic occasion. It was without doubt one of — if not the biggest — sporting occasion Ireland ever hosted.

We were mirrored to the world and later China copied our blueprint and everything that we had done. I would like to pay a very special thanks to all the families around Ireland who took in and hosted athletes from all parts of the world. You were fantastic.

Talking of homes and hosting I have also been in the residences of some of the most famous people in the world. Prince Bernhard of Holland, Bing Crosby and Bob Hope are just some that spring to mind.

Sport is such a huge part of my life and I have also met many sports personalities which are too numerous to mention. Two that spring to mind are two of the finest jockeys that Ireland ever produced — Mick Kinane and Tony 'AP' McCoy.

In fact, I shared a helicopter ride with Tony McCoy from Cheltenham in 2012. Tony, in his capacity as BBC Sports Personality of the Year, and my good self, flew to Manchester where we were both the recipients of a 'Pride of Erin' award.

Over the years I have also kept and collected so much golf memorabilia. I still have clubs and balls that I used in competition but I think that the pride of place in my collection must certainly go to one of Ben Hogan's rings.

Ben famously had 10 rings commissioned for his entourage. One was encrusted with 10 diamonds encircling a ruby and the other nine held nine diamonds encircling a ruby. I was given the 10 diamond ring as a gift from Orlimar whom I played under at one time.

The ring came with documentation which authenticated the fact that it belonged to Ben Hogan. I have always been a huge fan of his. He was a golfer who probably practised harder than anyone else in the history of the game.

I wear that ring on the little finger of my left hand and there is an inscription engraved upon it which says it all really:

'IN PURSUIT OF EXCELLENCE'

Ben is my hero. Similar to my motorbike and helicopter accidents, he also survived two car crashes. In one of those, his car collided with a train at a level crossing and Ben was so badly injured that he was not expected to survive.

The doctor who attended at the scene asked Ben if he had any last words to say to which Hogan replied: "I will win the US Open."

The doc thought he was hallucinating but would later find those words coming true.

Looking back on all the Irish players past and present, I would say that my uncle Christy O'Connor Senior was the best. He came out of Galway during very hard times and he had to fight every inch just to become a member of the PGA.

Apart from his outstanding Ryder Cup record and all the titles he won, his consistency over many decades was unbelievable. No Irish player past or present can match all of his achievements. Back in the 60s, 70s and early 80s he was the 'God of Golf' for all Irish players as we looked up to him and worshipped him. It was therefore very fitting that on November 2nd 2009 he was finally and rightfully inducted into the 'World Golf Hall of Fame'.

Because of not wanting to make a long journey, Senior could not attend the ceremony in St Augustine, Florida and he was so disappointed that he could not do so. He explained this in his acceptance speech which is fantastic and it can be watched on YouTube.

After viewing that three-minute speech you are left in no doubt as to the huge pride he felt as he says "I'm still walking on air." He also talked about how surprised he felt when George O'Grady rang to tell him the news saying, "I thought it was a joke."

At the end of it there was a tear in his eye. The extended O'Connor family travelled to America to accept the award on his behalf. When I was next in line to give a speech, I felt such immense pride as I sat there beside his daughter Marguerite and her husband Gerry.

I thought about the little area of Galway that we had all come from and it seemed so surreal to be there among the elite of world golf. It was a very fitting and final appreciation of what Christy did for the game he loves and still plays.

Thank you Christy for not only inviting me there for your very special night, but also for everything you have done for me down through the years. It is a plain fact that without you as an inspiration, I would never have become a professional golfer.

I am so glad that I did and I am also very grateful to all the people who helped me from my earliest beginnings. I have spoken at length about my father and my wife but without doubt the biggest influence on my career was my mother Elizabeth.

My father helped me indirectly through his total opposition to my game and in later years he saw the benefits and we became great friends. But my mother was always supportive of me in absolutely everything I did from the start. The shop close to the caravan park; my milk rounds; her paying for my golf membership fees as well as so many other things she helped me with. I may not have talked about her as much as the others but she was undoubtedly my rock.

In particular I must thank all the wonderful and ordinary golf fans that have supported not just me but all Irish golfers in every corner of the world. It is all fine and dandy mingled with celebrity but no famous or rich people gave me a leg up or inspired me. I had to do it myself and I was spurred on by the support of plain, hard-working Irish people — and actually, in remembering that lovely policeman from an earlier chapter, I received great support from people in so many countries.

When I try to remember the many moments I was out there on the course focussing on my next shot with my caddy and all of a sudden a shout of 'Come on Ireland' went up from someone in the crowd, I get goosebumps.

Or when I recall the Irish flag being hoisted and the Irish, or even those wanting to be Irish, all singing, I get very emotional and a tear comes to my eye. Those are the moments that I will never forget.

Strolling down the 18th fairway; knowing you have a few shots' cushion; tipping your cap to the thousands of cheering fans; getting the job done; the sweet smell of success and knowing you have conquered a top course and a top field — it speaks for itself.

Arriving home with clubs on one arm and the trophy in the other is the icing on the cake. Whether it is early junior events or senior events or whether it is amateur or professional, these are the memories which all of us golfers have and which are priceless.

I know that I will never go down in history as 'the greatest' golfer that ever played. It seems as if the requirements for that accolade rest with how many majors, how many titles and how many weeks were spent as World No.1. Who is counting? In the same way as a plumber, electrician or plasterer will never go down as the greatest in the world in their respective trades, I learned the intricacies of my game over many years.

I became as adept in my field as any human being in any job. There was never a putt, drive or chip that I could not perform precisely the same as the very best. Whether it was big hitting; holing an iron for eagle or making a monster 50ft birdie putt, I did it all.

In the spirit of doing any job over many years, I did mine to the best of my ability. I may not have performed consistently through my career and I may even have had to wait a little longer than most to eventually get there, but get there and perform I certainly did.

There were tough times; sad times; happy times and glorious times but there was never a dull moment along the way. I can honestly say that I enjoyed it all and I always tried to wear a smile under my cap as only we Irish can.

You only get one shot at it as they say and I will forever be remembered for that bit of magic I weaved at The Belfry with a 2-iron wand. RTE and the press have been very good to me and have constantly kept that moment fresh in people's minds.

However, from the rough and the fairways of the greatest golf courses that I have played around the world, I am filled with huge contentment and pride when I think of what I am leaving to future generations.

Something that is far more reaching and profound than any shot or greatness or titles are the courses which I have helped to create. These are my pitch marks. Marks that have been carved out of the earth by the many experiences I have enjoyed through my career.

Golf courses are little pieces of Heaven and something which every single one of us can use, enjoy and benefit from throughout our lives. What more can any person want — get out; keep fit; breathe fresh air; play a great game and marvel at the surrounding wildlife.

When myself and the great players such as my uncle, Palmer, Player, Nicklaus, Watson, Seve and Woods have long gone from this world, I hope that generations of people will enjoy the likes of Concra Wood and Headford and play the game that I have loved.

This should help in its own small way to ensure that the future of Irish golf will remain in a very healthy state for many decades to come. It is only in playing these affordable and accessible courses that the young boy and girl golfers of tomorrow will be unearthed.

After all, it is they who are our future. They are the treasures who will become the stars of tomorrow and carry on doing Ireland proud in major tournaments, Solheim Cups and Ryder Cups.

That is the real legacy which Christy O'Connor from Knocknacarra wishes to leave.

A Special Toast

19th Hole – Mount Wolseley Hotel, Co. Carlow. October 2005

From my office in Goatstown, County Dublin my daughter Ann has worked so hard for me for many years. She has organised countless numbers of my business dealings and meetings.

She also gave us one of our proudest days when she walked up the aisle to marry Mark Belton on the weekend of October 21st 2005. The wedding was held in a small parish church outside Tullow and later we gathered in Mount Wolseley for the reception.

There were around 450 guests and even though there were so many well known personalities present — Gay Byrne and his wife Kathleen Watkins; the late Joe Dolan; politicians; sportspeople — it was Ann's day and a real family one at that.

I gave my speech during which my uncle Christy had to stand to acknowledge a standing ovation from the assembled guests. But I was so proud of Mark joining the family.

A son of Frank and Marie Belton, in many ways I added another son to my family that day. As I sat there looking at Mark and Ann with so much pride, it seemed as if the O'Connor family of five was complete once more. But then along came a sixth.

In 2012 my daughter gave birth to Ava. She is a little princess who now rules the family. The newest generation of O'Connor as well as the first grandchild born to my wife and I.

May Ava and her proud parents — as well as all of you who have taken the time to read my story — lead long lives full of happiness, health and honesty. I toast and thank you all.

Christy O'Connor, July 2012

Index

A

Albert 2, 4, 19, 20, 26, 31, 169
Al Geiberger 75
Amen Corner 106, 109, 143, 157
Ann 38, 49, 50, 58, 61, 62, 63, 66,
        84, 94, 95, 118, 119, 122, 125,
        141, 150, 151, 152, 155, 157,
        158, 159, 160, 177, 180, 199,
        201, 205, 230
daughter Ann 202, 203, 204, 206,
        214, 217, 251
Antonio Garrido 94
Arnold Palmer 61, 70, 74, 75, 77,
        81, 89, 90, 132, 193, 249
A T&T Canada Open 221
Audi Senior Classic 238
Augusta 1, 13, 34, 66, 95, 98, 99,
        103, 107, 108, 109, 110, 111,
        113, 143, 157
Azalea 107, 109

B

Baldomero 34
Baldovino Dassu 68
Bannerman 71, 72
Barbados Open 239
Barnes 80
BBC 28, 33, 90, 148, 185
Beck 170
Bell South Senior Classic 238
Ben Crenshaw 93, 100, 110, 186
Ben Hogan' 245, 246
Benson & Hedges 37, 74, 93
Benson & Hedges International 127
Bernard Gallacher 74, 75, 78, 80,
        146, 175

Bernard Hunt 75, 77, 80, 149
Bernhard Langer 110, 124, 125, 127,
        130, 138, 140, 147, 159, 160,
        163, 164, 167, 188
Bill Rogers 126
Billy Casper 75, 78
Billy Foster 187, 194
Birkdale 125
Bobby Jones 99, 111
Bob Charles 28, 69, 215, 217
Bob Murphy 75
Bob Shearer 74
Bob Wallace 9, 11, 15, 16, 21-23
Bob Wynn 68
Bono 245
Bournemouth Echo 36
Brendan Bowyer 83
Brian Barnes 75, 78, 81
Brian Huggett 75, 79
Brian Smallwood 217
British Masters 189, 209
British Open 27, 33, 45, 53, 58, 59,
        61, 62, 64, 70-74, 83, 90, 91,
        93, 97, 99, 113, 124, 126,
        130--138, 140-144, 152, 154,
        221, 224, 229, 235, 237, 240,
        241
British PGA 82, 130
British Senior Open 213, 216, 228,
        229, 233, 235, 237-241
Bruce Fleisher 210, 212
Bruce Woodcock 116
Bubba Watson 155

C

Camellia 105
Car Care Plan event 129

Car Care Plan tournament 126
Cardinal Cushing 182
Carlow Golf Club 32, 75
Carnoustie 64, 91
Carroll's International 37, 40, 65, 67
Charles 216
Charlie Chawke 83
children Ann 123
Chip Beck 165, 167
Chris De Burgh 180
Chris Platts 183
Christy O'Connor Senior 2, 11, 12,
        21, 27, 29, 35, 37, 40, 57, 61,
        65, 66, 70, 84, 88, 90, 94, 98,
        119, 121, 132, 135, 141, 147,
        148, 168, 169, 177, 182, 195,
        197, 198, 201, 206, 207, 223,
        246, 249
Christy St George 10
City West Golf Club 190
Clarkey 237
Clifford Roberts 99, 112
Cliff Roberts 111
Connemara Crusher 116
Cotton 132
Craig Stadler 136
Curtis Strange 165

D

Dad 6, 12, 13, 15, 31, 144, 149, 151,
        152, 153, 156, 247
Dai Rees 75, 149
Darren 3, 48, 49, 119, 123, 200, 201,
        202, 203, 204, 206, 207, 208,
        209, 210, 211, 212, 214, 218,
        220, 221, 222, 228, 229, 237
Darren Clarke 90, 91, 137
Darren O'Connor 205
David Feherty 126, 129
David Graham 138
David Howell 190

David Jones 38
David J Russell 129
David Moore 45
David Quinn 205
Denis Durnian 126, 154
Denis O'Brien 244
Denis O'Sullivan 240
Denis Thatcher 181
Dermot Gilleece 217, 218
Des Smyth 124, 126, 127, 129, 237,
        240
Dick Hurst 218, 219
Doug Ford 102, 103
Doug Sanders 63
Duke of Edinburgh 243
Dunhill Cup 184, 197, 237
Dunhill Masters 130, 159
Dunlop Masters 37, 74, 93
Dutch Open 74, 93

E

Eamonn Darcy 42, 45-48, 56, 57, 68,
        75, 77, 78, 79, 80, 88-90, 117,
        121, 124, 129, 138, 146, 148,
        151, 153, 184, 191, 237, 240
Eddie Polland 40, 44, 88, 89, 90,
        117, 191
Edoardo Molinari 110, 183
Elizabeth Noone 1
El Paraiso Open 87
English Open 159
Ernie Els 236
Ernie Jones 184
Esker Hills Golf Course 190
Eugene 2, 15, 33, 34, 75, 83, 84,
        168, 181, 204
European money list 94
European Open 130
European Order of Merit 74, 84, 189
European PGA 147, 190
European Tour 1, 34, 39, 41, 44, 53,

74, 82, 85, 130, 155, 189, 207, 213, 215, 235

F

Fernandez 60
Firethorn 107
Flowering Peach 104
Floyd Geiberger 79
Foremost Insurance Championship 218, 221
Francisco Abreu 93
Frank 2, 14, 16, 19, 21, 22, 29, 30, 31, 32
Fred Couples 167-170, 172, 174, 175, 178-181, 185, 197, 241
Fred Daly 147
French Open 88, 94, 114
Fulford 37

G

Gallardo 114
Galway Fair 3
Garrido 114
Gary Cullen 50, 51
Gary Player 28, 58, 61, 88, 90, 100, 132, 215-217, 218, 249
Gay Brewer 66
Gay Byrne 251
Gene Littler 75
George O'Grady 246
German Open 40, 74, 157
Glasgow Classic 125
Glenn Day 188
Golden Bear 236
Golden Bell 106
Gordon Brand 165
Gordon Brand Junior 158, 181
Graeme McDowell 77, 110, 237
Greater Manchester Open 89
Greg Norman 110, 115, 137, 193

Guy Hunt 57, 75, 79

H

Hale Irwin 74, 75, 108, 228, 241
Harrington 90
Harry Bannerman 69, 70
Harry Bradshaw 147
Hassan Trophy 82
Headford Golf Club 191
Henry Cotton 55, 135, 137, 237
Home Depot Championship 222
Home Depot Invitational 210
Hospice Foundation 244
Howard Clark 165, 170
Hubert Green 91
Hugh Baiocchi 74

I

Ian Stanley 57, 68, 69
Ian Woosnam 46, 47, 165, 167, 181, 243
Irish Dunlop Masters 55, 191
Irish Hospitals Sweepstake 65
Irish Matchplay 38, 83, 115, 117, 239
Irish Open 64, 66, 72, 74, 93, 114, 118, 127, 130, 152, 159, 235
Irish Times 217
Isao Aoki 132
Italian Open 39, 93, 126
Ivor Robson 138

J

Jack Charlton 153
Jacklin 80, 90, 145, 163, 165, 167, 173, 178
Jack Newton 64, 73
Jack Nicklaus 13, 61-66, 75-78, 80, 81, 91, 93, 104, 111, 112, 132,

192, 193, 195, 209, 249
JC Snead 67, 68, 75, 78
Jeff Sluman 236
Jersey Airways European Open 155
Jersey Open 157, 158
Jim Mansfield 186, 187, 190, 232
Jim Mansfield Junior 204
Jimmy Bruen 54
Jimmy Kinsella 34, 37
Jimmy Martin 55, 147
Joe Carr 102
Joe Dolan 251
Joe Hayes 58
John Bland 41, 216, 219, 224, 225,
    226, 227
John Burke and his wife Peggy 121
John Daly 193
John McGuirk 115
John McTear 70
John Morrissey 39, 56, 87
John Mulholland 121, 228
Johnny Miller 75, 80, 91
John O'Leary 38, 75, 78, 79, 80, 88,
    89, 90, 117
John Player Trophy 37
Johnstone 189
Jones 132
Jose Maria Canizares 34, 94, 163,
    181
Jose Maria Olazabal 147, 153, 163,
    164, 165, 167
Jose Rivero 140, 144, 146

K

Kathleen Watkins 251
K Club 148, 194
Ken Brown 183
Ken Green 164
Kennemer Golf Club 29
Kenya Open 49, 183, 184
Kerrygold International 89, 113

Kirk Triplett 236
Knightsbrook Golf Club 192

L

Lancome Trophy 93
Lanny Wadkins 165
Larry Mize 110
Larry Walsh 118
Laurence Batley International 130
Lee Trevino 75, 77, 78, 98, 99
Lee Westwood 190
Liam Higgins 42, 89, 113, 184
Lopez 60
Lou Graham 75, 78, 79
Luke Donald 110

M

Madrid Open 34, 37, 74, 88, 93, 113
Magnolia 104
Malcolm Gregson 59
Manuel 34, 87
Manuel Pinero 93
Margaret Thatcher 181
Mark Belton 251
Mark Calcavecchia 136, 164, 167,
    170
Mark Haye 132
Mark James 91, 146, 149, 165
Mark McNulty 158
Mark O'Meara 138, 140, 164
Martini International 37, 56, 57, 64,
    66, 69, 89, 115, 124, 139
Martin Kaymer 110
Martin Thornton 115, 117
Mary Davis 244
Master Card Championship 222
Masters 99, 108, 110, 111, 114, 143,
    157
Matchplay 82
Matthew Byrne 170, 172, 174, 175,

176, 177, 184
Maureen 2
Maurice Bembridge 74, 75, 183
Michael Hoey 82
Michael Hynes 205
Mick Kinane 245
Mickleson 172
Mick O'Dwyer 89
Mike Ingham 44
Miles Murphy 220
Minister Frank Fahy 180
Mrs. Mellon 76
Muhammad Ali 245
Muirfield 241
Murphy's Irish Open 237
Myles Murphy 83

N

Nationwide Championship 210
Neil Coles 57, 88
Nelson Mandela 245
Niall Quinn 58
Nick Faldo 110, 124, 126, 137, 148,
        159, 163, 165, 167, 181, 188,
        192, 193, 194
Nicky English 58
Nigel 3, 49, 119, 123, 197, 199, 200,
        201, 202, 203, 204, 205, 206,
        214, 217, 221, 222, 223, 224,
        225, 226, 227, 228, 237
Noburu Sugai 233
Norio Suzuki 90
Norman Wood 75

O

Ove Sellberg 188

P

Paddy Casey 83, 85, 97, 99

Paddy McGuirk 35, 39, 40, 46, 115
Paddy O'Rourke 83, 84
Padraig Harrington 77, 91, 110, 202,
        237
Pascal 2, 15, 204, 230
Paul Azinger 165, 167, 170
Paul Casey 110
Paul Leonard 81
Paul McGinley 77, 91, 148
Payne Stewart 165, 167, 181
Penfold 36, 38, 39, 40, 74
Penfold Championships 88
Penfold Tournament 34, 167
Peter 37
Peter Alliss 141, 148
Peter Butler 69
Peter Oosterhuis 34, 35, 36, 75, 78,
        80, 110, 167
Peter Townsend 38, 81, 115, 191,
        239
PGA 1, 187
PGA National 190, 232
PGA Seniors 210
Philip Walton 126, 129, 148, 153
Phil Mickelson 66
Piccadilly Medal 34, 74
Pinero 94, 114
Pink Dogwood 13, 103
Portrush 214, 235
Portuguese Open 53, 54, 55, 88, 93
President John F Kennedy 182
President Kaunda 43, 44, 47, 48
President of Zambia 243
Prince Andrew 182, 209, 243

Q

Quail Hollow 210
Queen 243
Queens Park Club 167

R

R&A 136, 240
Rae's Creek 106, 107, 157
Ramos 114
Ray Floyd 75, 78, 136
Raymond 2, 15
Richard Joyce 207
Robert Rock 74
Rodger Davis 136
Roganstown Hotel and Golf C. 192
Roger Maltbie 108,110
Roker Park 24
Ronan 163, 168
Ronan Flood 202
Ronan Rafferty 126, 159, 163, 167,
    180
Ronnie Shade 57
Rory McIlroy 77, 90, 105, 110, 111,
    152, 203, 210
Ross Fisher 74, 110
Royal & Ancient Golf Association
    239
Royal Birkdale 27, 83, 90, 93, 124,
    221
Royal Caribbean Classic 238
Royal County Down 41, 224, 233,
    236
Royal Dublin 27, 130
Royal Lytham & St Annes 27, 58
Royal Portrush 213, 219, 233
Royal St George's 88, 129, 130, 132,
    134, 237, 240
Royal St Georges 57
Royal Troon 113
RTE 69, 90, 248
Ryder Cup 54, 55, 56, 70, 74, 75-77,
    78, 80, 81, 86, 90, 143, 144,
    145, 147, 148, 149, 151, 152,
    154, 156, 157, 159, 160, 162,
    163, 167, 183, 194, 197

S

Salvador Balbuena 93
Sam Snead 67, 102, 103
Sam Torrance 37, 69, 89, 125, 127,
    144, 149, 159, 165, 167, 168,
    181
Sandwich 131, 132, 137, 143
Sandy Lyle 129, 138-140
Sanyo Open 124, 127
SBC Senior Classic 229
Scandinavian Masters 125
Scottish Open 37
Sean 2, 4, 21, 22, 27, 29, 31, 65,
    169, 204, 228
Sean Quinn 149
Senior British Open 41, 223
Senior Open 240, 241
Senior Tour 190, 209, 213, 218, 238
Sergio Garcia 236
Seve Ballesteros 34, 85-94, 100, 101,
    110, 114, 115, 124, 130, 133,
    144, 145, 147, 158, 159, 163-
    167, 170, 183, 187, 199, 209,
    237, 249
Shane Lowry 74, 191
Siebel Classic 229
South Shields Golf Club 22
Spanish Open 34, 39, 74, 86, 88, 92,
    113, 124, 145
Special Olympics 244
St Andrews 53, 61, 62, 63, 97, 184,
    197, 224, 235, 236, 237, 239
State Farm Classic 210, 213, 222
Stephen Richardson 188
Steve Elkington 236
Steve Pate 136
Stewart 170
Stewart Cink 241
Sumrie Better Ball 89
Sun Alliance 57
Swiss Open 37, 82, 93, 114

T

Tea Olive 1
Ted Ray 147
Tenerife Open 153
The Belfry 130, 159, 163, 169, 174,
    179, 182, 183, 184, 185
The Postage Stamp 113
Thomas Bjorn 137, 236
Tiger Woods 194, 195, 199, 219,
    224, 236, 237, 249
Tomas Lopez 59, 63
Tom Cryan 55, 56
Tom Doak 186
Tom Fazio 186
Tom Kite 91, 165, 170, 237
Tom Lewis 137
Tom Morris 62
Tom Morris Junior 62
Tom Morris Senior and Junior 132
Tom O'Connor 71, 73, 202
Tommy Halpin 56, 81
Tommy Horton 75, 78, 80, 91, 100,
    101, 108, 110
Tom Watson 64, 70, 73, 74, 111,
    112, 125, 132, 136, 164, 167,
    234, 240, 241
Tom Weiskopf 75, 78
Tony 'AP' McCoy 245
Tony Jacklin 28, 34, 70, 75, 78, 79,
    89, 143, 144, 146, 147, 158-
    164, 175, 176, 180
Tony Johnstone 129, 188, 209
Tony O'Connor 81
Trevor Immelman 183
Turnberry 114, 240, 241

U

Uniroyal 114
US Masters 13, 34, 73, 95-98, 109,
    155

US Open 99, 152
US President Bill Clinton 1
US President George Bush Senior 76
US Senior Open 213, 222, 228
US Senior tour 213,217
US Tour 207, 220, 229

V

Vardon 132
Verizon Classic 229
Vicente Fernandez 59, 74, 91
Vijay Singh 153
Vincent 2, 15
Vincente 34
Volvo Open 153
Volvo PGA 158

W

Walton Heath 39
Watson 126, 249
WD & HO Wills 37
Weiskopf 79, 80
Wentworth 74, 184, 187
White Dogwood 106
wife 56, 198, 203, 204, 206, 214
wife Ann 217
William Jefferson Blythe III 1
Woodbrook 65, 66, 67, 127, 235
World Cup 24, 55
World Matchplay 74, 75, 158

Y

Yellow Jasmine 105

Z

Zambian Open 44, 53
Zandvoort 29
Zsa Zsa Gabor 229